SLAVERY'S LONG SHADOW

Slavery's Long Shadow

Race and Reconciliation in American Christianity

Edited by
James L. Gorman,
Jeff W. Childers,
and Mark W. Hamilton

WILLIAM B. EERDMANS PUBLISHING COMPANY
GRAND RAPIDS, MICHIGAN

Wm. B. Eerdmans Publishing Co.
4035 Park East Court SE, Grand Rapids, Michigan 49546
www.eerdmans.com

Printed in the United States of America

25 24 23 22 21 20 19   1 2 3 4 5 6 7

ISBN 978-0-8028-7623-2

Library of Congress Cataloging-in-Publication Data

Names: Gorman, James L., editor.
Title: Slavery's long shadow : race and reconciliation in American
    Christianity / edited by James L. Gorman, Jeff W. Childers, and Mark W.
    Hamilton.
Description: Grand Rapids : Eerdmans Publishing Co., 2019. | Includes
    bibliographical references and index.
Identifiers: LCCN 2018033132 | ISBN 9780802876232 (pbk. : alk. paper)
Subjects: LCSH: United States—Race relations. | Race relations—Religious
    aspects—Christianity. | Racism—United States—History. |
    Racism—Religious aspects—Christianity.
Classification: LCC E184.A1 S625 2019 | DDC 305.800973—dc23
    LC record available at https://lccn.loc.gov/2018033132

*This book is dedicated to Douglas A. Foster
in honor of his extraordinary service
to the causes of religious and racial unity*

Contents

Acknowledgments

The editors would like to thank Eerdmans Publishing and their team for taking on this project. Trevor Thompson and David Bratt have been helpful from the beginning. We are grateful to James Gorman's students at Johnson University who read and provided feedback on many chapters. We would also like to thank Jacob Payton and Ryne Parrish for their careful reading of the book and Charity Beam for her work on the index. Thanks to Johnson University for extra support of Gorman during fall 2017 and to Abilene Christian University for supporting the book in numerous ways. Special thanks go to Robert Rhodes and Ken Cukrowski at Abilene Christian for their help in bringing the book to fruition. We are grateful to Linda Foster for her helpful suggestions on this project. Above all, we are thankful for the life and witness of Doug Foster, whom this book seeks to honor.

Contributors

Tanya Smith Brice, Dean and Professor of Social Work, College of Professional Studies, Bowie State University

Joel A. Brown, PhD Candidate, University of Chicago

Lawrence A. Q. Burnley, Vice President for Diversity and Inclusion, University of Dayton

Jeff W. Childers, Carmichael-Walling Professor of New Testament and Early Christianity, Abilene Christian University

Wes Crawford, Preaching Minister, Glenwood Church of Christ, Tyler, Texas

James L. Gorman, Associate Professor of History, Johnson University

Mark W. Hamilton, Onstead Professor of Biblical Studies, Abilene Christian University

Richard T. Hughes, Scholar in Residence, Lipscomb University

Loretta Hunnicutt, Associate Professor of History, Pepperdine University

Christopher R. Hutson, Associate Dean and Associate Professor of Bible, Missions, and Ministry, College of Biblical Studies, Abilene Christian University

Kathy Pulley, Professor of Religious Studies, Missouri State University

Edward J. Robinson, Associate Professor of History and Religion, Texas College

Kamilah Hall Sharp, PhD Candidate, Brite Divinity School, Texas Christian University

Jerry Taylor, Associate Professor of Bible, Missions, and Ministry, Abilene Christian University

D. Newell Williams, President and Professor of Modern and American Church History, Brite Divinity School, Texas Christian University

Slavery's Long Shadow:
Race and Reconciliation in American Christianity

JAMES L. GORMAN, JEFF W. CHILDERS, AND MARK W. HAMILTON

Network anchors and political pundits covering the incoming election results on November 8–9, 2016, announced with surprise that Donald J. Trump would beat Hillary Rodham Clinton for the presidency. Almost no one expected him to win. Although Clinton led in most polls, states that everyone thought Clinton would win went to Trump.[1] Many questioned: How did the polls get it so wrong? The polls simply had not taken an accurate pulse of the American public. Against long odds, Trump had won the most powerful political office in the world. Although many new and contemporary factors such as economic hardship and fear of globalization influenced the surprising outcome of the election, other prominent factors such as race and religion had much deeper, older histories.

Exit polls demonstrated clear correlation between the voter's preferred candidate and the voter's gender, education, and age, but the categories of race and religion were among the most interesting—and they bring into focus a central question this book explores.[2] Although white individuals supported the Republican Party's candidate at a 20 percent margin (57 percent voted Republican and 37 percent Democrat), white people who self-identified as "born-again or evangelical Christians" supported Trump by a 65 percent margin (81 percent voted Republican and 16 percent Democrat). This margin of support infuriated some white evangelical millennials, who often opposed Trump for his vicious words during the campaign and his lifetime record of what they considered to be unethical living.[3] One young white evangelical stormed into one of

---

1. Matt Flegenheimer and Michael Barbaro, "Donald Trump Is Elected President in Stunning Repudiation of the Establishment," *New York Times*, November 9, 2016, https://www.nytimes.com/2016/11/09/us/politics/hillary-clinton-donald-trump-president.html.

2. For data arranged by these and other categories, see "Exit Polls," CNN, November 23, 2016, http://www.cnn.com/election/results/exit-polls.

3. For a list of Trump's racist statements, see David Leonhardt and Ian Prasad Philbrick,

our offices (Gorman's) on November 9 and proclaimed he wanted nothing to do with the evangelical label. He and his friends were shocked that
white evangelicals voted someone into office whose character and daily
living would have meant expulsion from their churches. But this view
represented only a small minority among voting white evangelicals. Most
white evangelical voters strongly preferred the Republican Party (even if
they did not like the candidate).[4]

In stark contrast to white people, black individuals voted for the Democratic Party by an 81 percent margin (89 percent Democrat and 8 percent
Republican).[5] Furthermore, according to a Pew Research Center study,
among "Historically Black Protestant Traditions" (HBPT), 80 percent lean
Democrat, 10 percent lean Republican, and 10 percent lean neither way.[6] Of
those in HBPT, 72 percent consider themselves "born-again or evangelical."[7]
That is, black evangelicals could not differ more sharply from their white
evangelical counterparts on political ideology. The relationship of race, religion, and politics has a long and deeply influential history, with a continued
impact on the shape and tenor of American society.[8]

So here is the question: How does one explain the stark contrast between
black and white evangelical political leanings? How can Christian sisters
and brothers of similar Christian DNA differ so sharply on this issue (and
others)? This is not an insignificant difference of opinion. We have black
evangelical friends who cannot comprehend how a Christian could vote Re-

---

"Donald Trump's Racism: The Definitive List," *New York Times*, January 15, 2018, https://www
.nytimes.com/interactive/2018/01/15/opinion/leonhardt-trump-racist.html.

4. For political leanings of Protestant evangelicals and other groups, see "America's
Changing Religious Landscape," Pew Research Center, May 12, 2015, http://www.pewforum
.org/2015/05/12/americas-changing-religious-landscape/, and the interactive database at http://
www.pewforum.org/religious-landscape-study/. According to Pew's study, among "Protestant
evangelicals" (a category including some nonwhite evangelicals), who constitute one-fourth
of the American population, 56 percent lean Republican, 28 percent lean Democrat, and 16
percent lean neither way.

5. "Exit Polls." Similarly, though not as decisive, the Latino community had a 38 percent
margin for the Democratic Party (66 percent Democrat and 28 percent Republican).

6. See "America's Changing Religious Landscape," where one can download the full
report in a PDF. For this and similar statistics on Historically Black Protestant Traditions,
see http://www.pewforum.org/religious-landscape-study/religious-tradition/historically
-black-protestant/.

7. "America's Changing Religious Landscape," 32, of the full report.

8. Mark A. Noll, *God and Race in American Politics: A Short History* (Princeton: Princeton University Press, 2008); Peter Goodwin Heltzel, *Jesus and Justice: Evangelicals, Race, and
American Politics* (New Haven: Yale University Press, 2009).

publican, and we have white evangelical friends who cannot fathom voting Democrat. How can this be? In historical terms, how did this happen?

The central argument of this book is that at the center of the story of American Christianity is the inextricable connection of race relations and Christian unity.[9] This connection provides a coherent theme and question that runs throughout the essays: How have race relations and Christian unity interacted and shaped both the church and the larger American culture? Encounters of white and black people in the Christian community have produced some of the most heinous ideas and actions in history, but they have also incited beautiful acts of love, kindness, and sacrifice for the marginalized. Interactions of black and white Christians have sometimes prompted interracial cooperation in pursuit of justice for all people, but they have also led to the greatest racial divide in American society today—segregated worship services on Sunday morning. The way race relations have proceeded within Christianity often shaped American culture, and vice versa. When pundits and pollsters sought answers for the surprising 2016 Trump victory, race and religion were among the factors under consideration because polls revealed that historical Christian divisions along the lines of race drastically altered one's approach to American culture and politics.[10]

This book is designed especially for undergraduate students wishing to understand how historical realities of race relations and Christianity have formed American history up to the twenty-first century. The book is meant to supplement survey college courses in American history and religion. The book's three sections offer users three entry points into the conversation—five chapters covering major historical periods, four case studies, and three chapters exploring ways forward. While some essays may break new ground, the purpose of the essays is to synthesize and present scholarly consensus and debate for the student, teacher, and lay reader.

9. David W. Wills, "The Central Themes of American Religious History: Pluralism, Puritanism, and the Encounter of Black and White," *Religion and Intellectual Life* 5, no. 1 (September 1987): 30–41, persuasively argues that the encounter of black and white should be added to the central themes of pluralism and Puritanism that have governed American religious historiography.

10. Alec Tyson and Shiva Maniam, "Behind Trump's Victory: Divisions by Race, Gender, Education," Pew Research Center, November 9, 2016, http://www.pewresearch.org/fact-tank/2016/11/09/behind-trumps-victory-divisions-by-race-gender-education/; Gregory A. Smith and Jessica Martínez, "How the Faithful Voted: A Preliminary 2016 Analysis," November 9, 2016, http://www.pewresearch.org/fact-tank/2016/11/09/how-the-faithful-voted-a-preliminary-2016-analysis/.

Race Relations and Christian Unity

"Race" and "religion" are impossibly broad topics, so we have chosen to focus here primarily on Christian unity and black-white race relations in the history of the United States of America.[11] Equally rich histories could be written that engage other eras of North American history, other religions, and the many race relations that shaped history in the Americas. We have chosen the two primary foci of Christian unity and black-white race relations not only because they together have exerted enormous influence in shaping American history and culture,[12] but also because they have been at the center of religious historian Douglas A. Foster's academic and ecclesiastical work, which this book seeks to honor. Whereas the five chapters covering major historical periods take stock of American Christianity broadly, the four case studies and three essays on ways forward focus on Foster's own Christian tradition, the Stone-Campbell Movement, which includes the Churches of Christ, Christian Churches, and Christian Church (Disciples of Christ). The first section will introduce readers to the construct of race and Christian unity, while the Stone-Campbell Movement will be discussed in the last two sections.

"Race" is a social construct or idea; it is not a biological reality.[13] Scholar of race and religion James Bennett explains, "As an idea, race claims people can be sorted into distinct and exclusive groups that are marked by unalter-

11. For an erudite examination of the terms "race" and "religion," see K. Merinda Simmons, "Identifying Race and Religion," in *The Oxford Handbook of Religion and Race in American History*, ed. Kathryn Gin Lum and Paul Harvey (New York: Oxford University Press, 2018), 25–39.

12. Wills, "The Central Themes," 30–41; Judith Weisenfeld, "On Jordan's Stormy Banks: Margins, Center, and Bridges in African American History," in *New Directions in American Religious History*, ed. Harry S. Stout and D. G. Hart (New York: Oxford University Press, 1997), 418–19; Richard Delgado and Jean Stefancic, *Critical Race Theory: An Introduction*, 3rd ed. (New York: New York University Press, 2017), 63-84. Wills argues that the encounter of black and white should be seen as a central theme of American religious history. Weisenfeld notes the ways in which African American experience has occupied both the margins and the center of American religious history, and in both places African Americans' interaction with white Christians has been very important. Nonetheless, the editors do not intend to suggest that the black-white binary is the essential racial binary in American history. With critical race theorists Delgado and Stefancic, we stress the importance of the differential racialization thesis, which holds that "each disfavored group in this country has been racialized in its own individual way and according to the needs of the majority group at particular times in its history" (79).

13. Colin Kidd, *The Forging of Races: Race and Scripture in the Protestant Atlantic World, 1600-2000* (Cambridge: Cambridge University Press, 2006), chap. 1.

able, physical characteristics that are a result of ancestry and genetics (ethnicity, in contrast, describes characteristics attributed to culture rather than biology)."[14] Historian of race George Frederickson highlights "unalterable" biological characteristics as the line of differentiation between ancient tribalism or xenophobia and modern racism: "It is when differences that might otherwise be considered ethnocultural are regarded as innate, indelible, and unchangeable that a racist attitude or ideology can be said to exist."[15] For example, Bennett explains that the protoracism of early colonization often viewed indigenous American and African people as inferior because of their religions, so the inferiority could ostensibly be altered through conversion. Some correlated skin color with the religious inferiority of heathenism. That is, "black" skin was associated with slave status and "heathen" religion in contrast to "white" skin, which represented freedom and Christianity.

On the other hand, in the colonial processes of racialization, skin color of Africans (and Native Americans) eventually shifted from signifying religious inferiority of their "races" to signifying biological inferiority.[16] Early colonists of British North America began developing what eventually became a rigid black-white racialization of American society. As African slaves came to the colonies, colonial legislatures passed laws in the seventeenth and eighteenth centuries not only to legalize slavery but also to establish a racial hierarchy and guard against the mixing of races. The influential (and persuasive to white colonists) equation of skin color with innate, biological, or religious difference proved a stubborn idea to upturn. Indeed, the creation of and struggle against this narrative of difference and inequality are a central theme of this book. The perception that skin color or other inherited physical characteristics represented an unalterable biological inferiority or superiority has been the most prominent racist ideology driving black-white race relations in American history.

As several chapters in the book flesh out, the origins of the idea of race are multifaceted. Although some similarities existed in ancient societies, the modern construct of race had origins in fourteenth- and fifteenth-century western Europe, receiving elaboration and ostensible "scientific" justifica-

14. James B. Bennett, "Race and Racism," in *Encyclopedia of Religion in America*, ed. Charles H. Lippy and Peter W. Williams (Washington, DC: CQ Press, 2010), 4:1825.

15. George M. Frederickson, *Racism: A Short History*, Princeton Classics (Princeton: Princeton University Press, 2002), 5.

16. Bennett, "Race and Racism," 1826. Of course, conversion of slaves and free black individuals to Christianity in the eighteenth and nineteenth centuries complicated the perceived race-religion binary.

tion in the contexts of exploration, colonization, the Enlightenment, and African slavery.[17]

Christians searched the Scriptures for answers about race and for justifications of the institution of slavery. The curse of Canaan (Gen. 9:18-27) proved influential for many slave owners. In that passage, Ham's son Canaan (the grandson of Noah) was cursed into perpetual service to Ham's brothers because he apparently acted inappropriately when he encountered his naked, drunk grandfather, or so they read the Genesis story, which in fact is more ambiguous. Slave owners often added a racial gloss to suggest that the curse (whose mark, according to them, was black skin) made Canaan the progenitor of the African "race," even though Genesis said nothing of the sort. This passage and others persuaded many white Christians to see black slavery as a God-ordained institution that should dominate social relations between white and black people. Both proslavery and white supremacist Christians also rallied to Genesis 4:15, suggesting the murderous mark of Cain was black skin.[18] These political, social, and religious developments together created the contexts for the construction of several types of modern racism that reached their climax in the twentieth century, most famously anti-Semitic racism in Germany and antiblack racism in the American South and South Africa, as well as other forms.[19]

Racism exists when one self-identified racial group excludes or oppresses another group it deems biologically inferior. That is, as Frederickson puts it, racism is "not merely a set of beliefs; it also expresses itself in the practices, institutions, and structures that a sense of deep difference justifies or validates. . . . It either directly sustains or proposes to establish *a racial order*, a permanent group hierarchy that is believed to reflect the laws of nature or the decrees of God."[20] The racist idea of difference is typically coupled with a theory of inequality. In America, the racist ideology that "white" people are biologically superior to "black" people has fueled antiblack racism, which has been at the heart of the nation's 240 years of history.

---

17. Frederickson, *Racism*, chap. 1; Bennett, "Race and Racism," 1825-28; Kidd, *The Forging of Races*, chaps. 2-4.

18. Bennett, "Race and Racism," 1827.

19. Frederickson, *Racism*, chap. 1; Bennett, "Race and Racism," 1826. This is not to say that many other groups were not the target of racist language and actions in the modern world. Natives where European countries colonized were often considered both religiously and biologically inferior to European colonizers, and this racism often materialized in brutal treatment of many groups beyond Semitic or black individuals.

20. Frederickson, *Racism*, 6, 151-70.

As new groups entered the United States, their relative "whiteness" became part of the overall racialized discussion. Being white meant being treated with dignity. Being nonwhite or "black" meant the opposite. These racial categories have been fluid, constantly changing and being renegotiated in light of new concerns.[21] Yet the effects of antiblack racism in America run deep into American culture: American city, state, and federal institutions have usually advantaged the white individual and disadvantaged the black (among other minorities) individual. The structures of Christian churches in America also bear the wounds of racism.

We should emphasize that racism need not be present to sustain and perpetuate a racialized society, a point that Michael Emerson and Christian Smith drive home in their book *Divided by Faith*. They define a "racialized society" as *"a society wherein race matters profoundly for differences in life experiences, life opportunities, and social relationships,"* or *"a society that allocates differential economic, political, social, and even psychological rewards to groups along racial lines; lines that are socially constructed."*[22] The racialization of society and Christianity does not require racism or prejudice as typically defined because practices that reproduce racial division in society "(1) are increasingly covert, (2) are embedded in normal operations of institutions, (3) avoid direct racial terminology, and (4) are invisible to most Whites."[23]

For example, highly educated white people (who are less likely to be racist than poorly educated white people) are more likely than poorly educated white people to live in racially homogenous neighborhoods and send their children to schools that are racially homogenous. This is not necessarily because they are racist; instead, they tend to have the resources to buy houses in quiet neighborhoods with good schools, which typically means living in "whiter" neighborhoods. In this way, neighborhoods continue to be racially segregated even without overt racism.[24] The same processes are

21. Matthew Frye Jacobson, *Whiteness of a Different Color: European Immigrants and the Alchemy of Race* (Cambridge, MA: Harvard University Press, 1999).

22. Michael O. Emerson and Christian Smith, *Divided by Faith: Evangelical Religion and the Problem of Race in America* (Oxford: Oxford University Press, 2000), 7.

23. Emerson and Smith, *Divided by Faith*, 9. They quote these four characteristics from an unpublished study, Eduardo Bonilla-Silva and Amanda Lewis, "The 'New Racism': Toward an Analysis of the U.S. Racial Structure, 1960s–1990s" (1997), 476. See also Bonilla-Silva, *Racism without Racists: Color-Blind Racism and the Persistence of Racial Inequality in America*, 5th ed. (Lanham, MD: Rowman and Littlefield, 2017).

24. Emerson and Smith, *Divided by Faith*, chap. 1.

at work in the segregation of today's Christian congregations. White and black people need not be overtly racist to perpetuate the segregation of the Christian church; rather, they make seemingly reasonable decisions that inadvertently prolong a racialized church. Obviously, racism does exist and does contribute to the racialization of American Christianity. We simply highlight that the racialization of societies or institutions does not happen only by the efforts of traditional racists.

Inextricably intertwined in the American story of race and racism are Christian unity and division. Christians throughout history have seen Christian unity as an important end in itself as well as a means to other ends. Jesus's prayer recorded in John 17 (especially vv. 20–23) established the apostolic grounds, Trinitarian nature, and evangelistic ends of the unity of the church. In the centuries after Jesus's prayer, the ancient churches gathered in "ecumenical" councils, which by definition appealed to the authority of the unified witness of the worldwide church, though they also divided ancient Christianity. As history moved on, and Christians accommodated and shaped Christianity to be meaningful in their different social and intellectual contexts, Christians formally and informally divided. Yet they often also displayed an innate ambivalence about division, resisting it or even asserting a redefined unity, seeking to soften the harsh edges of fragmentation. By the time of America's founding, the Christian church existed in many worldwide traditions that often did not share fellowship with one another. Distinct and even exclusive forms of religious community found fertile soil in an American context that nurtured the ideals of individual expression. Christians pursuing unity throughout American history have constructed unprecedented ecumenical efforts, which always were in tension with divisions along theological and practical lines. Race relations have persistently intensified a desire for unity and, conversely, exacerbated Christian division.

A History of Race and Reconciliation in American Christianity

The history of race relations covered in this book focuses not only on the ways Christians created, enforced, and sometimes opposed racism, but also on how the relationships between black and white people have shaped American Christianity and culture. In the early American republic, white and black individuals related to one another largely within the institution of slavery. Despite a new political atmosphere that stressed the sanctity of the (white, male) individual, the founding documents of America contained only the implicit suggestion that all people (including black people and women) had rights such as owning property and voting. Americans have been working out the implications of all people having inalienable rights ever since the founders put their signatures to the Declaration of Independence. In many cases, race relations, Christian unity and division, and the founding ideals of equality have combined or conflicted to push and prod American cultural and religious developments.

Evangelical revivalism provided one of the earliest challenges to inherited race relations during the early national era. Evangelicals in the revivals from the 1790s to the 1830s, collectively referred to as the Second Great Awakening, interpreted their times through eschatological lenses. They applied the new ideals of political liberty to the gospel, poignantly expressed in Elias Smith's religious periodical the *Herald of Gospel Liberty*. Christians from different denominations united in prayer and even cooperated in missionary endeavors around the world. Baptists, Presbyterians, Methodists, and others started massive revivals together, leading many people to experience new birth conversions during which they often engaged in religious experiences like falling, running, barking, and the jerks. They interpreted these unitive efforts in missions and revival in the context of new political freedoms as clear signs that they lived during the last days, a time when God would pour out his Spirit on his people. Furthermore, evangelical conversions challenged traditional boundaries, as some argued that individuals who experienced new birth became spiritual equals regardless of sex or race. Black people were converted alongside white people, and both "races" exhorted those around them to seek the same cathartic cleansing that made them all one before Christ. Both the American ideals enshrined in the Declaration of Independence and the energetic evangelical awakenings became foundations from which Christians challenged antiblack racism.

Freedom of religion in the new nation created a competitive religious marketplace, but a simultaneous postmillennial optimism fostered a broad ecumenical consensus in the form of a pan-Protestant "benevolent empire" that exerted enormous influence in American culture and transatlantic evangelicalism.[25] Capturing the energy of the Second Great Awakening

25. Charles I. Foster, *An Errand of Mercy: The Evangelical United Front, 1790–1837* (Chapel Hill: University of North Carolina Press, 1960); Roger H. Martin, *Evangelicals United: Ecumenical Stirrings in Pre-Victorian Britain, 1795–1830* (Metuchen, NJ: Scarecrow, 1983). The term "postmillennial" describes the view common in the nineteenth century according to which sweeping human progress would lead to Jesus's return in glory. The betterment of the world

and the activist impulse of evangelicals, an antebellum reform movement sought to Christianize American culture and win the world to Western Christianity.[26] The unitive efforts of optimistic Christians targeted practices they saw as contrary to the gospel. One social ill these benevolent reformers sought to eradicate was slavery; that reform both united the church against slavery and divided the church largely into opposing North-South identities.

Among the most famous individuals to offer prophetic critique of Christianity from within the Christian tradition as well as illustrate the interconnection of race relations and Christian unity was Frederick Douglass. Douglass drew a careful distinction:

> What I have said respecting and against religion, I mean strictly to apply to the *slaveholding religion* of this land, and with no possible reference to Christianity proper; for, between the Christianity of this land, and the Christianity of Christ, I recognize the widest, possible difference—so wide, that to receive the one as good, pure, and holy, is of necessity to reject the other as bad, corrupt, and wicked. To be the friend of the one, is of necessity to be the enemy of the other. I love the pure, peaceable, and impartial Christianity of Christ: I therefore hate the corrupt, slaveholding, women-whipping, cradle-plundering, partial and hypocritical Christianity of this land.[27]

Douglass and many of his contemporaries used Christianity to critique the racist institution of slavery, and in doing so, they drove a sharp wedge between Christians who supported slavery and Christians who opposed it. Although they led the abolition movement and struggle for racial equality, the pursuit of justice led to the division of the churches. In American churches, on the one hand, there has been no greater challenge to Christian unity than the struggle with antiblack racism. On the other hand, there has been no greater catalyst of interracial effort for justice against racism.

---

seemed to such thinkers to anticipate the greater glory that God would bring to a perfected creation.

26. Donald G. Mathews, "The Second Great Awakening as an Organizing Process, 1780–1830: An Hypothesis," *American Quarterly* 21, no. 1 (1969): 23–43; William R. Hutchison, *Errand to the World: American Protestant Thought and Foreign Missions* (Chicago: University of Chicago Press, 1987).

27. *Narrative of the Life of Frederick Douglass, an American Slave. Written by Himself* (Boston: Anti-Slavery Office, 1845), 118, http://docsouth.unc.edu/neh/douglass/menu.html.

Despite the heroic efforts of individuals like Douglass, as Christians engaged a society that defined white and black people as different and unequal, the Christian church often accommodated or helped construct the racialized society emerging in America. In the years leading up to the Civil War, Christians largely separated into sectional constituencies—the South invoking the Bible to support slavery, and the North, to oppose it. As historian Mark Noll has argued, the Civil War was a theological crisis.[28] Denominations formally and informally divided over the issue of slavery in the 1840s and 1850s, foreshadowing the nation's bloody conflict of the 1860s.[29]

As the Civil War developed into the eras of Reconstruction and Jim Crow segregation, most African American Christians sought independence from white denominations by founding independent African American congregations and denominations.[30] In the American South, many white Christians combined their faith with Southern culture to form "Lost Cause" civil religion,[31] a response to the spiritual and psychological need among Southerners to reaffirm their identity after defeat in the Civil War. The hopes of political autonomy were lost, but the South fought for their cultural identity. The Lost Cause identified the Confederate cause as God's cause, Southern people as God's people, and the Southern way of life as virtuous and ideal. The South had lost the war not because of the impropriety of slavery or their way of life, but because God was chastening them for being a sinful people; if they responded faithfully, the South might rise again. The Lost Cause retained the thoroughgoing racism of previous American history, and therefore its advocates sought to minimize freedoms for black people and keep them as near to bondage as possible.[32] In this atmosphere, and with continued racism also in the North, black

28. Mark A. Noll, *The Civil War as a Theological Crisis* (Chapel Hill: University of North Carolina Press, 2006).

29. See excerpts illustrating these divisions among the Baptists, Methodists, and Presbyterians in Edwin S. Gaustad and Mark A. Noll, eds., *A Documentary History of Religion in America Since 1877*, 3rd ed. (Grand Rapids: Eerdmans, 2003), 1:489–500.

30. Paul Harvey, *Through the Storm, through the Night: A History of African American Christianity* (Lanham, MD: Rowman and Littlefield, 2011), chaps. 4–5; Lawrence H. Mamiya, "African American Religion: From the Civil War to Civil Rights," in Lippy and Williams, *Encyclopedia of Religion in America*, 1:33–42.

31. For an illustration of this powerful amalgamation, see Thomas Nast, "The Union as It Was," *Harper's Weekly* 18, no. 930 (October 24, 1874): 878, https://www.loc.gov/item/2001696840.

32. Charles Reagan Wilson, *Baptized in Blood: The Religion of the Lost Cause, 1865–1920*, 2nd ed. (Athens: University of Georgia Press, 2009).

Christians in the North and South usually left white denominations and started their own.

Since this time, a "color line" has divided most Christians even in the same denominational families. Martin Luther King Jr. highlighted this reality in 1960: "It is one of the tragedies of our nation, one of the shameful tragedies, that eleven o'clock on Sunday morning is one of the most segregated hours, if not the most segregated hours [sic], in Christian America."[33] Although separation into different communities is not necessarily anti-Christian, the stark division of the Christian church along racial lines continues to be a pressing question for Christians in the twenty-first century.[34]

The civil rights era and the varied responses to it have largely shaped race relations and diverging religious and political alignments up to the present. While King made successful overtures to the Christian church and the American public to unite in their pursuit of civil rights for black people in the 1950s and 1960s, white evangelical leader Bob Jones used Acts 17:26–27 (i.e., God determined the boundaries of the nations' dwelling places) to argue that God planned and desired racial segregation so that each race could fulfill its God-ordained purpose. He said advocates for desegregation were satanic forces working against God's plans. Seeking to preserve the whites-only enrollment at his university (many Christian universities were whites-only at that time), Jones used Christian Scripture to justify segregation.[35] Historian Randall Balmer has demonstrated that the issue of segregation (rather than abortion) was the primary catalyst for the rise of the Religious Right.[36] The Religious

33. Martin Luther King Jr., "Interview on 'Meet the Press' (April 17, 1960)," in *The Papers of Martin Luther King, Jr.*, vol. 5, *Threshold of a New Decade, January 1959–December 1960* (Berkeley: University of California Press, 2005), 5:435, https://kinginstitute.stanford.edu/king-papers/documents/interview-meet-press.

34. For explorations of this issue and potential responses, see Emerson and Smith, *Divided by Faith*; Curtiss Paul DeYoung et al., *United by Faith: The Multiracial Congregation as an Answer to the Problem of Race* (Oxford: Oxford University Press, 2003).

35. Both Taylor and Strickland provide a transcript of the sermon: Justin Taylor, "Is Segregation Scriptural? A Radio Address from Bob Jones on Easter of 1960," *The Gospel Coalition*, July 26, 2016, https://blogs.thegospelcoalition.org/evangelical-history/2016/07/26/is-segregation-scriptural-a-radio-address-from-bob-jones-on-easter-of-1960/; Nathanael Strickland, "Is Segregation Scriptural?" *Faith and Heritage*, August 28, 2013, http://faithandheritage.com/2013/08/is-segregation-scriptural/; Paul A. Freund, "The Supreme Court, 1973 Term," *Harvard Law Review* 88, no. 1 (1974): 220–21.

36. Randall Balmer, "The Real Origins of the Religious Right," *Politico*, May 27, 2014, http://politi.co/1tn6Viz; Randall Balmer, *The Making of Evangelicalism: From Revivalism to Politics and Beyond* (Waco: Baylor University Press, 2010), chap. 4.

Right and its numerous sister institutions have captivated white evangelical Christians since the late 1970s, and therefore, they have been instrumental in shaping the current black-white evangelical dichotomy in politics.

It is already clear that twenty-first-century American culture will continue to be shaped by the long history of the relationship of race relations and Christian unity. Among the best-known events culminated in March 2008 when presidential hopeful Barack Obama had to respond to his pastor's 2003 words, "God damn America." Jeremiah Wright, pastor at Trinity United Church of Christ in Chicago, where the Obamas attended, had spoken from the pulpit that God would damn America for her sins of injustice, for killing her citizens, and for treating her citizens as less than human beings. The "righteous jeremiad," as historian Paul Harvey calls Wright's words, was a common theme in the African American Christian experience and in the Bible, but the racial divide in the churches meant that most white people had no idea what Wright's comment meant in the black Christian vernacular. Therefore, Obama found himself explaining the black Christian tradition to the public as he sought to win the Democratic nomination over Hillary Rodham Clinton. In this moment, African American prophetic protest steeped in Christian tradition became a major issue in the 2008 presidential race.[37] Whereas Wright utilized the jeremiad, Obama in his first inaugural address appealed to what Harvey calls "the gospel of hope," another central theme in the black Christian tradition: "Because we have tasted the bitter swill of civil war and segregation, and emerged from that dark chapter stronger and more united, we cannot help but believe that the old hatreds shall someday pass; that the lines of tribe shall soon dissolve; that as the world grows smaller, our common humanity shall reveal itself; and that America must play its role in ushering in a new era of peace."[38]

Obama's subsequent eight-year presidency certainly ushered in a new era, but the black-white binary constructed in America's history continued to shape the experiences of many Americans. Rather than a "postracial" America, the eight years under the first black president were a period of extraordinary racial tension in which Christians often took sides based on their political leaning, the color of their skin, or both (and the two factors often correlated).

37. For a survey of the event and primary sources of Wright and Obama, see Harvey, *Through the Storm*, 133–35, 180–82.

38. "President Barack Obama's Inaugural Address," The White House, January 21, 2009, https://obamawhitehouse.archives.gov/blog/2009/01/21/president-barack-obamas-inaugural-address; Harvey, *Through the Storm*, 135.

In 2017, when the United States transitioned from its first black president to Donald J. Trump, who made inflammatory racial remarks during his campaign for the presidency, Americans braced for a seemingly difficult period for race relations. It is our hope that this book provides a rich context from which Christians today might engage the issues of race relations and Christian unity. Perhaps it is again time for Christians to provide an example of what reconciliation and unity might look like in American culture by modeling it in their churches. At a time when American society seems at an impasse, perhaps Christians will find a way to work for Christian unity among the diverse "races" in their neighborhoods. As the world grows smaller, will Christians choose to highlight national and "racial" tribal lines to construct an "us-them" posture of fear and defense, or will Christians lead efforts to help American culture find a common humanity upon which not only Christians in local congregations but all people everywhere unite for the common good? We hope this book illuminates our Christian and national past to guide us into a future that is less divided and more united.

Developing the Case

To make that illumination possible, the contributors to this book consider the issues from several angles. The first section provides readers with an overview of race and Christian unity or division in major eras of American history. First, James L. Gorman studies evangelical revivalism and race relations in the early years of the American republic, showing that some of the basic patterns of racial division and resistance to it date to the period before and just after independence from Great Britain. Although for a brief time it appeared as if evangelicals would lead an emancipation movement in the late eighteenth century, evangelicals proved incapable of resisting powerful pro-slavery groups that opposed emancipation in the early nineteenth century. Then Wes Crawford picks up the story for the antebellum and immediate post-Civil War eras, demonstrating the complex story of the construction of race and subsequent racial division in Christianity. Crawford's essay offers an introductory examination of perhaps the most formative years in American history for setting the trajectory of the impact of race relations on Christian unity and division.

Christopher R. Hutson next explores the complex, and often disturbing, relationship between religion and lynching during the era of Jim Crow at the end of the nineteenth and beginning of the twentieth century. Hutson's chapter offers important analysis of lynching culture and Christian use of the Bible to support it. Kathy Pulley provides an accessible introduction to both the civil rights movement and the Religious Right, with insightful analysis of opportunities both movements had to pursue interracial unity. Pulley shows convincingly that the rise of the Religious Right in the mid- to late twentieth century, with all its attendant political ramifications, depended greatly on preexisting racial attitudes and racialized practices. To finish mapping the historical trail, Joel A. Brown surveys the state of race and Christianity in America today. Brown's incisive chapter delineates ways white Christians have often been complicit in the broader white American resistance to black civil rights, even while these white Christians typically believe themselves not to be racist.

One profitable angle into the study of race relations and Christian unity consists of singling out Christian traditions for examination. The four case studies in the book's second section utilize this approach by focusing on the Stone-Campbell Movement (SCM), which serves as an interesting example because it began as a movement focused on Christian unity. The founders of the SCM saw Christian unity as a vital and attainable aim, proposing that if Christians took only the clear teachings of the New Testament as a basis for Christian fellowship, Christian unity would be forthcoming.[39] Although SCM adherents succeeded in their advocacy for Christian unity in many ways, they also failed, most visibly (and ironically) in their division into multiple denominations that themselves are mostly racially segregated.

Drawing from ideas and practices of the transatlantic evangelical missionary movement, political and philosophical currents emphasizing the innate potential of all people (regardless of family or education), and the democratic revolutions, the SCM arose on the US frontier in the early national era (1780s to 1810s) of American history. Barton Stone led the "Christians" in Kentucky and surrounding states, whereas Thomas Campbell and his son Alexander led a group of "Reformers" in Pennsylvania. Although Stone Christians and Campbell Reformers were distinct, many in each group found enough in common to merge some of their congregations and unite for other endeavors by the 1830s.[40]

---

39. Focus on the SCM for the case studies is also fitting because Douglas Foster, whom this book honors, has been a lifelong adherent of the SCM and an advocate for Christian and interracial unity.

40. D. Newell Williams, Douglas A. Foster, and Paul M. Blowers, *The Stone-Campbell Movement: A Global History* (Saint Louis: Chalice, 2013), 9–29; James L. Gorman, *Among the*

The commonalities between Christians and Reformers were rooted in their proposal to the Christian world, which began with the firm conviction that denominational divisions were evil because they precluded the unity Christ prayed for in John 17 and therefore obstructed Christ's plan for conversion of the world (i.e., Christian unity would lead the world to believe). To heal this division and unite the church, SCM leaders proposed using the New Testament as the only rule for faith and practice of the church (rather than divisive creeds). Once Christians jettisoned their creeds and confessions as terms of fellowship, Christians would begin to unite on the ostensibly clear teachings of the New Testament. As they examined the Bible, SCM leaders came to agree on some common features of what they believed to be the New Testament church: a plan of salvation rooted in an individual's choice to obey the testimony of the gospel (which culminated in believer's baptism by immersion for the forgiveness of sins),[41] weekly practice of the Lord's Supper, congregational polity (or church government), rejection of creeds, and a belief that using proper, "commonsense" rules to interpret the Bible would lead all people to the same conclusions about the clear (or "express") teachings of Scripture.

Although enough Americans found the SCM's proposal persuasive to make it the fifth-largest Protestant denomination in the United States by 1900, it simultaneously became increasingly difficult for SCM members to agree on the purportedly clear teachings of the New Testament church, which resulted in two major divisions in what had started as a unity movement.[42] On the one hand, in response to the sharp divisions thrown into focus by the Civil War, SCM leaders insisted that the church must not divide because of its essential unity in Christ. The notion that SCM churches had remained united after the Civil War, when so many Christian denominations had formally divided, became a point of pride in the movement's self-understanding. On the other hand, SCM churches had not remained as unaffected by the powerful forces of disunity as they supposed.[43] Complex

---

Early Evangelicals: Transatlantic Origins of the Stone-Campbell Movement (Abilene, TX: Abilene Christian University Press, 2017).

41. SCM leaders pointed to Acts 2:38, in which Peter instructed his hearers: "Repent, and be baptized every one of you in the name of Jesus Christ so that your sins may be forgiven; and you will receive the gift of the Holy Spirit" (NRSV).

42. Edwin Scott Gaustad and Philip L. Barlow, eds., *New Historical Atlas of Religion in America*, 3rd ed. (New York: Oxford University Press, 2001), 374.

43. See Douglas A. Foster, "The Effect of the Civil War on the Stone-Campbell Movement," *Stone-Campbell Journal* 20, no. 1 (Spring 2017): 5-16.

divisions arose that were rooted in America's sectional conflict, post-Civil War development, and various social and theological developments in the twentieth century. After less than two hundred years of existence, the SCM unity movement divided into three distinct streams. The largely southern group became known as the Churches of Christ, easily identified by their a cappella congregational singing. In the North, the more conservative group became known as "independents," or Christian Churches/Churches of Christ (because some congregations are called Church of Christ and others Christian Church), and the theologically progressive group as the Christian Church (Disciples of Christ). Although these groups retained their regional majorities, each has congregations today throughout the United States and the world. Despite their agreement on the ideal of unity, the SCM reflected the broader American Christian trend of dividing at times of social (e.g., Civil War) and theological (e.g., liberalism) change.[44]

SCM history also illuminates and corroborates the broader American Christian story of racism and reconciliation through interracial unity. For the most part, white SCM members did not oppose slavery until it became politically acceptable to do so. But there were important exceptions. Also, with important exceptions, white SCM members generally continued to exhibit racism after the abolishment of slavery, and, also with major exceptions, black SCM members and institutions sought independence from white SCM members and institutions because of the racism black people experienced when working with whites. For the most part, SCM members were divided about the propriety of participating in the civil rights movement.

Authors of the four case studies in the book's second section help readers learn from both the tragic and the encouraging stories of the SCM's history of race and Christian unity, revealing the often subtle ways in which race and religion interact. Loretta Hunnicutt considers how Churches of Christ understood white women and women of color at the intersection of race, gender, and Christian unity. While some aspects of the problems she describes are unique to these Restorationist churches, most elements play out much more widely. Similarly, Lawrence A. Q. Burnley describes how the Disciples of Christ related to the twentieth-century civil rights movement, which is a story of both courage and failure. Edward J. Robinson takes a very broad view as he considers attempts at racial reconciliation during the era of Jim Crow and the subsequent civil rights movement, demonstrating that

---

44. For narratives of these divisions, see Williams, Foster, and Blowers, *The Stone-Campbell Movement*, chaps. 2 and 5.

oppression could also stimulate courageous efforts at redemption. Robinson's case study reveals the complexity involved in interracial cooperation through his analysis of one white and one black individual whose valiant and countercultural work together provides an inspiring example of interracial unity even as it reveals the influence of America's racial history on even the most well-intended Christians. And finally, D. Newell Williams and Kamilah Hall Sharp find twelve ways the Disciples of Christ have combated racism before providing results from a recent survey of Disciples of Christ leaders. The survey results reveal that, despite Disciples' efforts to combat racism and the election of an African American woman as their general minister and president on July 9, 2017, minoritized individuals continue to experience racism in the churches.

In the book's third section, three authors offer proposals for the future. Each writes from deep personal experience and commitment, seeking to bring an understanding of the gospel to bear on the challenges of race and religion. From different points of view, each calls all of us to a new way of being. Together they argue that while we must know the past in order to understand the present, we need not be enslaved to it; critical examination can lead to liberation for both the oppressed and the oppressor. Richard T. Hughes diagnoses the history of racial disunity in SCM churches as the result of the SCM's legacy of faulty understandings of salvation, and calls for a deliberate reappropriation of the gospel of grace as its remedy. Tanya Smith Brice reflects on key events from the history of race relations in Churches of Christ, suggesting that the way forward entails not only learning from the past but may sometimes include revisiting it and seeking to fulfill its promises. Jerry Taylor analyzes the career of Douglas A. Foster, distinguished scholar and churchman dedicated to racial reconciliation, commending him to readers as a concrete model of professional and personal practice.

Each of the authors has contributed to this volume to honor Douglas A. Foster for his academic and ecclesial work for Christian and interracial unity.

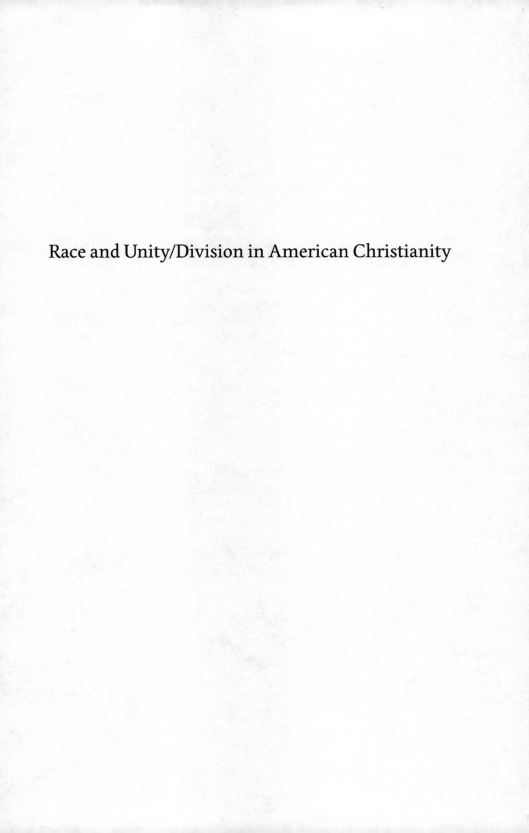

Race and Unity/Division in American Christianity

Evangelical Revivalism and Race Relations in the Early National Era

JAMES L. GORMAN

Barton Stone filed papers to free his slaves in 1801 because he believed God detested slavery and it would be abolished due to the revivals of his day. A minister of two frontier Presbyterian congregations in central Kentucky, Stone had encountered a type of slavery near Charleston, South Carolina, in 1797 that he identified as the "exciting cause of my abandonment of slavery." "My soul sickened," he recounted forty years later, "at the sight of slavery in more horrid forms than I had ever seen it before; poor negroes! some chained to their work—some wearing iron collars—all half naked, and followed and driven by the merciless lash of a gentleman overseer—distress appeared scowling in every face."[1] A few years after that experience, Stone filed a deed of manumission for his two slaves, Ned and Lucy, whom he had received from his mother at her death. Stone later recalled, "I had emancipated my slaves from a sense of right, choosing poverty with a good conscience, in preference to all the treasures of the world." But Stone acknowledged more at work than his personal moral choice; the revival had become an active emancipator: "This revival cut the bonds of many poor slaves."[2] Some evangelicals believed that the goal of Christian unity in the revivals and the renunciation of slavery were harbingers of the imminent millennium and the end of slavery.[3] For many evangelicals, the revivals were a sign of the last days that made urgent the abolition of slavery and conversion of enslaved people.

African Americans did not become Christians in substantial numbers until the awakenings of the mid-eighteenth and especially the early nine-

---

1. *The Biography of Eld. Barton Warren Stone, Written by Himself; with Additions and Reflections*, ed. John Rogers (Cincinnati: J. A. & U. P. James, 1847), 27–28.

2. *The Biography of Eld. Barton Warren Stone*, 44.

3. D. Newell Williams, *Barton Stone: A Spiritual Biography* (Saint Louis: Chalice, 2000), 76–77.

teenth century, and both the spatial arrangements and the message of revivals shaped black-white race relations in American Christianity.[4] Amid revolutionary ideology that suggested that all people had unalienable rights to life, liberty, and happiness, evangelical revivals in the early national era of American history (1780s–1810s) gathered black and white people together for shared divine encounters where revivalists preached an egalitarian message of freedom from spiritual bondage. As historian Peter Heltzel avers, "Revivals were sites for increased spiritual interaction between blacks and whites, functioning as new space for racial integration where all were equal at the altar of God. . . . Revivals provided African Americans with both a message of equality before God and a physical space where they were free to express themselves through singing, shaking, running, dancing, chanting, and shouting."[5] Historian Paul Harvey argues that the awakenings of the eighteenth and nineteenth centuries "effectively implanted the seeds of a biracial culture of popular evangelicalism into the ground of American religious expression."[6]

This chapter interacts with scholarship and primary sources to explore several questions and issues related to evangelical revivalism and race relations in the early national era. After describing evangelical revivalism and the political context, the chapter explores major questions historians have engaged:[7] What was the nature of evangelical opposition to slavery and why did it change by 1810? Why did enslaved African Americans critically appropriate evangelicalism at that time, and in what ways did they contribute to the construction of it? What continuity existed between evangelical revivalism and traditional African religions? How did enslaved people experience evangelical Christianity in general and revivalism in particular, and in what ways did these religious, cultural, and racial exchanges shape race relations in American Christianity? How did those exchanges lead to

4. Paul Harvey, *Through the Storm, through the Night: A History of African American Christianity* (Lanham, MD: Rowman and Littlefield, 2011), chap. 2; Albert J. Raboteau, "African-Americans, Exodus, and the American Israel," in *African-American Christianity: Essays in History*, ed. Paul E. Johnson (Berkeley: University of California Press, 1994), 4.

5. Peter Goodwin Heltzel, *Jesus and Justice: Evangelicals, Race, and American Politics* (New Haven: Yale University Press, 2009), 19.

6. Paul Harvey, *Christianity and Race in the American South: A History*, Chicago History of American Religion (Chicago: University of Chicago Press, 2016), 39.

7. For an overview of central historical questions and works, see Judith Weisenfeld, "On Jordan's Stormy Banks: Margins, Center, and Bridges in African American History," in *New Directions in American Religious History*, ed. Harry S. Stout and D. G. Hart (New York: Oxford University Press, 1997), 417–44.

unity or division in the church? Although evangelical revivalists of the era did at times break down some barriers—between free and slave, poor and rich, male and female, black and white, Baptist and Methodist—due to the egalitarian and democratic effects of conversion (i.e., spiritual equality no matter the sex, race, or denomination), and though some did advocate for enslaved people, they failed to create a lasting biracial unity in their Christian tradition.

Revivalist and Revolutionary Contexts

The "evangelical" movement arose in the eighteenth century, especially in the heat of the Great Awakening revivals of the middle of the century.[8] Evangelicals located on both sides of the Atlantic Ocean de-emphasized denominational creeds and confessions, pointing instead to the new birth conversion experience as the essential marker of Christian identity.[9] Therefore, evangelicals conducted revivals primarily to lead people to conversion. Revivals ostensibly created space for what evangelicals called the "outpouring of God's Spirit," manifested primarily in God's work of "new birth" conversion—a moment when God changed a person's corrupt nature and saved the person from eternity in hell.[10] This new birth had potentially subversive ends, as some evangelicals used its egalitarian message of spiritual equality to challenge or momentarily transcend gender, racial, and other social constructs and mores. That certainly became the case for many enslaved people who experienced conversion.

Revivals occurred between what historians call the Great Awakening that flourished in the 1740s and the Second Great Awakening of the early nineteenth century; therefore, historians debate when the Great Awakening stopped, when the Second Great Awakening began, and whether the labels

8. The best treatment of the Great Awakening is Thomas S. Kidd, *The Great Awakening: The Roots of Evangelical Christianity in Colonial America* (New Haven: Yale University Press, 2007).

9. For an introduction to the origins and definition of evangelicalism, see Mark Hutchinson and John Wolffe, *A Short History of Global Evangelicalism* (Cambridge: Cambridge University Press, 2012), chap. 1; David W. Bebbington, *Evangelicalism in Modern Britain: A History from the 1730s to the 1980s* (London: Routledge, 1989), 1–19.

10. Mechal Sobel, *Trabelin' On: The Slave Journey to an Afro-Baptist Faith*, Contributions in Afro-American and African Studies 36 (Westport, CT: Greenwood Press, 1979; Princeton: Princeton University Press, 1988), 97.

are even helpful.[11] Nonetheless, most historians describe the Second Great Awakening as a nationwide series of revivals from the 1790s to the 1830s with several geographic centers—the Great Revival in the West (1797-1805), New England revivals (1790s-1800s), and New York revivals (1820s-1830s).[12] The Great Revival in the West became known for its multiple-day revivals sparked especially by Presbyterian sacramental occasions, Methodist camp meetings, and Methodist quarterly meetings. These revivals, which were often interdenominational (Baptists, Methodists, and Presbyterians) and biracial, included religious exercises such as falling, barking, running, dancing, laughing, singing, and jerking.[13]

Revivals under consideration in this chapter occurred in the wake of the Revolutionary War and the formation of the new nation's government, which led to heightened rhetoric of liberty, assumed "unalienable rights" of all people, and a thoroughgoing democratization of American society. These ideas and practices of freedom, equality, common sense, natural rights, popular sovereignty, and religious liberty drastically shaped Christianity, even as Christianity informed many of these sociopolitical ideals, as illustrated in Nathan Hatch's classic study *The Democratization of American Christianity*.[14] Evangelical revivals often became sites where political and religious egalitarianism combined to forge powerful challenges to hierarchies and assumptions about children, women, and black people.

Evangelical Opposition to Slavery

Although antislavery sentiment began on both sides of the Atlantic in the middle of the eighteenth century, the American Revolution, with assertions that all individuals had unalienable rights, unintentionally intensified the public debate about slavery and abolition in America. The idea that "all men are created equal" and are imbued with natural rights was difficult to

11. Kidd, *The Great Awakening*, xviii-xix.

12. Bret E. Carroll, *The Routledge Historical Atlas of Religion in America* (New York: Routledge, 2000), 62-63; Kidd, *The Great Awakening*, xix.

13. For overviews of the exercises and the Great Revival in the West, see *The Biography of Eld. Barton Warren Stone*, 39-42; John B. Boles, *The Great Revival: Beginnings of the Bible Belt* (Lexington: University Press of Kentucky, 1996); Paul Keith Conkin, *Cane Ridge: America's Pentecost*, Curti Lectures (Madison: University of Wisconsin Press, 1990).

14. Nathan O. Hatch, *The Democratization of American Christianity* (New Haven: Yale University Press, 1989).

reconcile with involuntary lifetime slavery, unless black people could be construed as less than human. That is one reason all northern states had either abolished slavery or set in place laws for gradual emancipation by 1804. In the South, however, economic interests and whites' racial anxieties precluded abolition. The two sections of the country justified their positions with differing political, social, racial, and theological arguments, setting the stage for the American Civil War (1861-1865). From colonial times to the eve of the Civil War, some evangelicals were leaders in the antislavery cause.[15]

An important factor contributing to the conversion of African Americans to evangelical Christianity in the early national era was evangelical opposition to slavery, even if evangelicals were always divided on the issue. John Wesley and the Methodists led evangelical opposition to slavery. Wesley unequivocally condemned slavery in *Thoughts upon Slavery* (1774): slavery could not be reconciled with justice, mercy, or Christianity, and God would atone for the blood of the slaves with the blood of traders and owners.[16] Bishops Francis Asbury and Thomas Coke advanced an antislavery platform in America, though proslavery Methodists persistently rejected it. The 1780 Baltimore Methodist conference declared slavery "contrary to the laws of God, man, and nature, and hurtful to society" and encouraged all Methodists to free their slaves.[17] The 1784 conference even voted to expel those who bought or held slaves if they had been previously warned and if they lived where emancipation was legal. This rule created a firestorm among Methodists until another Baltimore conference in 1785 suspended it. Still, in Maryland between 1783 and 1799, for one example, 1,800 slaves were freed in predominately Methodist territory. And Methodist ministers in the South, such as Virginian James O'Kelly in 1789, continued to condemn slavery, calling slave overseers "devils incarnate."[18]

15. George M. Frederickson, *Racism: A Short History*, Princeton Classics (Princeton: Princeton University Press, 2002), 64-65; Mark A. Noll, *In the Beginning Was the Word: The Bible in American Public Life, 1492-1783* (Oxford: Oxford University Press, 2016), 315-21; Kenneth Morgan, *Slavery and the British Empire: From Africa to America* (Oxford: Oxford University Press, 2007), chap. 7; David Brion Davis, *The Problem of Slavery in the Age of Revolution, 1770-1823* (Ithaca: Cornell University Press, 1975).

16. John Wesley, *Thoughts upon Slavery* (Philadelphia: Joseph Crukshank, 1774), 55-57.

17. American Methodist statements on slavery from this era are compiled in the appendix in Donald G. Mathews, *Slavery and Methodism: A Chapter in American Morality, 1780-1845* (Princeton: Princeton University Press, 1965), 293-303. The quote here is from 295.

18. James O'Kelly, *Essay on Negro Slavery* (Philadelphia: Prichard Hall, 1789), 11, http://digitalcommons.acu.edu/crs_books/77; Mathews, *Slavery and Methodism*, 3-18, 295-98; Morgan, *Slavery and the British Empire*, 151-52; John B. Boles, introduction to *Masters and Slaves*

In 1800, the Methodist General Conference unequivocally condemned the hypocrisy of proclaiming liberty of all people and owning slaves in their broadside "Address of the General Conference" (1800), which bore the signatures of bishops Coke, Asbury, and Richard Whatcoat. "The Address" "lamented the great national evil of NEGRO-SLAVERY" because it was "repugnant to the unalienable rights of mankind, and to the very essence of civil liberty, but more especially to the spirit of the Christian religion." Methodist leadership attempted to hasten the "universal extirpation of this crying sin" by leveraging Methodist social capital to change US laws.[19] "The Address" infuriated slaveholders, who found new ways to challenge leaders: many stopped letting their slaves attend meetings. In South Carolina in early 1801, for example, Asbury wrote that the "rich among the people never thought us worthy to preach to them: they did indeed give their slaves liberty to hear and join our Church; but now it appears the poor Africans will no longer have this indulgence."[20] In the wake of this opposition, the Methodists softened their emancipationist voice.

Baptist churches and associations in Virginia, Kentucky, New York, Indiana, Illinois, and Ohio also publicly opposed slavery, though Baptist opposition usually followed. John Leland, a leading Baptist pastor in Virginia, produced an antislavery resolution for the Baptist General Committee in Virginia in 1790, resolving that slavery was a "violent deprivation of the rights of nature, and inconsistent with a republican government." The resolution encouraged members to use "every legal measure, to extirpate this horrid evil from the land, and pray Almighty God, that our Honourable Legislature may have it in their power, to proclaim the general Jubilee."[21] Such antislavery movements sometimes led people to free their slaves: Virginian Robert Carter III freed more than 450 slaves beginning in 1791, though his action was not typical of elite evangelicals. Leading Baptists Shubal Stearns and El-

---

in the House of the Lord: Race and Religion in the American South, 1740–1870, ed. John B. Boles (Lexington: University Press of Kentucky, 1988), 8.

19. General Conference of the Methodist Episcopal Church, "The Address of the General Conference of the Methodist Episcopal Church to All Their Brethren and Friends in the United States" (General Conference of the Methodist Episcopal Church, 1800), https://www.loc.gov /item/rbpe.02900100.

20. The Journal of the Rev. Francis Asbury, Bishop of the Methodist Episcopal Church (New York: Lane & Scott, 1852), 3:7.

21. Baptist General Committee (Virginia), Minutes of the Baptist General Committee, at their yearly meeting, held in the city of Richmond, May 8th, 1790, 7. Digital facsimile available through Early American Imprints (series 1, no. 45820).

hanan Winchester carried Baptist antislavery revivalism to slaves and poor whites in the South, accelerating the Christianization of enslaved people. In England, Baptist leader William Carey argued that missions were becoming successful in the 1790s in part because of an increase in efforts to "abolish the inhuman Slave-Trade."[22] Like Methodists, however, some Baptists immediately opposed resolutions like the one in 1790. In fact, after much debate, the General Committee in Virginia refused to discuss slavery in 1793 because it claimed such a discussion belonged to the legislative body.[23]

Congregationalist evangelicals also worked against slavery in this period, and none were more vocal than Jonathan Edwards's student, Samuel Hopkins. In 1776, he published an antislavery work that argued that slavery was "contrary to the whole tenor of divine revelation" and urged Americans to free their slaves.[24] In a 1793 sermon to the Providence Society for Abolishing the Slave Trade, he said slavery was an instrument of Satan and an obstacle to Christ's command to spread the gospel. Supporters of slavery were the "emissaries of satan." Slavery would be abolished anywhere the gospel was preached and obeyed. Hopkins advocated for colonization (sending freed black people to black colonies in Africa) because he believed white racism so permeated the United States that black people would never be treated equally.[25]

Presbyterian leaders also opposed slavery. Leading Kentucky Presbyterian David Rice published a 1792 speech in which he argued that involuntary slavery was unjust.[26] As noted in the introduction, Stone's antislavery views led him to free his slaves in 1801. And Stone's Cane Ridge congregation

22. William Carey, *An Enquiry into the Obligations of Christians, to Use Means for the Conversion of the Heathens* (Leicester, UK: Printed and Sold by Ann Ireland, 1792), 79.

23. Monica Najar, *Evangelizing the South: A Social History of Church and State in Early America*, Religion in America (New York: Oxford University Press, 2008), 145–48; Harvey, *Christianity and Race*, 53; Kidd, *The Great Awakening*, 250; Sylvia R. Frey and Betty Wood, *Come Shouting to Zion: African American Protestantism in the American South and British Caribbean to 1830* (Chapel Hill: University of North Carolina Press, 1998), 100–103.

24. Samuel Hopkins, *A Dialogue concerning The Slavery of the Africans; Shewing It to Be the Duty and Interest of the American Colonies to Emancipate All Their African Slaves* (Norwich, CT: Judah P. Spooner, 1776), 18.

25. Samuel Hopkins, *A Discourse upon the Slave-Trade, and the Slavery of the Africans* (Providence: J. Carter, 1793), 11, 21–22, appendix; Noll, *In the Beginning*, 317–18; James L. Gorman, *Among the Early Evangelicals: Transatlantic Origins of the Stone-Campbell Movement* (Abilene, TX: Abilene Christian University Press, 2017), 69–71.

26. David Rice, *Slavery Inconsistent with Justice and Good Policy* (Philadelphia: Parry Hall, 1792).

actively pursued the antislavery cause: an elder at Cane Ridge, David Purviance, was elected to the Kentucky legislature as an antislavery representative in the late 1790s; in 1800, Stone presented a resolution on behalf of his Cane Ridge and Concord congregations to the West Lexington Presbytery stating that slavery was a moral evil, and those who continued the practice should be removed from the church; and emancipations in Bourbon County, led by members of the Cane Ridge congregation, increased during the Great Revival in the West. Some Presbyterian revivalists, such as Rice, believed that the goal of Christian unity in the revivals and the renunciation of slavery were harbingers of the imminent millennium. Commenting on the Great Revival in the West, Paul Conkin wrote that "antislavery sentiment became almost synonymous with the revival."[27]

Although evangelicals were not ultimately successful in upending the institution of slavery, public opposition to slavery in the wake of the American Revolution, along with numerous features of evangelical revivalism explored below, made evangelicalism the most attractive new religious home for free and enslaved African Americans in the nation's early history.

Evangelical Revivalism and Race Relations

The revivals were the central occasions for black and white interaction, expression, and biracial construction of religious meaning. Although revivals were often segregated, black and white people brought unique backgrounds to the revivals, and both shaped the evangelicalism that emerged.[28] Scholars debate the extent of continuity between West African religious practices and evangelical revival practices, but since the work of Albert Raboteau, Eugene Genovese, and Mechal Sobel in the 1970s, nearly all agree that some similarities between the African past and evangelical revivalism made the latter palatable even to those enslaved by Christians.[29] Among the overlap-

27. Conkin, *Cane Ridge*, 118; Williams, *Barton Stone*, 77–78; D. Newell Williams, Douglas A. Foster, and Paul M. Blowers, eds., *The Stone-Campbell Movement: A Global History* (Saint Louis: Chalice, 2013), 14; Andrew E. Murray, *Presbyterians and the Negro: A History* (Philadelphia: Presbyterian Historical Society, 1966), 12–28.

28. On segregation, see Conkin, *Cane Ridge*, 91; Frey and Wood, *Come Shouting to Zion*, 110, 140–48; Kenneth O. Brown, *Holy Ground: A Study of the American Camp Meeting*, Garland Reference Library of Social Science 717 (New York: Garland, 1992), 8–9, 21.

29. Albert J. Raboteau, *Slave Religion: The "Invisible Institution" in the Antebellum South* (Oxford: Oxford University Press, 1978); Eugene D. Genovese, *Roll, Jordan, Roll: The World the*

ping beliefs and practices, scholars highlight the idea of death and spiritual rebirth at initiation; instantaneous regeneration; and ecstatic bodily exercises, clapping, stomping, dancing, and singing.[30] Emphasizing the agency of enslaved people and the influence of biracial revivalism, historian Sylvia Frey highlights the "dialectical" process of black and white people shaping evangelical revivalism and its rituals, especially the conversion ritual. That is, one should not imagine a simple process of black cultural adaptation to white, but a biracial construction and reinterpretation of revivalism's rituals.[31] The biracial nature of revivalism "decisively shaped black and white religious culture."[32]

Evangelicals held revivals to procure new birth conversions that ostensibly made the convert spiritually equal to all other Christians, at least in the eyes of God. Therefore, conversion could have profound effects on race relations. As historian Donald Mathews explains, because evangelicals accepted conversions as "authentic signs of God's grace and blacks' humanity," the conversion experience "could not be denied all its egalitarian implications for blacks, despite racial stereotypes, anxieties, and fears."[33] For example, James McGready, a leading revivalist of the era, argued that "an ignorant negro, who had never learned his letters, but had embraced Christ, understands [the Bible] unspeakably better than the wisest man in an unregenerate state."[34] Even if black people never experienced full equality in the revivals and churches, as white and black experienced divine grace together in conversion and other common religious rituals (baptism, communion, love

---

Slaves Made (New York: Vintage Books, 1976); Sobel, *Trabelin' On*; Weisenfeld, "On Jordan's Stormy Banks," 420–23; Harvey, *Christianity and Race*, 42.

30. Sobel, *Trabelin' On* (1988), chaps. 4–5; Raboteau, *Slave Religion*, 64–65; Curtis J. Evans, "African American Christianity and the Burden of Race," in *American Christianities: A History of Dominance and Diversity*, ed. Catherine A. Brekus and W. Clark Gilpin (Chapel Hill: University of North Carolina Press, 2011), 105; Frey and Wood, *Come Shouting to Zion*, 101.

31. Sylvia R. Frey, "Shaking the Dry Bones: The Dialectic of Conversion," in *Black and White Cultural Interaction in the Antebellum South*, ed. Ted Ownby and Charles W. Joyner (Jackson: University Press of Mississippi, 1993), 35; Winthrop D. Jordan, *White over Black: American Attitudes toward the Negro, 1550–1812*, 2nd ed. (Chapel Hill: University of North Carolina Press, 2012), 212–15.

32. Frey and Wood, *Come Shouting to Zion*, 140.

33. Donald G. Mathews, *Religion in the Old South*, Chicago History of American Religion (Chicago: University of Chicago Press, 1977), 70–71; Sobel, *Trabelin' On* (1988), 102.

34. James M'Gready, "Sermon XXI: The Qualifications and Duties of A Minister of the Gospel," in *The Posthumous Works of the Reverend and Pious James M'Gready*, ed. James Smith (Louisville: Printed by W. W. Worsley, 1831), 1:314.

feast, right hand of fellowship, kiss of charity), new forms of racial interaction emerged.[35] Forced migration and the slave trade commodified human beings, but revivalist new birth theology sometimes worked to reverse this commodification, reasserting the humanity of black people.[36] Born-again Christians, white and black, stood equally before God, even if they experienced great disparity in society.

Conversions at the revivals were often accompanied by ecstatic experiences, and African American experiences were often held out as exemplary or perceived as divine sanction of the revivals. Revival broke out at a 1774 Methodist quarterly meeting in Virginia, where Thomas Rankin said there were more black and white participants for the love feast than ever before. During worship, Rankin exhorted hearers to look at the black section of the gathering: "See the number of the black Africans who have stretched out their hand and heart to God!" Directly after that, it "seemed as if the very house shook with the mighty power and glory of Sinai's God." God's presence overwhelmed the people, so that "they were ready to faint and die under his almighty hand. For about three hours the gale of the Spirit thus continued to breathe upon the dry bones."[37] In the Kentucky revivals of 1801, one eyewitness reported that black experiences were a sign of God's favor: "several poor black people [were converted], some of whose experiences have astonished me—This is the work of the Lord, and it is marvelous in our eyes."[38] Richard McNemar, another minister at the Kentucky revivals that year, highlighted that "no sex nor color, class nor description, were exempted from the pervading influence of the spirit."[39]

Revivals were also the primary place where black and white evangelicals created new forms of music and dance. Distinctive aspects of camp meeting songs that emerged in this era were "the chorus, the folksong-style melodies,

35. Frey and Wood, *Come Shouting to Zion*, 101, 108.

36. Kevin Gaines, "African-American History," in *American History Now*, ed. Eric Foner and Lisa McGirr (Philadelphia: Temple University Press, 2011), 404.

37. P. P. Sandford, ed., *Memoirs of Mr. Wesley's Missionaries to America: Compiled from Authentic Sources* (New York: G. Lane & P. P. Sandford, for the Methodist Episcopal Church, 1843), 231; Frey and Wood, *Come Shouting to Zion*, 110–11.

38. In letters from Lexington, Kentucky, dated March 8 and 9, in William W. Woodward, ed., *Surprising Accounts of the Revival of Religion, in the United States of America, in Different Parts of the World, and among Different Denominations of Christians . . . Collected by the Publisher* (Philadelphia: William W. Woodward, 1802), 55–56.

39. Richard McNemar, *The Kentucky Revival; or, A Short History of the Late Extraordinary Out-Pouring of the Spirit of God, in the Western States of America* (Cincinnati: John W. Browne, 1807), 23.

and the rough and irregular couplets that referred to scriptural concepts and to everyday experiences."[40] And some of the songs printed in the songbooks for camp meetings came from the African American musical tradition.[41]

Opponents sometimes racialized and attacked the new music and dance that were associated with the emotional worship of the camp meetings. The Reverend John E. Watson opposed certain Methodist "errors," such as songs composed by black people and the dancing that went along with them. He argued that the songs were erroneous not only because they contained bad poetry and poor content, but also because they were "most frequently composed and first sung by the illiterate *blacks* of the society."[42] Watson expressed disdain toward the all-night hymn sings, which were apparently common: they kept "singing tune after tune . . . scarce one of which were in our hymn book."[43]

Watson also charged that the bodily movements and noises that accompanied such songs were "a most exceptionable error, which has the tolerance at least of the rulers of our camp meetings."[44] Writing in 1819, after Methodist revivals had converted many from the African American community, Watson provides a fascinating account of ways the black-white "dialectical" process had already shaped evangelical revival culture. He also illustrates at least one negative response to the new racial interactions prompted by biracial revivalism:

> In the blacks' slave quarter the coloured people get together, and sing for hours together, short scraps of disjointed affirmations, pledges, or prayers, lengthened out with long repetition *choruses*. These are all sung in the merry chorus-manners of the southern harvest field, or husking-frolic method, of the slave blacks; and also very greatly like the Indian dances. With every word so sung, they have a sinking of one or other leg of the body alternately; producing an audible sound of the feet at every step, and as manifest as the steps of actual negro

40. Eileen Southern, *The Music of Black Americans: A History* (New York: Norton, 1971), 97.
41. Southern, *Music of Black Americans*, 97–98.
42. A Wesleyan Methodist and John L. Watson, *Methodist Error; or, Friendly, Christian Advice to those Methodists who indulge in extravagant religious emotions and bodily exercises* (Trenton, NJ: D. & E. Fenton, 1819), 28–30, http://archive.org/details/methodisterroror00wesl; Frey and Wood, *Come Shouting to Zion*, 144.
43. A Wesleyan Methodist and Watson, *Methodist Error*, 31; Southern, *Music of Black Americans*, 95.
44. A Wesleyan Methodist and Watson, *Methodist Error*, 30.

dancing in Virginia, etc. If some, in the meantime sit, they strike the sound alternately on each thigh. What in the name of religion, can countenance or tolerate such gross perversions of true religion! but the evil is only occasionally condemned, and the example has already visibly affected the religious manners of some whites.[45]

This may be an early description of the "ring shout," though scholars disagree on the developments of this ritual dance of African origin. It may have developed in part at camp meetings, though African American meetings hidden from white view were also utilized for the creation of such religious rituals. As early as 1809, contemporary accounts mention black revivalists dancing in ways unfamiliar to white revivalists, sometimes all through the night.[46]

Historians Sylvia Frey and Betty Wood argue that revivalist liturgical traditions "formed an important nexus in race relations within the biracial evangelical community," yet white reactions set a trajectory for the separation of white and black Christian music and dance.[47] White evangelicals increasingly sided with Watson in his condemnation of black song and dance as erroneous. The analysis of Frey and Wood on this point is worth quoting at length:

> Despite its mixed origins, emotional worship was increasingly characterized as "black" and, therefore, culturally inferior. Such an identification worked to reinforce the growing consciousness of racial distinction developing behind the rising wall of spiritual separation. White Christians rejected rituals that had an apparent African style or feeling or were associated with supposed racial inferiority in favor of the more carefully controlled European cadences with which they were familiar. For black Christians ritual music and dance became important cultural foci, symbols of their cultural independence and of their identity as a black group.[48]

Also important in the biracial revival culture created during this era were black preachers. Black preachers and leaders flourished among Meth-

45. A Wesleyan Methodist and Watson, *Methodist Error*, 30–31.
46. Frey and Wood, *Come Shouting to Zion*, 145–47; Southern, *Music of Black Americans*, 98–99.
47. Frey and Wood, *Come Shouting to Zion*, 147–48.
48. Frey and Wood, *Come Shouting to Zion*, 147–48.

odists. Among the most famous was Harry Hosier, who itinerated with Asbury, Coke, Whatcoat, and Freeborn Garrettson. The stage they shared drew large crowds of black and white people, even as some objected to black people preaching to white audiences. The revivals also encouraged females to join in preaching. Female, African American, and free, Jarena Lee heard the voice of God several years after experiencing evangelical conversion: "Go preach the Gospel!"[49] After she spent years seeking the blessing of Richard Allen, cofounder of the African Methodist Episcopal Church, her powerful sermon in 1818 convinced him and others that God had gifted her to preach.[50] From that time to the 1840s, she preached in black, white, and biracial congregations, camp meetings, and revivals. Many other black Baptist and Methodist preachers could be mentioned, some of whom served biracial congregations.[51]

Ubiquitous in eyewitness accounts of the Great Revival in the West were African American exhorters and preachers. McNemar highlighted the egalitarian nature of exhortation at the revivals: "All distinction of names [i.e., denominations] was laid aside," and all were "welcome to sing, pray, or call sinners to repentance. Neither was there any distinction of age, sex, color, or any thing of a temporary nature: old and young, male and female, black and white, had equal privilege to minister the light which they received, in whatever way the spirit directed."[52] McNemar reasoned that egalitarian experiences witnessed at revivals were proof of the divine origin of the revivals: "To see a bold Kentuckian (undaunted by the horrors of war) turn pale and tremble at the reproof of a weak woman, a little boy, or a mean African; to see him sink down in deep remorse, roll and toss, and gnash his teeth, till black in the face . . . —who would say the change was not supernatural and miraculous?"[53] More than two dozen Methodist, Baptist, and Presbyterian preachers spoke at the Cane Ridge Revival (at least one unidentified black minister preached to a separate assembly of African Americans), though many laypeople exhorted after conversion.[54] In his recollection of these revivals, McGready wrote, "It is a common case, for illiterate Negroes, and

---

49. *Religious Experience and Journal of Mrs. Jarena Lee, Giving An Account of Her Call to Preach the Gospel* (Philadelphia: Printed and Published for the Author, 1849), 10.

50. *Religious Experience and Journal of Mrs. Jarena Lee*, 17.

51. Hatch, *Democratization of American Christianity*, 105–7; Harvey, *Through the Storm*, 42–43.

52. McNemar, *The Kentucky Revival*, 29–30.

53. McNemar, *The Kentucky Revival*, 34.

54. Conkin, *Cane Ridge*, 90–91.

little children of 5, 6, 7 and 8 years old, when they get their first comforts, to speak of their views of [Christ, salvation, and other theological topics] with an eloquence and pathos that would not disgrace a preacher of the Gospel."[55]

James M'Corkle brought together many of these characteristics in his description of a North Carolina revival in 1802. Suddenly, "as if by an electric shock, a large number in every direction men, women, children, white and black, fell and cried for mercy." M'Corkle described "a poor black man with his hands raised over the heads of the crowd, and shouting 'Glory to God on high.'" M'Corkle sought to get closer to this man but was stopped by "another black-man prostrate on the ground, and his aged mother on her knees at his feet in all the agony of prayer for her son." He described a nearby scene, where "a black-woman, grasp[ed] her mistress' hand, and cr[ied] 'O mistress you prayed for me when I wanted a heart to pray for myself. Now thank God he has given me a heart to pray for you and every body else.'"[56] These and similar accounts illustrate the biracial nature and egalitarian effects of the revivals.

A Failed Experiment in Biracial Unity

Despite evangelical positions against slavery and for unalienable natural rights, despite biracial revivals and churches, and despite egalitarian conversion, white evangelicals leading revivals in the early national era were unable to create a lasting biracial unity. I see at least two major explanations for this. First, biracial unity—a genuine unity between black and white participants—never really existed in evangelical revivalism. Perhaps nothing illustrates this more than the segregated revivals and churches. Most white evangelicals believed the "poor Negros" were biologically inferior to white people—physically separating black from white reified this belief. The racialization and gendering of religious space (that is, physically separating black and white, men and women) could symbolically destroy the revolutionary ideology and egalitarian theology evangelicals preached. Separating people at meetings "delineated the fault lines of race, class, and gender and

55. James M'Gready, "A Narrative of the Revival of Religion in Logan County, Etc.," *Western Missionary Magazine*, June 1, 1803, 172.

56. Letter from James M'Corkle dated January 8, 1802, documenting a revival in Randolph, North Carolina, in James Hall and James M'Corkle, *A Narrative of A Most Extraordinary Work of Religion in North Carolina by the Rev. James Hall. Also A Collection of Interesting Letters from the Rev. James M'Corkle* (Philadelphia: William W. Woodward, 1802), 21.

physically structured the idea that for men and women, and for blacks and whites, spiritual equality operated on different terms," say historians Frey and Wood. As evangelicals preached new birth egalitarianism, "the spatial arrangements of the meeting argued differently, reproducing as they did [society's] race and gender hierarchies." Furthermore, "beyond these new social and psychological walls, divergent forms of ritual behavior and a different constellation of worship patterns began to emerge."[57] That is, the racialization of space set a trajectory of division among black and white evangelicals, both in their meetings and in their religious rituals, that continues to shape evangelical churches today.

If separate seating illustrates a lack of biracial unity and foreshadows future racial divisions, then the exodus of African Americans from white congregations as soon as it was possible more clearly evinces the persistent racial inequity black people experienced in white revivals and churches in both the North and the South. Historian David Wills highlights the realities at work here: "black evangelicals, eager for autonomy in administering their own affairs, discovered that when it came to questions of the exercise of leadership or control over property, white power was the almost invariable rule of ecclesiastical as well as civil order. The result of these developments—which undermined the sharing of both meaning and power—was racial schism."[58] For example, when Richard Allen, Absalom Jones, and others experienced overt racism at a Philadelphia Methodist church in the 1790s, they left and started an independent church, which eventually became the African Methodist Episcopal Church (1816). In the North, black Christians created other independent Baptist, Methodist, Episcopal, and Presbyterian congregations and denominations in the early national era. In the South before the Civil War, some black Baptists and Methodists created independent congregations, but many were forced to worship with or be supervised by whites. Many found authentic worship only in the "brush harbors," meeting spaces where enslaved people worshiped, away from the supervision of whites. After the abolition of slavery, nearly all black Christians left white churches for independent evangelical congregations and denominations. That is, black Christians rejected white racism, but many embraced evangelicalism.[59]

57. Frey and Wood, *Come Shouting to Zion*, 141.

58. David W. Wills, "The Central Themes of American Religious History: Pluralism, Puritanism, and the Encounter of Black and White," *Religion and Intellectual Life* 5, no. 1 (Fall 1987): 38.

59. Carroll, *Routledge Historical Atlas*, 84–87.

Second, and closely connected to the first explanation, even the most vigorous white opponents of slavery backed away from their earlier positions by the second decade of the 1800s. Historians have given multiple explanations for the antislavery movement's weakening in the early nineteenth century. First, the revolutionary ideology of inalienable rights waned as white leaders turned to nation building in the early national era, which required compromise between slave and free states. Second, as the antislavery movement won emancipationist laws in all Northern states by 1804 and the United States outlawed the international slave trade on January 1, 1808, the reformist zeal lost momentum. Also, economic developments throughout the South saw an increase in demand for slave labor as cotton became king, entrenching the institution in Southern society.[60]

Furthermore, what Sobel highlights about Baptists also applies to other evangelical groups: the evangelicals' quick growth rapidly moved them from the religious margins to the mainstream, which brought social respectability. They "became more conformist and less concerned with opposition to the establishment. As they themselves were improving their social position, they became less interested in the downtrodden and were less likely to oppose established institutions, such as slavery."[61] For example, Methodists removed the chapter on slavery from the *Discipline* in 1804 and 1808.[62] And by 1809, Asbury journaled about the propriety of amelioration instead of emancipation: "We are defrauded of great numbers by the pains that are taken to keep blacks from us; their masters are afraid of the influence of our principles. Would not an *amelioration* in the condition and treatment of slaves have produced more practical good to the poor Africans, than any attempt at their *emancipation*? . . . What is the personal liberty of the African which he may abuse, to the salvation of his soul; how may it be compared?"[63]

Likewise, in 1808, when Christian Church leaders from Ohio said slavery was inconsistent with Christianity and thus slaveholders should be disfellowshiped (i.e., excommunicated), Stone and Purviance, two antislavery proponents who in 1800 proposed the same idea, took a different position. According to one report, Stone argued that every slaveholder among the Christian Churches that he knew had exemplary conduct, and since they had endured persecution for the "Christian" cause, "to declare them out of

60. Jordan, *White over Black*, vii–ix. ‧
61. Sobel, *Trabelin' On* (1988), 88–89.
62. Hatch, *Democratization of American Christianity*, 106–7.
63. *Journal of the Rev. Francis Asbury*, 3:298.

fellowship would be ungenerous and cruel in the extreme."[64] Like so many other evangelical antislavery proponents, Stone had softened his position on the hard line of fellowship he had drawn only eight years earlier.

Just as white political leaders who focused on nation building in this era compromised to appease the slave states, so white evangelical leaders, who focused on building their quickly-growing denominations, compromised to conciliate their newly won slaveholding adherents; what they condemned as satanic in 1800, they had learned to tolerate by 1810. As Mathews explains, evangelicals "could not create a long-lasting abolition movement where the social context could not support it. The social realities of slavery and the psychological realities of racial prejudice simply could not be counterbalanced by religious commitment—they could be affected but not destroyed."[65]

As white evangelicals gave up their earlier, more prophetic antislavery views, black evangelicals felt the sting of betrayal in white evangelical accommodation of slavery and the continued "paternalism and prejudice of the best-intentioned whites." As Raboteau argues, "Blacks could accept Christianity because they rejected the white version with its trappings of slavery and caste for a purer and more authentic gospel."[66] They found allies among many white evangelicals in the 1780s and 1790s, but the first two decades of the new century saw a decisive shift that deeply damaged evangelical race relations and impeded biracial unity.

To summarize: evangelical revivalism in the early national era led to the Christianization of African Americans. Channeling revolutionary ideology and egalitarian theology of new birth, evangelical biracial revivals offered ideas and practices that had some continuity with the African religious past and attractive meaning and experience for their American present. Although this combination of variables led African Americans to embrace evangelical Christianity, it did not lead to a lasting biracial unity among evangelicals. Evangelicals preached spiritual equality in biracial revivals and churches, but entrenched views about the inferiority of black people, the racialization of religious space that corroborated these racial views, and the negative experiences of black people in white churches led most black Christians to leave white congregations as soon as it was legally possible.

---

64. William Lamphier, "Letter to the Editor, Dated Alexandria, (Vir.), April 25th, 1809," *Herald of Gospel Liberty* 1, no. 19 (May 12, 1809): 74; Williams, *Barton Stone*, 131.

65. Mathews, *Religion in the Old South*, 75.

66. Albert J. Raboteau, "The Black Experience in American Evangelicalism: The Meaning of Slavery," in *The Evangelical Tradition in America*, ed. Leonard I. Sweet (Macon, GA: Mercer University Press, 1984), 190.

The biracial experiment of evangelical revivals in the early national era did not lead to prolonged biracial unity; rather, it contributed to the "color line" dividing evangelical churches today. But the revivals incubated a vibrant African American Christianity that continues to shape American society and culture. Sylvia Frey summarizes the era well: "During the era of the Second Awakening black and white spiritual destinies converged more frequently and intensely than ever before. Paradoxically the period also marks the beginning of their spiritual journeys on widely separate tracks."[67]

67. Frey, "Shaking the Dry Bones," 34.

Racism and Division in Christianity during the Antebellum and Reconstruction Eras

Wes Crawford

Slavery. The Middle Passage. Nat Turner. The Invisible Institution. Richard Allen. Frederick Douglass. Harriet Beecher Stowe. The Civil War. Reconstruction. W. E. B. Du Bois. Booker T. Washington. Rosa Parks. Martin Luther King Jr. Birmingham, Alabama. The Civil Rights Movement. Fannie Lou Hamer. The Long Hot Summer. Watts Riots. Trayvon Martin. Freddie Gray. Ferguson, Missouri. Charlottesville, Virginia. Racism.

This short litany of names, events, places, and terms brings to the surface the strong emotions associated with racism in America. The destruction created by racism in American culture generally has proved just as damaging in American Christianity specifically. Just as socially constructed racial categories helped to support American laws aimed at keeping African Americans in their proper hierarchical place within society, and just as those same categories provided justification for separate and unequal school systems, faulty perceptions of race also have divided the church in America. In a 1987 essay, David W. Wills rightly included "the encounter of black and white" as one of three defining themes of American religious history.[1] Along with pluralism and Puritanism, the uneasy and sometimes volatile relationship between African American and white Christians has given shape to a divided American church. This essay seeks to shine a light on that unfortunate narrative, illuminating the ways in which racism has created and supported a segregated church in America.

Race and Racism

Race is a socially constructed category. One is incorrect, therefore, to speak of the "white race" or the "black race" as if skin color necessarily or by na-

---

1. David W. Wills, "The Central Themes of American Religious History: Pluralism, Puritanism, and the Encounter of Black and White," *Religion and Intellectual Life* 5, no. 1 (Fall 1987): 30–41.

ture separates these two groups of human beings. Certainly, skin color does provide one distinguishing physical characteristic among humans, but why has so much meaning been applied to this single physical characteristic? Although people have all sizes of feet and shapes of ears, those physical features are not used to classify one race from another.[2] In reality, society has elevated skin color as the primary racial determinant. Not only does this physical feature rise above the rest in society's effort to classify individuals, but society has also attached specific meaning only to certain physical characteristics. A person with blue eyes or red hair does not have to defend himself or herself against stereotypes of mental inferiority or financial hardship. Some people born with black skin, however, spend their lives defending against both.

Unfortunately, pseudoscience has provided the basis for incorrect and often detrimental connotations for darker skin color. One explanation for black complexion is the Phaethon myth from Ethiopia, which rested upon the belief that Phaethon, a young boy who drove his chariot too close to the sun, doomed his progeny to black skin. Other proponents of more naturalistic explanations have posited the theory that darker skin originated from the strong heat of the African sun.[3] More common and tragic scientific studies on skin color centered on the great chain of being. In the eighteenth century, scientists made it their joint mission to classify all kinds of matter, including planets, diseases, animals, and humans. For example, François Berneir and Carolus Linnaeus poured themselves into the task of classifying human beings. Though they could have used any physical feature to serve as the basis for their classification system, these two men focused their attention on skin color. As other scientists had done with plants and animals, these scientists ranked the various classifications of human beings from lower to higher orders. In their research, darker-skinned individuals consistently ranked toward the bottom of the great chain of being, while lighter-skinned individuals remained consistently toward the top.[4] According to their research, therefore, darker-skinned people were by nature less refined and less intellectually able than lighter-skinned people.

In his book *The Forging of Races: Race and Scripture in the Protestant Atlantic World, 1600–2000*, Colin Kidd shatters such nonsensical conclusions.

2. Michael O. Emerson and Christian Smith, *Divided by Faith: Evangelical Religion and the Problem of Race in America* (New York: Oxford University Press, 2000), 7.

3. Winthrop D. Jordan, *White over Black: American Attitudes toward the Negro, 1550–1812* (Chapel Hill: University of North Carolina Press, 1968; New York: Norton, 1977), 11–13. Citations are to the Norton Library edition.

4. Jordan, *White over Black*, 219–28, 482–511.

Through his excellent summary of the many ways in which historians, scientists, and scholars have sought to classify various kinds of human beings in recent centuries, Kidd shows that the geographical region of one's ancestry has more bearing on the biological makeup of a human being than skin color.[5] For example, in a close examination of fingerprint patterns, scientists determined that most Europeans, black Africans, and east Asians have loops in their fingerprints; whorls are more common among Mongolians and Australian Aborigines; and arches are more common among those native to southern Africa and central Europe. Another study examining the relationship of blood type to geographical ancestry concluded that Baffin Eskimos, Australian Aborigines, Basques, Polynesians, and the Shoshone of Wyoming had large populations of people with the A blood type and very few people with the B blood type. Conversely, the Welsh, Italians, Thai, Finns, Japanese, Chinese, and Egyptians had nearly equal numbers of people with A and B blood types. Kidd's research debunks the conclusions offered by pseudoscientists that skin color provides an adequate basis for human classification. In fact, skin color has less to do with one's biological makeup than a host of other factors. Further, contrary to some popular, historic, and racist viewpoints, skin color has no bearing upon intellectual capacity or moral tendencies.

Even more tragic than scientific theories that devalued dark-skinned people were the religious justifications for racism centered on Scripture. According to the Hamite myth, black skin resulted from God's curse on Ham, following his sin against his father, Noah, in Genesis 9. In that narrative, God cursed Ham's descendants, the Canaanites, dooming them to a life of slavery under the authority of Ham's brothers. Early Jewish scholars believed the descendants of Ham, those doomed to lifetime servitude, were black. For example, although scholars point to various points of origin of the Hamite myth,[6] some early Jewish sources suggest that Ham was "smitten in his skin," that Noah told Ham "your seed will be ugly and dark-skinned," and that Ham was the father "of Canaan who brought curses into the world, of Canaan who was cursed, of Canaan who darkened the faces of mankind."[7]

---

5. Colin Kidd, *The Forging of Races: Race and Scripture in the Protestant Atlantic World, 1600-2000* (Cambridge: Cambridge University Press, 2006), 1-18. For additional information on this subject, see also Ibram X. Kendi, *Stamped from the Beginning: The Definitive History of Racist Ideas in America* (New York: Nation Books, 2016).

6. E.g., see discussion in Christopher R. Hutson's chapter, pp. 58-88, below.

7. *The Babylonian Talmud*, trans. I. Epstein et al., 35 vols. (London: Soncino, 1935-1960), Sanhedrin, II, 745; *Midrash Rabbah*, trans. H. Freedman and Maurice Simon, 10 vols. (Lon-

Historian Winthrop Jordan argues that this myth gained traction within Christian circles in the sixteenth century, as Christian theologians became more interested in Jewish writings and, at the same time, European Christians initiated numerous overseas expeditions into Africa.[8]

James B. Bennett agrees with Jordan's assessment, writing, "The concept of race emerged from the confluence of numerous developments, including the age of exploration and colonization, the Protestant Reformation, the Enlightenment, and the emergence of African slavery."[9] In other words, Europeans developed their concept of race and added meaning to skin color in order to justify the Atlantic slave trade. Over time, these scientific and religious explanations for skin color aided in the construction of an injurious and prejudicial image of black people, giving new meaning to blackness. Light-skinned Europeans viewed dark-skinned Africans as savages. As they might treat beasts of the field, Europeans packed Africans on ships in extremely tight quarters and sent them across the Atlantic Ocean to be sold as slaves.

Europeans viewed Africans as savages. Even more, they viewed Africans as sexual savages who, left to their own devices, would engage in all kinds of sexual debauchery, including rape and incest. Leo Africanus, sixteenth-century explorer of Africa and author of *Descrittione dell'Africa*, reveals another component of blackness created by Europeans. He depicts Africans as savages with "great swarmes of Harlots among them; whereupon a man may easily conjecture their manner of living."[10] In the mid-sixteenth century, another author, Jean Bodin, wrote that Ethiopia and lust went hand in hand.[11] Armed with "scientific" conclusions based upon the great chain of being and biblical justification from theories such as the Hamite myth, Europeans attached these and other negative connotations to blackness, thereby justifying their inhumane treatment of their fellow human beings.

As European settlers arrived in America, these negative connotations of blackness shaped American culture and Christianity. In the early eighteenth century, Puritan preacher Samuel Willard declared in a sermon, "All servi-

---

don: Soncino, 1939), 1:293; *The Zohar*, trans. Harry Sperling and Maurice Simon, 5 vols. (London: Soncino, 1931), 1:246-47.

8. Jordan, *White over Black*, 18.

9. James B. Bennett, "Race and Racism," in *Encyclopedia of Religion in America*, ed. Charles H. Lippy and Peter W. Williams (Washington, DC: CQ Press, 2010), 1825-32.

10. Leo Africanus, *History and Description of Africa*, trans. John Pory, ed. Robert Brown (London: Printed for the Hakluyt Society, 1896), 1:180.

11. Jean Bodin, *Method for Easy Comprehension of History*, trans. Beatrice Reynolds (Paris: Martinem Iuuenem, 1566; reprint, New York: Norton, 1969), 103-6, 143.

tude began in the curse."[12] Decades later, Thomas Jefferson, an American founder who himself looked down upon the institution of slavery, wrote, "In reason they [blacks] are much inferior, as I think one could scarcely be found capable of tracing and comprehending the investigations of Euclid; and that in imagination they are dull, tasteless, and anomalous."[13] Using Euclid, the so-called father of geometry, as a synonym for mathematics itself, Jefferson implies black-skinned individuals are inferior in both their mathematical and imaginative skills. Negative connotations of blackness shaped American political leaders and church leaders, creating an American culture wherein dark-skinned individuals were devalued, disregarded, and even feared.

In the years following the Emancipation Proclamation, as former slaves began to move freely across the American landscape, Harvard professor Nathaniel Southgate Shaler added to the false narrative by promoting his theory of retrogression, which utilized the caricature of African Americans created by centuries of faulty scientific studies and poor exegesis. According to his theory, once they were freed from the strong disciplinary control of white society, African Americans would regress into their natural barbaric state.[14] Shaler's theory found widespread support and stirred a fear among whites that perpetuated racism and segregation. One may witness this popular depiction of African American men in D. W. Griffith's 1915 silent film, *Birth of a Nation*. This movie, based upon Thomas Dixon's *The Clansman* (1905), which glowingly portrays the Ku Klux Klan as the protectors of Christian virtue and characterizes black men as criminals, rapists, and animalistic barbarians, was one of the first so-called blockbuster films in American history. The book and movie underscored the negative connotations of blackness and gave rise to the reemergence of the Ku Klux Klan in the early twentieth century.

In his book *The Crucible of Race*, Joel Williamson helps contemporary students of American history understand better the implications of Shaler's theory of retrogression by describing what he terms the "Southern, organic society." Williamson writes, "In that order there would be various parts in the social body, and every part would have its place and

---

12. Samuel Willard, "Sermon CLXXIX [August 24, 1703]," in *A Compleat Body of Divinity in Two Hundred and Fifty Expository Lectures on the Assembly's Catechism* (Boston: B. Eliot and D. Henchman, 1726; New York: Johnson Reprint, 1969), 613.

13. Thomas Jefferson, *Notes on the State of Virginia*, ed. William Peden (Chapel Hill: University of North Carolina Press, 1955), 139–40.

14. Nathan Shaler, "The Negro Problem," *Atlantic Monthly* 54 (November 1884): 703; Shaler, "Science and the African Problem," *Atlantic Monthly* 66 (June 1890): 42.

function."[15] In the Southern, organic society, white men viewed themselves as the patriarchal protectors of white women, shielding them from the sexual savagery of African American men. For the society to properly function, each member of that society needed to stay in his or her assigned place. Slaves had to assume the role of slave; masters had to assume the role of master. Women took charge of the home, and men took charge of the women. Following the days of slavery, whites perpetuated this system by keeping African Americans in their place through segregation and Jim Crow laws. The greatest offense in the Southern, organic society occurred when individuals moved outside of their assigned places in the social order.

In the minds of many white people, the Southern social order provided protection for all members of society—African American and white. By the last generation of slavery, whites had developed a stereotypical image of all black people known as Sambo. Williamson describes this fictional character: "The Sambo of imagination was a child adopted into the white family, an adult black body with a white child's mind and heart, simultaneously appealing and appalling, naturally affectionate and unwittingly cruel, a social asset and a liability. Sambo had within him, then, two terrific and opposite capacities. Improperly cared for, he became bestial, an animal in human form and all the more dangerous because of his human capabilities. Properly managed, on the other hand, he was like a child—and dear."[16]

In the antebellum period (between the War of 1812 and the American Civil War), whites controlled the potentially destructive Sambo through the iron fist of slavery. Following the Civil War, whites continued their efforts to tame Sambo through Jim Crow segregation. From the colonial period through Reconstruction (1865–1877), white Europeans and Americans constructed a theory of race that worked to demean and demoralize African Americans. These socially constructed racial categories had profound negative implications for America.

Consider, for example, the Supreme Court opinion penned by Chief Justice Robert B. Taney in the landmark case *Dred Scott v. John F. A. Sandford* (1857). In justifying the court's decision, Taney writes:

> In the opinion of the court, the legislation and histories of the times, and the language used in the Declaration of Independence, show, that

15. Joel Williamson, *The Crucible of Race: Black-White Relations in the American South Since Emancipation* (New York: Oxford University Press, 1984), 24.
16. Williamson, *The Crucible of Race*, 23–24.

neither the class of persons who had been imported as slaves, nor their descendants, whether they had become free or not, were then acknowledged as a part of the people, nor intended to be included in the general words used in that memorable instrument.

It is difficult at this day to realize the state of public opinion in relation to that unfortunate race, which prevailed in the civilized and enlightened portions of the world at the time of the Declaration of Independence, and when the Constitution of the United States was framed and adopted. But the public history of every European nation displays it in a manner too plain to be mistaken.

They had for more than a century before been regarded as beings of an inferior order, and altogether unfit to associate with the white race, either in social or political relations; and so far inferior, that they had no rights which the white man was bound to respect; and that the negro might justly and lawfully be reduced to slavery for his benefit. He was bought and sold, and treated as an ordinary article of merchandise and traffic, whenever a profit could be made by it. This opinion was at that time fixed and universal in the civilized portion of the white race. It was regarded as an axiom in morals as well as in politics, which no one thought of disputing, or supposed to be open to dispute; and men in every grade and position in society daily and habitually acted upon it in their private pursuits, as well as in matters of public concern, without doubting for a moment the correctness of this opinion.

And in no nation was this opinion more firmly fixed or more uniformly acted upon than by the English Government and English people. They not only seized them on the coast of Africa, and sold them or held them in slavery for their own use; but they took them as ordinary articles of merchandise to every country where they could make a profit on them, and were far more extensively engaged in this commerce than any other nation in the world.

The opinion thus entertained and acted upon in England was naturally impressed upon the colonies they founded on this side of the Atlantic. And, accordingly, a negro of the African race was regarded by them as an article of property, and held, and bought and sold as such, in every one of the thirteen colonies which united in the Declaration of Independence, and afterwards formed the Constitution of the United States. The slaves were more or less numerous in the different colonies, as slave labor was found more or less profitable. But no one seems to have doubted the correctness of the prevailing opinion of the time.[17]

Centuries of slave trade built upon racist ideologies cemented in the minds of many Americans, including the chief justice in America's highest court, an incorrect, dangerous, and injurious image of black-skinned human beings. The *Dred Scott* case declared that African Americans could not attain citizenship in America. More fundamentally, however, the decision declared black-skinned people fundamentally inferior to white-skinned people. The same racist ideologies that scarred American society also caused deep divisions within the American church.

Racism in the American Church during the Antebellum Period

The socially constructed racial categories and the negative connotations of blackness created in previous centuries by scientists and religious leaders provided the foundation for a fractured church in antebellum America. In the decades preceding the Civil War, free African Americans in the North, frustrated by white racism, founded their own independent denominations. White Christian preachers in the South, motivated by racism and the compulsion to protect the Southern, organic society, preached sermons aimed at creating better slaves and masters. This racially charged climate resulted in the formation of the invisible institution, an underground Christian movement created and perpetuated by African American slaves. Though many African Americans continued to worship in predominantly white congregations in the South, most did so out of compulsion by white leaders, and those biracial congregations maintained the racialized social structure of the American South, thereby relegating their African American attendees to second-class citizenship. Whether in the North or the South, then, American Christians remained separated by a color line in the days preceding the Civil War.

As one might expect, the move toward independent African American denominations occurred much earlier in the North than in the South. The well-known story of Richard Allen and Absalom Jones has long been recognized as the genesis moment of the black church in America.[18] In 1787, these

17. Dred Scott v. Sandford, 1857, The 'Lectric Law Library, accessed September 22, 2017, http://www.lectlaw.com/files/case23.htm.

18. For a fuller account of this event, see C. Eric Lincoln and Lawrence H. Mamiya,

two men, along with several other African Americans, planned to worship at Saint George's Methodist Episcopal Church in Philadelphia. Arriving late for the service, they moved to the balcony, descended to their knees, and began praying with the congregation. Unbeknownst to them, the balcony was closed to black Christians; therefore, during the prayer, white ushers pulled them from their knees and escorted them down the stairs. This moment became the proverbial straw that broke the camel's back, for Allen, Jones, and many other African American Christians left Saint George's church that Sunday and never returned. This contingent poured their energies into the Free African Society, a group they had incorporated seven months prior to their exodus from Saint George's church. Allen, who had been ordained a deacon by Francis Asbury in 1799, assumed leadership of this group. In 1816, Allen united four African American Methodist congregations in Pennsylvania, New Jersey, Delaware, and Maryland to form a new African American denomination, the African Methodist Episcopal Church. On April 10, 1816, the other ministers from this new denomination elected Allen as their first bishop.

African American Baptists also separated from their white counterparts, but their independence occurred much less formally due to the congregational autonomy Baptists practice. African American Baptists did establish their own independent congregations in the North in the early nineteenth century, but they did not create independent African American denominations until the late nineteenth and early twentieth century. The African Baptist Church in Boston was established in 1805, and the Abyssinian Baptist Church in New York was founded three years later in 1808. The Reverend Thomas Paul, an African American minister from Boston, helped to organize both congregations. In 1809, Henry Cunningham helped organize another historic African American Baptist church, First Baptist Church in Philadelphia.[19] Even though these congregations had African American leadership and membership, white Baptists continued to exercise some level of control over them. For example, white Baptist associations still appointed preachers for African American congregations in both New York and Philadelphia.[20] Notwithstanding this level of white control, African American

---

The Black Church in the African American Experience (Durham, NC: Duke University Press, 1990), 50–51.

19. Lincoln and Mamiya, *The Black Church*, 25.

20. Miles Mark Fisher, "What Is a Negro Baptist?," *Home Mission College Review* 1, no. 1 (May 1927): 1–2.

Christians in the North did experience far greater independence than their counterparts in the South.

In the antebellum South, whites discouraged slaves from forming their own, independent congregations or denominations, and in some cases, laws were passed prohibiting it. In some locations, African American slaves were not even allowed to meet separately for religious gatherings.[21] Fearing slaves might orchestrate revolts, Southern whites passed legislation restricting African American religious services. One of many such laws was passed in South Carolina at the turn of the nineteenth century. It forbade slaves "even in company with white persons to meet together and assemble for the purpose of religious worship, either before the rising of the sun or after the going down of the same."[22] History has shown that these white legislators had reason to worry; many of the best-known slave revolts in the American South were initiated under religious auspices and were led by African American religious leaders.[23] In August of 1831, for example, Nat Turner, a slave in Southampton County, Virginia, led a revolt that culminated in the killing of over fifty white people, making it the largest and deadliest slave revolt in American history. According to white lawyer Thomas Gray, Turner declared that he had seen a vision from God directing him to take up arms against his enemies.[24] Following this slave revolt, many Southern states passed even stricter legislation that kept African Americans from becoming preachers. The *Richmond Enquirer* summarized well the sentiment of Southern whites following Turner's revolt: "The case of Nat Turner warns us. No black man ought to be permitted to turn a preacher through the country. The law must be enforced—or the tragedy of Southampton appeals to us in vain."[25] During the same period, one New Orleans newspaper complained that an African

21. Exceptions certainly existed to this rule. Some slaves were permitted a measure of independence from white control. See, for example, John B. Boles, ed., *Masters and Slaves in the House of the Lord: Race and Religion in the American South, 1740–1870* (Lexington: University Press of Kentucky, 1990), and Mechal Sobel, *Trabelin' On: The Slave Journey to an Afro-Baptist Faith*, Contributions in Afro-American and African Studies 36 (Westport, CT: Greenwood Press, 1979; Princeton: Princeton University Press, 1988).

22. Quoted in Vincent Harding, "Religion and Resistance among Antebellum Slaves, 1800–1860," in *African-American Religion: Interpretive Essays in History and Culture*, ed. Timothy E. Fulop and Albert J. Raboteau (New York: Routledge, 1997), 111–12.

23. Harding, "Religion and Resistance," 111–19.

24. Thomas R. Gray and Nat Turner, *The Confessions of Nat Turner* (Boston: Thomas R. Gray, 1831).

25. Quoted in George Washington Williams, *History of the Negro Race in America* (New York: G. P. Putnam's Sons, 1883), 2:90.

American church was "the greatest of all public nuisances and den for hatching plots against masters."[26]

Efforts to keep slaves in their assigned place did not end in the courthouse; Southern Christian congregations did their best to perpetuate racism as well. In their effort to protect their Southern, organic society, white Christian preachers of the South returned again and again to Ephesians 6 and Colossians 3 in their preaching calendars. These texts admonished Christians to maintain hierarchical order within society: wives should submit to husbands, children should obey parents, and slaves should obey masters. The actions of Southern courts and congregations to keep African Americans in their place had the effect of further dividing the Christian church along the color line.

In response to white racism, some slaves undoubtedly acquiesced out of fear by obeying the laws and staying firmly within the place assigned to them in the Southern, organic society. Others, however, ignored these new laws or rebelled against them, refusing to accept the status quo. In 1830, as one white preacher was recounting the biblical story of Onesimus, lauding the ancient slave's obedience in returning to his master, half of the slaves in the audience walked out of the church building.[27] Still others refused to obey the laws restricting their private assemblies of worship. C. Eric Lincoln eloquently describes the religious impulses of Southern African Americans in the antebellum period:

> Often, when the white man's worship service was over, the black man's might truly begin, for neither his heart nor his private membership was in the white church, where he was scorned and demeaned. There was that other church, that invisible institution which met in the swamps and the bayous, and which joined all black believers in a common experience at a single level of human and spiritual recognition. Deep in the woods and safely out of sight of the critical, disapproving eyes of the master and the overseer, the shouts rolled up—and out. The agony so long suppressed burdened the air with sobs and screams and rhythmic moans. God's praises were sung. His mercy enjoined. His justice invoked. There in the Invisible Church the black Christian met God on his own terms and in

---

26. Quoted in Richard C. Wade, *Slavery in the Cities* (New York: Oxford University Press, 1964), 83.

27. Harding, "Religion and Resistance," 120.

his own way without the white intermediary. That invisible communion was the beginning of the Black Church, the seminal institution which spans most of the history of the black experience. It offers the most accessible key to the complexity and the genius of the black subculture, and it reflects both a vision of the tragedy and an aspect of hope of the continuing American dilemma.[28]

Albert Raboteau's seminal work, *Slave Religion*, provides a detailed examination of the invisible institution.[29] Outside of the purview of their white masters, slaves met in brush harbors and practiced a religion that fused Christianity with worship traditions from Africa. In the invisible institution, Christian sermons centered on the biblical narrative of the exodus, and African American preachers cast slaves as the new Israelites on the cusp of receiving their long-awaited freedom.

The invisible institution, slave revolts, and the degree to which numerous African Americans refused to accept the place in society assigned to them by white masters, politicians, and church leaders allow contemporary students of history to recognize the depth of division between African American and white Christians in the antebellum period. As the Civil War approached, that division grew even wider.

Not only did the topic of race divide individual African American and white Christians from each other, it also caused official separation among the largest Christian bodies in America. In 1857, New School Presbyterians divided over slavery, with the Southern faction forming the United Synod of the Presbyterian Church. In the summer of 1861, Old School Presbyterians also divided on the question of slavery. The predominantly white Methodist Episcopal Church divided in 1844 with the emergence of the Methodist Episcopal Church South. A year later, largely as a result of questions surrounding slavery, the Southern Baptist Convention was formed as Southern Baptist leaders broke away from national Baptist organizations.

The political and cultural breach between Northern and Southern states certainly had ecclesiastical implications, and Mark Noll correctly charac-

28. C. Eric Lincoln, "The Racial Factor in the Shaping of Religion in America," in *African American Religious Thought: An Anthology*, ed. Cornel West and Eddie S. Glaude Jr. (Louisville: Westminster John Knox, 2003), 164–65.

29. Albert Raboteau, *Slave Religion: The "Invisible Institution" in the Antebellum South* (New York: Oxford University Press, 1978); see also Raboteau, *Canaan Land: A Religious History of African Americans*, Religion in American Life (New York: Oxford University Press, 1999), 42–60.

terizes the Civil War as a theological crisis.[30] Northern Christians supported their abolitionist position by appealing to the Bible. Likewise, Southern Christians supported their proslavery position by quoting chapter and verse. One witnesses this strong allegiance to Scripture by both Union and Confederate Christians in a revealing exchange between two Presbyterian leaders, one from the North and the other from the South. Each man staked his position firmly on the Bible. Albert Barnes, a graduate from Princeton Seminary and pastor of the First Presbyterian Church in Philadelphia, argued that Christians who use the Bible to support slavery bring calamity and ridicule down upon the entire Christian enterprise.[31] In response to Barnes, Fredrick Ross, pioneer preacher from Tennessee and then pastor of a Presbyterian church in Huntsville, Alabama, used the same Bible to elevate his proslavery position. He wrote, "The Southern slave-holder is now satisfied, as never before, that the relation of master and slave is sanctioned in the Bible; and he feels, as never before, the obligations of the word of God."[32] Unable to reconcile these kinds of hermeneutical issues centered on slavery, the largest Christian denominations in America divided in the decades preceding the Civil War.

Slavery generally and racism specifically divided America, and the church proved itself powerless to repair this massive fissure. In fact, the church proved itself culpable in the racist activities that precipitated the Civil War. As the antebellum period drew to a close, the divisions within the church in America mirrored the divisions of the nation itself.

Racism in the American Church during the Period of Reconstruction

As the Civil War ended and the nation began the long process of putting North and South back together again, politicians, generals, and other national leaders soon realized the enormity of that task. The animosity between these two geographically defined regions was so great that it led to the assassination of a president in the days following the end of the conflict,

30. Mark Noll, *The Civil War as a Theological Crisis* (Chapel Hill: University of North Carolina Press, 2006).

31. Albert Barnes, "The Church and Slavery," in *A Documentary History of Religion in America to 1877*, ed. Edwin S. Gaustad and Mark A. Noll, 3rd ed. (Grand Rapids: Eerdmans, 2003), 496-98.

32. Frederick A. Ross, "Slavery Ordained of God," in Gaustad and Noll, *A Documentary History of Religion in America to 1877*, 500.

and even today one notices a significant cultural divide between the north and the south. Church leaders, too, experienced the difficulties associated with trying to put divided denominations back together again. Some of those efforts lasted decades before unification resulted, as with the Methodists. Other faith groups, such as the Baptists, never became one again. In reality, racism caused and perpetuated a deep division within America and the American church. A careful look at the Reconstruction period allows students of history to see the depth of that chasm.

Historian Charles Reagan Wilson's landmark publication, *Baptized in Blood*, provides a picture of the Reconstruction period by describing the "religion of the Lost Cause" among Southerners following the Civil War.[33] Most Southerners believed God was on their side during the conflict between the states, and they needed a way to make sense of their defeat. Wilson argues that Lost Cause civil religion was a confluence of Christianity and Southern Confederate culture. Ministers such as Baptist John Williams Jones led the construction of Lost Cause religion, complete with sacred stories (revivals in the Confederate camps, the holiness of Confederate leaders, and stories of heroes, "martyrs," and models of Southern identity), saints (Lee, Davis, Jackson), hymns, holy days (Confederate Memorial Day, celebrated on Davis's birthday), symbols (Confederate flag, monuments to the Confederate saints, Confederate saints portrayed in church stained glass windows), and organizations (churches and their clergy, United Daughters of the Confederacy, United Confederate Veterans). The cultural narrative adopted by many Southerners posited the belief that God used their defeat in the Civil War to discipline God's chosen people. After all, God only disciplines those God loves!

In similar fashion, Abraham Lincoln sought to make sense of the Civil War through his understanding of God's providence. In his "Second Inaugural Address," Lincoln said:

> If we shall suppose that American slavery is one of those offenses which, in the providence of God, must needs come, but which, having continued through His appointed time, He now wills to remove, and that He gives to both North and South this terrible war as the woe due to those by whom the offense came, shall we discern therein any departure from those divine attributes which the believers in a living

---

33. Charles Reagan Wilson, *Baptized in Blood: The Religion of the Lost Cause, 1865–1920* (Athens: University of Georgia Press, 1980).

God always ascribe to Him? Fondly do we hope, fervently do we pray, that this mighty scourge of war may speedily pass away. Yet, if God wills that it continue until all the wealth piled by the bondsman's two hundred and fifty years of unrequited toil shall be sunk, and until every drop of blood drawn with the lash shall be paid by another drawn with the sword, as was said three thousand years ago, so still it must be said "the judgments of the Lord are true and righteous altogether."[34]

Both North and South, then, read their situations through the lens of God's will. As Lincoln said in the same speech, "Both read the same Bible and pray to the same God." Northerners and Southerners, praying and believing in the same God, believed God set their pasts, presents, and futures in motion.

Wilson's description of Lost Cause religion grants students of history a glimpse of the ways in which Southerners made sense of their defeat following the Civil War. In response to God's tough love, Southerners poured themselves into creating the perfect society, one modeled after Victorian ideals. Wilson describes one aspect of this society as the "cult of chivalry" that focused on "manners, women, military affairs, the ideal of Greek democracy, and Roman oratory."[35] In many ways, the society described by Wilson bears a striking resemblance to the Southern, organic society described by Williamson. In both societies, law and order stand as prime virtues. In both societies, chivalry reigns as men seek to protect women. In order for both societies to function properly, each member of the society must stay in his or her place. Though Abraham Lincoln's Emancipation Proclamation outlawed slavery in America, Southerners found new ways to keep African Americans in their place within the Southern, organic society. Sharecropping, violence, racial terrorism, and Jim Crow segregation ensured that white men and women would continue to stand above African Americans in the South.

During the earliest days of Reconstruction, the South appeared to be on its way to significantly curbing the negative impact of racism. Concerned citizens of the North made their way south to help in the rebuilding process. Union troops offered protection in the streets and at the ballot box. The

34. Abraham Lincoln, "Second Inaugural Address of the Late President Lincoln" (1865), Library of Congress, accessed January 5, 2018, https://www.loc.gov/item/scsm000283.

35. Wilson, *Baptized in Blood*, 3.

protection and aid offered by the North had immediate political impact. Lerone Bennett describes the tremendous strides taken by former slaves during Reconstruction:

> A former slave named Blanche Kelso Bruce was representing Mississippi in the United States Senate. Pinckney Benton Stewart Pinchback, young, charming, daring, was sitting in the governor's office in Louisiana. In Mississippi, South Carolina, and Louisiana, black lieutenant governers [sic] were sitting on the right hand of power. A black was secretary of state in Florida; a black was on the state supreme court in South Carolina. In these and other Southern states, blacks were superintendents of education, state treasurers, adjutant generals, solicitors, judges and major generals of militia. Robert H. Wood was mayor of Natchez, Mississippi, and Norris Wright Cuney was running for mayor of Galveston, Texas. Seven blacks were sitting in the [United States] House of Representatives.[36]

As Emerson and Smith point out, this rapid change on the political and cultural landscape proved too much for many white Americans, Northern or Southern, to accept.[37] Within a few years of the war, Northern troops and citizens had returned home, allowing Southerners to deal with the race problem on their own.

Left to their own devices, many Southerners turned to violence as a tool to protect their society. Between 1882 and 1885, there were 227 reported lynchings of African Americans. Between 1889 and 1899, that number increased to 1,240. In 1898 alone, white mobs seized and murdered 104 African Americans.[38] Afraid of a society influenced by African American voters, white legislators passed stringent laws restricting uneducated former slaves from voting. Those who did meet the legal requirements were discouraged from exercising their new right, guaranteed by the Fifteenth Amendment, by mobs of white people at voting stations or by the fear of being lynched when the sun went down.

In response to such blatant racism, much of it extended by white citizens who also held positions of authority in Christian congregations, most Afri-

---

36. Lerone Bennett, *Before the Mayflower: A History of Black People in America*, 6th rev. ed. (New York: Penguin Books, 1993), 215.

37. Emerson and Smith, *Divided by Faith*, 38–39.

38. Raboteau, *Canaan Land*, 72.

can Americans fled the white churches of their former masters as soon as they were able. During the Reconstruction period, independent black denominations emerged in the South and many independent black denominations that had been born in the North also moved southward. Between 1860 and 1872, the African Methodist Episcopal Zion Church increased from 27,000 members to over 200,000 members, with most of its growth coming from African Americans in the South. By 1880, the African Methodist Episcopal Church had grown to 400,000 members. In South Carolina alone, African American membership in the white-led Southern branch of the Methodist church fell from 42,469 in 1860 to just 653 in 1873. Following the war, African Americans also swarmed out of white-led congregations aligned with the Southern Baptist Convention. In 1858, there were 29,211 African Americans associated with the Southern Baptist Convention in South Carolina. By 1874, there were only 1,614. An independent African American Baptist denomination, the National Baptist Convention, was formed in 1895.[39]

In addition to joining African American denominations or establishing new, independent ones, some African Americans found ways to distance themselves from their white counterparts without leaving predominantly white Christian denominations. One branch of the Stone-Campbell Movement, the Churches of Christ, provides an excellent example of this phenomenon. To an even greater extent than Baptist churches, Churches of Christ lack any overarching denominational structures to bind individual congregations together; they have historically found cohesion through Christian colleges, religious periodicals, and lectureships associated with leaders and members of their congregations.[40] Baptists, Methodists, and Presbyterians initiated their sectional divisions in the antebellum period through official means—denominational meeting votes or the formation of new conventions. The Stone-Campbell Movement lacked any vehicle for such official pronouncements; therefore, Northern and Southern members of the movement divided, over a period of decades, into sectional bodies, known eventually as Disciples of Christ (in the North) and Churches of Christ (in the South). By the late nineteenth century, each group had developed its own means of cohesion and identity formation: each independent tradition had its own colleges, journals, and lectureships. Within

39. Raboteau, *Canaan Land*, 68–69.

40. For a fuller explanation of the way these three entities have provided cohesion among Churches of Christ congregations, see Wes Crawford, *Shattering the Illusion: How African American Churches of Christ Moved from Segregation to Independence* (Abilene, TX: Abilene Christian University Press, 2013), 27–53.

the Stone-Campbell Movement, the emergence of independent channels of cohesion signals separation.[41]

Though still considered members of the same denomination, African American members of Churches of Christ began to develop their own, independent systems for cohesion in the decades following the Civil War. By the time of the American civil rights movement in the mid-twentieth century, African American members of Churches of Christ had their own religious periodical (the *Christian Echo*), their own school (Southwestern Christian College), and their own lectureship (the Annual National Lectureship).[42] Throughout this same period (and even today), African American and white members of Churches of Christ interacted only occasionally, and African Americans were engaged by whites primarily through paternalistic gestures or outright racism. The vast majority of African American and white members of this denomination worship separately in racially defined congregations each Sunday morning. Even though these congregations exist across the South with the common label "Church of Christ" on their signs, the racist interactions between African American and white members of this denomination have caused a fissure every bit as deep as the gap between African American and white Presbyterians, Methodists, or Baptists.

Throughout the period of Reconstruction, white Christians in the North and the South kept African Americans at arm's length through laws, segregated school systems, and racially defined congregations. African Americans, in response to continuous and pervasive white racism, established their own independent congregations and denominations. At the height of the civil rights movement, Martin Luther King Jr. stated: "It is one of the tragedies of our nation, one of the shameful tragedies, that eleven o'clock on Sunday morning is one of the most segregated hours, if not the most segregated hour, in Christian America."[43] This study has shown the truth of King's assessment, and also that America was infected with the virus of racism in its infancy.

---

41. This topic has been treated in much greater detail in Douglas Foster, "The Struggle for Unity during the Period of Division in the Restoration Movement, 1875-1900" (PhD diss., Vanderbilt University, 1987); David Edwin Harrell, "The Sectional Origins of the Churches of Christ," *Journal of Southern History* 30 (1964): 261-77; and Richard Hughes, *Reviving the Ancient Faith: The Story of Churches of Christ in America*, 2nd ed. (Abilene, TX: Abilene Christian University Press, 2008).

42. Crawford, *Shattering the Illusion*, 143-77.

43. "Dr. Martin Luther King, Jr. Discusses Sit-In Demonstrations," interview by Frank Van Der Linden et al., *Meet the Press*, April 17, 1960, https://archives.nbclearn.com/portal/site /k-12/browse/?cuecard=5093, at 23:46.

Regardless of the era in American history, race has been a central character in the story of American Christianity, and it has left division in its path. David W. Wills was correct in his assessment: the encounter between black and white is one of the defining themes of American religious history. From the earliest decades of the sixteenth century to the first decades of the twenty-first century, the power of the Christian gospel in the hands of American Christians has been unable to challenge the drastic effects of pseudoscience and faulty exegesis. In Galatians 3:28, the apostle Paul writes: "There is neither Jew nor Greek, there is neither slave nor free, there is no male and female, for you are all one in Christ Jesus" (ESV). Paul's words serve as a reminder that Christ's gospel has the power to bridge the many social divides of our world, no matter how deep or wide those chasms may be. May God speed the day when this dream of unity, rather than the present reality of division, is the witness of the American church.

The Role of Religion in the Lynching Culture of Jim Crow America

CHRISTOPHER R. HUTSON

In 1890 the state of Louisiana passed a law that black and white passengers could not ride together in the same railroad cars. Segregation by law and custom had been well established in Northern free states in the decades before the Civil War, when most Southern blacks still lived on plantations in close proximity to their white owners. But after the war, white Southerners began to emulate the Northern practice.[1] Railroad cars for black passengers were dubbed "Jim Crow" cars, a term borrowed from African American folk culture popularized among whites by minstrels who performed in blackface, caricaturing African Americans.[2] In Louisiana, Homer Plessy challenged the railroad segregation law all the way to the United States Supreme Court, which in 1896 upheld the Louisiana law. The landmark *Plessy v. Ferguson* decision (1896) established the phrase "separate but equal" as the law of the land and opened the way for waves of new segregation laws across the South, as Southern states tried to outdo each other in mandating segregation in every aspect of society.[3] This situation continued until the landmark decision

1. C. Vann Woodward, *The Strange Career of Jim Crow*, 3rd ed. (Oxford: Oxford University Press, 1974), 17–29.

2. Ken Padgett, "Origins of Jump Jim Crow," Blackface!, accessed December 4, 2017, http://www.black-face.com/jim-crow.htm.

3. For a representative sample of segregation laws, see a list of Jim Crow laws compiled by the National Park Service, accessed December 4, 2017, https://ferris.edu/HTMLS/news/jimcrow/pdfs-docs/origins/jimcrowlaws.pdf. For oral histories of black experiences, see William H. Chafe, Raymond Gavins, and Robert Korstad, eds., *Remembering Jim Crow: African Americans Tell about Life in the Segregated South* (New York: New Press, 2001). For a range of

I am pleased to dedicate this essay to Doug Foster, who over the years has believed that African American history is American history and not an appendix to it. Some of this material was presented at the Pepperdine Bible Lectures, Pepperdine University, Malibu, California, in 2017. Thanks to Tanya Hart, Don Haymes, and Horace Means for reading earlier drafts and improving my argument.

Brown v. Board of Education of Topeka, Kansas (1954), when the Supreme Court found that "separate educational facilities are inherently unequal" and unconstitutional. The *Brown* decision paved the way for the civil rights movement. This chapter explores a time when racial segregation laws were legal, a period framed by the two Supreme Court decisions, of 1896 and 1954, respectively, with the understanding that some segregation laws were in place throughout the country decades before 1896 and some continued for decades after 1954. Also, even though de jure segregation began to collapse after 1954, there remained de facto segregation and the fear and loathing and misunderstanding that "Jim Crow" represented.

This chapter describes the role of Christianity in the Jim Crow era, a period characterized by segregation laws and by cultural attitudes that undergirded those laws. The first section of the chapter describes one specific lynching in Waco, Texas, as a case study, then the historical context of the lynching culture in America. The next section describes how white Christians twisted the Bible to rationalize their prejudices; this is followed by a description of the resurgence of a genuinely Christian critique of the problem and orientation to a better way of life.

The Lynching of Jesse Washington (1916)

On the afternoon of Monday, May 8, 1916, a fifty-three-year-old white woman, Lucy Fryer, was found in a shed on her farm near Waco, in Mc-Lennan County, Texas, dead from multiple blows to the head with a blunt object.[4] A rumor spread that she may also have been raped. Within hours, Sheriff Sam Fleming arrested a seventeen-year-old black boy named Jesse Washington, a field hand on the Fryer farm. Washington had blood on his clothes, which he said was his own, from a nosebleed. Immediately, word spread that the murderer had been caught, and cries went up for swift justice. Fearing mob violence, Fleming moved the suspect to neighboring Hill County for questioning in the Hillsboro jail. Washington was illiterate, but

---

African American religious responses to the circumstances, see Milton C. Sernett, ed., *African American Religious History: A Documentary Witness*, 2nd ed., C. Eric Lincoln Series on the Black Experience (Durham, NC: Duke University Press, 1999).

4. Quotations and other information in the following paragraphs come from Patricia Bernstein, *The First Waco Horror: The Lynching of Jesse Washington and the Rise of the NAACP*, Centennial Series of the Association of Former Students, Texas A&M University 101 (College Station: Texas A&M University Press, 2005); it is based on exhaustive examination of primary sources.

while he was in custody, the McLennan County sheriff's deputies coaxed him to place his X on a detailed and graphic confession that he obviously did not write.[5] Afterward, he was transferred to Dallas, again to keep him safe from mob violence.[6] Sheriff Fleming, who was running for reelection at the time, heeded the cries for swift "justice" and scheduled a trial for the following Monday, only one week after the murder.

On the morning of May 15, the city of Waco was buzzing with excitement. By 9:00 a.m., the courtroom was overflowing, and people were cramming the hallways and stairwells of the courthouse. Meanwhile, three blocks away, photographer Fred Gildersleeve was setting up his camera in the mayor's office on the second floor of city hall, from which he anticipated a sweeping view of action later in the day. Another crowd, "the largest ever seen," according to the Waco Morning News, was milling about the jail, hoping to catch a glimpse of a murderer. One teenage girl declared, "I would just give anything to see that negro." The crowd at the jail did not know the accused had been moved to the judge's office in the courthouse late Sunday night. There, six young, inexperienced, court-appointed defense attorneys had met Washington for the first time and told him there was no possibility of acquittal, that he should spend the night in prayer.

At 10:00 a.m., the sheriff cleared spectators from the jury box and forced the courtroom crowd to clear a path for the judge. When the defendant was brought in, one of the spectators pulled a gun and said, "Might as well get him now." But a cooler head admonished, "Let them have their trial. We'll get him before sundown." It took thirty-five minutes to empanel a jury, some jurors being lifted over the crowd to the jury box.

The trial took another forty minutes and consisted mainly of the medical examiner's testimony on the cause of death and the testimony of law enforcement officers about their investigation and the defendant's confession. There was no mention of rape. Only one of Washington's defense attorneys spoke, asking a single question: Did you do it? Washington responded that he had and mumbled that he was sorry. After deliberating only four minutes, the jury returned a verdict of guilty. One person said it was "as fair as any ever given in this courtroom." Someone else yelled, "Get him!" And the

5. Bernstein, The First Waco Horror, 94–95, reproduces the full text of the confession from the trial transcript and from the Waco Semi-Weekly Tribune, May 13, 1916, 2.
6. Fleming's fears were warranted. Since the end of Reconstruction in 1877, already seven black men had been lynched in McLennan County, according to William D. Carrigan, The Making of a Lynching Culture: Violence and Vigilantism in Central Texas, 1836–1916 (Urbana: University of Illinois Press, 2004), appendix A.

crowd surged forward before the judge could finish writing the verdict in his docket.

People had been waiting all morning to see a good lynching, and this was the time. The sheriff's deputies did not interfere as spectators seized Washington, hustled him down a back stairway and up the street, stripping him naked along the way. The crowd surged first toward the Brazos River, intending to hang their victim from the Washington Avenue Bridge, as they had done in a previous lynching in 1905. But the ringleaders steered them toward city hall. Onlookers, eager to participate in the death of a murderer, beat the boy with clubs and stabbed him with knives. Under a tree in front of city hall, crates and packing materials appeared. They put a chain around Washington's neck and threw it over a branch. They doused the crates and the boy with fuel oil and struck a match. When Washington tried to climb the chain, they cut off his fingers, then his toes and ears as souvenirs. Someone cut off his penis and reportedly wrapped it in a handkerchief to show his friends later. Boys in the branches climbed down to escape the billowing smoke. Men hoisted Washington by his neck and began lowering him into the flames, raising and lowering him again and again for over an hour. While the well-dressed men and women on the lawn jostled to see, the mayor watched from his office, along with the chief of police and the photographer.

When it was over, a man on a horse lassoed the charred torso and dragged it through the streets. The skull broke off, and children pried out teeth for souvenirs. More professional souvenirs appeared in the form of postcards hastily produced by Fred Gildersleeve.

The Jesse Washington lynching became a sensation, because it was so well documented, beginning with those photographs. Also, the NAACP (National Association for the Advancement of Colored People) hired a white suffragette activist named Elisabeth Freeman to visit Waco under cover and gather information. She collected the postcards; interviewed Waco citizens and civic leaders, including the mayor and trial judge; and even sweet-talked her way to a copy of the official trial transcript. From her letters and detailed report, W. E. B. Du Bois compiled a vivid account in a special issue of the NAACP journal, *Crisis*.[7] As a result, this particular lynching was reported in newspapers as far away as Chicago, New York, and London.

7. W. E. B. Du Bois (unsigned), "The Waco Horror," supplement to the *Crisis* 12, no. 3 (July 1916), accessed December 4, 2017, http://credo.library.umass.edu/view/full/mums312 -b163-i124.

Newspapers in Waco editorialized against a mob taking the law into their own hands and against the desecration of the corpse, and then they hastened to put the story aside as the work of a few rabble-rousers from the lower classes. But Gildersleeve's photographs tell a different story. The spectators were men and women in fashionable attire, dressed as if for church. They were estimated at fifteen thousand when Waco's population at the time was only twenty-five thousand. They were not the dregs. They were society. And Waco in those days was a society town, home of a dozen colleges, including Baylor University, the oldest college in the state. Waco was a center of cotton processing, boasted the tallest skyscraper in Texas, and counted some thirty-nine white and twenty-four black churches. No doubt most of the spectators were churchgoing people.

In the aftermath, no one questioned whether the trial was in fact "as fair as any ever given in this courtroom." The alleged perpetrator was a minor. He was illiterate, and one teacher reportedly said he was unable to learn. Was he mentally competent to understand what was happening to him or the contents of the "confession" that he signed with an X? We cannot apply modern criminal justice standards to an arrest and trial that happened fifty years before *Miranda*, but it is worth noting that a teenage boy was interrogated without a lawyer by a sheriff who needed a quick conviction to boost his chances for reelection. Whose blood was on his clothes? Was the "confession" coerced? Did the defendant have adequate representation for his defense? Did the deputies plant evidence—the hammer allegedly used to kill Mrs. Fryer? Why did law enforcement not make any effort to stop the lynching?

Sadly, there was hardly a detail in the Jesse Washington story that was not repeated hundreds or thousands of times.[8] Lynching, or vigilante justice, the action of private citizens to execute alleged criminals outside the processes of the judicial system, was widespread in America in the nineteenth and early twentieth centuries. On the western frontier in the mid-nineteenth century, where populations were thin and law enforcement thinner, lynching was a common response to thefts of livestock. But in 1896, the *Chicago Tribune*'s annual tally of lynchings in America reported for the first time more black victims than white, and in subsequent years their records showed lynching as "mostly southern and directed almost exclu-

8. Christopher Waldrep, ed., *Lynching in America: A History in Documents* (New York: New York University Press, 2006); Grace Elizabeth Hale, *Making Whiteness: The Culture of Segregation in the South, 1890–1940* (New York: Pantheon, 1998), 199–239.

sively at blacks,"[9] a phenomenon that historian William Carrigan describes as the "racialization of lynching."[10] Between 1882 and 1968, the Tuskegee Institute documented 4,743 lynchings in America, of whom 3,446 victims were black.[11] In McLennan County, Texas, between 1885 and 1921, there were 10 confirmed lynchings and 8 more unconfirmed, and all the victims were black.[12]

How could the white Christians of Waco turn blind eyes to the brutalities, dismissing them as anomalous, minor disturbances, or approving them, or even participating? It is impossible to understand the Jim Crow era without taking stock of the role religion played in America to justify segregation in both North and South and to create a climate in which lynching was seen as something regrettable, perhaps, but inevitable, excusable, even necessary. What we need to see is how Christians co-opted the Bible in support of the white supremacy that pervaded American culture, North and South alike.

The Historical Context of the Waco Horror (1865–1954)

In the half-century before the Civil War, Christians staked out various positions on slavery. At one extreme, a few argued that slavery was immoral and antithetical to the gospel and should be abolished immediately. Proponents of this abolitionist view were primarily in the North, and included such prominent activists as William Lloyd Garrison (Episcopal), president of the American Anti-Slavery Society and editor of the *Liberator*; Frederick Douglass and Harriet Tubman (both African Methodist Episcopal Zion [AME Zion]); and John Boggs (Disciples of Christ), editor of the *North-western Christian Magazine*. Abolitionists in the South were scarce, but notables

9. Waldrep, *Lynching in America*, 115.

10. Carrigan, *Making of a Lynching Culture*, 132–61, quotation from 133; for contemporary observations on the national trend, see Ida B. Wells, *A Red Record: Tabulated Statistics and Alleged Causes of Lynching in the United States, 1892–1893–1894* (Chicago: Donohue & Henneberry, 1895), excerpted in Waldrep, *Lynching in America*, 4–6; Charles M. Bishop, "The Causes, Consequences, and Cure of Mob Violence," in *Democracy in Earnest*, ed. James E. McCulloch (Washington, DC: Southern Sociological Congress, 1918), 191–200. On the rise of the NAACP and its journal *Crisis* in response to the rising tide of black lynchings, see Bernstein, *The First Waco Horror*, 29–62.

11. "022 Lynching Information," Tuskegee University, accessed December 4, 2017, http://archive.tuskegee.edu/archive/handle/123456789/507.

12. Carrigan, *Making of a Lynching Culture*, appendices A and B.

included Denmark Vesey (African Methodist Episcopal Church), who organized a slave revolt in South Carolina in 1822, and Levi Coffin (Quaker) of Greensboro, North Carolina, who became the unofficial "president" of the Underground Railroad.

At the other extreme, many argued that it was God's grand design for Europeans to dominate the world and black Africans to be their slaves. Indeed, most Christians in the South found abolitionist views so intolerable that in the 1840s the largest denominations split along sectional lines. The Methodist Episcopal Church South, the Presbyterian Church in the United States, and the Southern Baptist Convention all embraced slavery as divinely authorized. After these splits, Southern clergy developed increasingly elaborate and ingenious rereadings of the Bible in defense of slavery, which they routinely preached to Southern churchgoers, and they adapted their arguments for pro-segregation sermons in the next century.

In the broad middle, most Christians of all denominations North and South agreed that the Bible recognized both slaves and slave owners as faithful people of God, as long as owners treated their slaves fairly and justly, according to biblical mandates. For example, an anonymous South Carolina Episcopalian argued in 1823: "Slavery is found not to be contrary to the laws of God, so it is left to our own judgement, whether to hold slaves, or not. But the same God who permits slavery, has required of us, in his holy word, their religious instruction. And it certainly appears to a religious man, to be inconsistent, to say the least of it, to claim the authority of God, in one case, and to reject it in another."[13]

While moderates took comfort in their Christian piety, they disagreed on whether slavery was essential to the economy of the South or bad economic and political policy that should be phased out over time. Even so, whether one adopted a moderate position that God *allowed* slavery or a hardline position that God *mandated* slavery, the practical effect in the South was that the vast majority of Christians saw no contradiction between their faith and their "peculiar institution." At the outbreak of the Civil War, several Confederate states formally stated the reasons why they seceded. In its

---

13. *Practical Considerations Founded on the Scriptures Relative to the Slave Population of South-Carolina* (Charleston, SC: A. E. Miller, 1823), 37. For a similarly "moderate" position in the thought of prominent Northern editor and educator Alexander Campbell, see Christopher R. Hutson, "Middle Ground? Alexander Campbell on Slavery and Carroll Osburn on Gender," in *Restoring the First-Century Church in the Twenty-First Century: Essays on the Stone-Campbell Restoration Movement (in Honor of Don Haymes)*, ed. Warren Lewis and Hans Rollmann, Studies in the History and Culture of World Christianities 1 (Eugene, OR: Wipf and Stock), 335–54.

"Declaration of Causes" in 1861, the state of Texas asserted the importance of slavery and the right of each state to self-determination. But then Texas went further than other states in spelling out the ideological underpinnings of their argument:

> We hold as undeniable truths that the governments of the various States, and of the confederacy itself, were established exclusively by the white race, for themselves and their posterity; that the African race had no agency in their establishment; that they were rightfully held and regarded as an inferior and dependent race, and in that condition only could their existence in this country be rendered beneficial or tolerable.
>
> That in this free government *all white men are and of right ought to be entitled to equal civil and political rights*; that the servitude of the African race, as existing in these States, is mutually beneficial to both bond and free, and is abundantly authorized and justified by the experience of mankind, and the revealed will of the Almighty Creator, as recognized by all Christian nations; while the destruction of the existing relations between the two races, as advocated by our sectional enemies, would bring inevitable calamities upon both and desolation upon the fifteen slave-holding states.[14]

The anticipated "inevitable calamities" and "desolation" were financial, as the economies of most slave-holding states, including Texas, were based on cotton produced by slave labor. The declaration of secession of the state of Georgia made explicit the economic consequences of abolition, estimating the total value of slaves in the Southern states as $3 billion in 1861.[15] Indeed, after the Civil War, property tax receipts in McLennan County, Texas, dropped 73 percent, half of which was the loss of slaves, and the local economy remained depressed for a decade.[16] We should not underestimate the

---

14. The full text is at "The Declaration of Causes of Seceding States: Texas," Civil War Trust, accessed December 4, 2017, https://www.civilwar.org/learn/primary-sources/declaration-causes-seceding-states#Texas.

15. "The Declaration of Causes of Seceding States: Georgia," Civil War Trust, accessed December 4, 2017, https://www.civilwar.org/learn/primary-sources/declaration-causes-seceding-states#Georgia.

16. Vivian Elizabeth Smyrl, "McLennan County," *Handbook of Texas Online*, Texas State Historical Society, modified September 2, 2016, http://www.tshaonline.org/handbook/online/articles/hcm08.

ability of human beings to rationalize anything on which they believe their economic security depends.

After the Civil War, it might appear that the abolitionist arguments had carried the day. During the period of Reconstruction (1865–1877), the former Confederate states were administered by the Union army under a military occupation, and Congress created the Freedmen's Bureau within the Department of War to oversee the transition of former slaves into free society. Congress enacted a series of new laws granting civil rights to the former slaves. Those laws were buttressed by the Thirteenth Amendment of the US Constitution (1865), abolishing slavery; the Fourteenth Amendment (1866), guaranteeing "due process of law" and "equal protection of the laws" to all citizens; and the Fifteenth Amendment (1869), prohibiting discrimination in voting rights "on account of race, color, or previous condition of servitude." Furthermore, since blacks were a majority of the populations of Mississippi and South Carolina, as well as a majority population within some congressional districts of a number of other states, blacks began to hold local, state, and federal offices. During Reconstruction, fourteen blacks were elected to the US House of Representatives from seven Southern states, and two to the Senate, both from Mississippi.

On the surface, therefore, it might seem that Reconstruction was a time when America was moving toward racial integration. With the abolition of slavery, white Christians in the South experienced a crisis of faith, but not because they recognized how grossly they had misread their Bibles. Consider, for example, the entry for Sunday, October 8, 1865, from the diary of Gertrude Clanton Thomas of Augusta, Georgia:

> About one year ago I came up the Avenue & selecting a seat in the Pine Woods I leaned against a tree and read *Nelly Norton* and tried to solve the vexed problem of "Whether Slavery was right?" I came with my Bible in my hand to consult and refer to and hoped to be convinced of what I doubted—I little thought then that the question would be so summarily disposed of in less than nine months from that time. Today Slavery as it once existed is a thing of the past & has no longer an existence in the Southern States.
>
> We owned more than 90 Negroes with a prospect of inheriting many more from Pa's estate—By the surrender of the Southern army slavery became a thing of the past and we were reduced from a state of affluence to comparative poverty—so far as I individually am concerned to utter beggary for the thirty thousand dollars Pa gave

me when I was married was invested in Negroes alone— . . . I did not know until then how intimately my faith in revelations and my faith in the institution of slavery had been woven together—true I had seen the evil of the latter but if the *Bible* was right then slavery *must be*—Slavery was done away with and my faith in God's Holy Book was terribly shaken. For a time I doubted God. . . . When I opened the Bible the numerous allusions to slavery mocked me. Our cause was lost. Good men had had faith in that cause. Earnest prayers had ascended from honest hearts—Was so much faith to be lost? I was bewildered—I felt all this and could not see God's hand—

The Negroes suddenly emancipated from control were wild with their newly gained and little understood freedom. Cap Bryant of the Freedman's Bureau aided as much as was possible in sowing broadcast the seed of dissention between the former master and slave and caused what might have continued to be a kind interest to become in many cases a bitter enmity. The Negro was the all absorbing theme which engaged all minds. The Negro and Cap Bryant!—The Negroes regard him as a Savior (They are just beginning to discover the cloven foot).[17]

In the waning months of the war, Thomas resolved to settle in her mind a biblical doctrine of slavery, taking as her guide the recently published novel *Nellie Norton* by Baptist pastor Ebenezer W. Warren.[18] The novel tells how beautiful, young Nellie travels from her home in New England to visit her wealthy uncle in Savannah, Georgia. All the slaves she encounters are well dressed and profess that they are happy, enjoy their work, and are grateful that their masters have taught them Christianity. When she expresses disapproval of the "laws and sentiments" that perpetuate slavery, her uncle replies that "you abominate the law of God, and the sentiments inculcated by his holy prophets and apostles."[19] Nellie's educated and genteel uncle is a formidable advocate on all aspects of slavery in history, in law, and above all in the Bible.

17. Virginia Ingraham Burr, ed., *The Secret Eye: The Journal of Ella Gertrude Clanton Thomas, 1848–1889*, rev. ed. (Chapel Hill: University of North Carolina Press, 1990), 276–77.

18. E. W. Warren, *Nellie Norton. Or, Southern Slavery and the Bible: A Scriptural Refutation of the Principal Arguments upon which the Abolitionists Rely. A Vindication of Southern Slavery from the Old and New Testaments* (Macon, GA: Burke, Boykin & Co., 1864). In her diary Thomas misspelled the name of the title character.

19. Warren, *Nellie Norton*, 6.

The novel is a series of contrived conversations in which "Uncle T" discusses every relevant Bible verse from Ham to Philemon, taking account of the views of the illustrious Bible scholars of the day, so that Nellie is thoroughly disabused of "the usual prejudices against slavery which Northern birth and education instill."[20] Uncle T's grand summation of all the arguments concludes "that abolitionism unavoidably tends to infidelity."[21] When Nellie's own pastor, an erudite doctor of divinity well versed in abolitionist views, visits from New England, even he is unable to answer arguments in favor of the proposition that "Slavery was not only permitted but absolutely decreed" in the Bible.[22] Later, he is caught helping a young slave escape to the North, and he is callow in his denials, lying in court to save himself and abandoning the boy to his fate. Subsequently, as chaplain of a Massachusetts regiment, he proves cowardly on the battlefield. Meanwhile, Nellie marries a gallant Southern gentleman and embraces the happy life of the Georgia planters. The novel can be read both as a response to Harriet Beecher Stowe's *Uncle Tom's Cabin* (1852) and as a handbook for anyone who, like Gertrude Thomas, wanted to believe that the Bible endorsed the slave society.

As her diary makes clear, Thomas was convinced that slavery met divine approval, which led to a crisis of faith when emancipation came. Yet she did not question whether she or Warren had misinterpreted the Bible. Rather, the source of her depression was her loss of financial security in that her fortune had been bound up almost entirely in human chattel.[23] She was in Georgia living through the "calamities" that the state of Texas had predicted if the slaves were freed. She questioned the capacity of African Americans to cope with their new freedom, and she pilloried "Cap Bryant," the local administrator of the Freedmen's Bureau, in language that anticipated the novels of ordained Baptist minister Thomas Dixon Jr.[24]

20. Warren, *Nellie Norton*, 8. For a similar systematic treatment of slavery from a Southern Presbyterian minister, see George D. Armstrong, *The Christian Doctrine of Slavery* (New York: Charles Scribner, 1857).

21. Warren, *Nellie Norton*, 197.

22. Warren, *Nellie Norton*, 33.

23. Burr, *The Secret Eye*, 276n11, notes that, according to her father's will, Thomas received from her father $25,000, mainly in slaves, and her husband another $5,000.

24. Thomas Dixon Jr., *The Leopard's Spots: A Romance of the White Man's Burden—1865–1900* (New York: Doubleday, Page & Co., 1902); Dixon, *The Clansman: An Historical Romance of the Ku Klux Klan* (New York: Doubleday, Page & Co., 1905); Dixon, *The Traitor: A Story of the Fall of the Invisible Empire* (New York: Doubleday, Page & Co., 1907).

Dixon's first novel, *The Leopard's Spots* (1902), describes beleaguered, genteel Southerners harried by "marauding bands of negroes armed to the teeth terrorising the country, stealing, burning and murdering,"[25] aided by scurrilous Yankee scalawags and carpetbaggers and by Republican politicians, including a malevolent agent of the Freedmen's Bureau named Simon Legree. As Dixon tells it, the heroic Ku Klux Klan imposes vigilante justice against the "reign of terror." In the novel, when the North Carolina Supreme Court strikes down a law forbidding intermarriage between blacks and whites, the KKK responds by lynching Tim Shelby, a black school commissioner and candidate for chief justice of the North Carolina Supreme Court.[26] Dixon's novel was so successful that he followed up with *The Clansman* (1905) and *The Traitor* (1907). This "Reconstruction Trilogy" became the basis for D. W. Griffith's wildly popular silent movie *Birth of a Nation* (1915), which idolized the Ku Klux Klan.

Gertrude Thomas's diary shows that Dixon was not creating a new ideology but reflecting sentiments simmering in Southern souls since the time of his own childhood in Reconstruction-era North Carolina. In particular, we should note the Southern perspective that abolitionism was opposed to the will of God. Confederates had viewed the war as an infidel invasion that called for killing Yankees in defense of gospel truth. Thus, James Warley Miles, an Episcopal priest and professor in the College of Charleston, could preach in 1863 that "certain races are permanently inferior in their capacities to others," namely, "the African entrusted to our care," and he could proclaim that the Confederate states "have a mission of peace and benefaction to the world."[27] Similarly, James R. Wilmeth, chaplain (Churches of Christ) in the Thirty-First Texas Cavalry under General Richard M. Gano (also a Churches of Christ minister), was disgusted to see blacks in the Union army near Camden, Arkansas: "There was the Gen. [Steele] with colored official inferiors but social and political equals. How humiliating to any man of moral dignity and refined taste!"[28] And yet, in appealing for his own perma-

25. Dixon, *The Leopard's Spots*, 100.

26. Dixon, *The Leopard's Spots*, 147–50.

27. Robert R. Mathisen, ed., *Religion and the American Civil War: A History in Documents* (New York: Routledge, 2015), 235–36. Mathisen collects numerous examples of wartime sermons and religious documents from North and South.

28. James R. Wilmeth, "Thoughts and Things as They Occurred in Camp A.D. 1864," diary, transcribed by Martha Carroll (2002), Abilene Christian University Special Collections, Microfilm-929.2, Wilmeth Family Papers, 1837–1925, entry for April 24, 1864. At the time, Major General Frederick Steele commanded the VII Corps of the Union army

nent appointment to the post of chaplain, Wilmeth affirmed without irony that "there is a holy & just God who presides over the destinies of Nations & armies . . . no Nation nor army can, as a body, enjoy His benign appro-bation while habitually disregarding His sovereign authority & indulging in a course of conduct repugnant to His divine will, but that in order to the enjoyment of this blessing, His authority must be recognized & the precepts of His moral government inculcated."[29]

Confederate soldiers internalized such sentiments from their religious leaders. Sergeant William Pitt Chambers of the Forty-Sixth Mississippi Vol-unteer Infantry, for example, was confident in God's providence: "relying on God's protecting mercy, I went forward," and "inwardly, commending my soul to my Savior, I mounted the crest of the hill."[30] He mused in his diary about the possible "nominal freedom" of an "inferior race," about Yankee prisoners who switched sides and enlisted in the Confederate army as "the lowest and most debased looking set of men I ever saw . . . a discredit to any civilized army."[31] By 1865, Chambers saw defeat as inevitable, but rather than considering that God might have favored the abolitionist cause, he rationalized Confederate defeat as God's chastisement of his people, thus embracing the religion of the Lost Cause that would become a bulwark of Southern segregation.[32] Thus it was a "Christian faith . . . molded during the conflict [that] 'contributed to the rhetoric of white religious and cultural separatism.'"[33] Defeat in battle only deepened the roots of Southern religious resolve. From the hewn tree sprang forth a shoot that would blossom in the lynching culture of the Jim Crow era.

---

in Arkansas, which included the First Kansas (Colored) Brigade and the Second Kansas (Colored) Brigade.

29. Wilmeth diary, October 29, 1864.

30. William Pitt Chambers, *Blood and Sacrifice: The Civil War Journal of a Confederate Soldier*, ed. Richard A. Baumgartner (Huntington, WV: Blue Acorn Press, 1994), 175–76, entry for October 1864.

31. Chambers, *Blood and Sacrifice*, 119, entry for February 15, 1864; 190, January 1, 1865.

32. Charles Reagan Wilson, *Baptized in Blood: The Religion of the Lost Cause, 1865–1920* (Athens: University of Georgia Press, 1980).

33. Kurt O. Berends, "Confederate Sacrifice and the 'Redemption' of the South," in *Religion in the American South: Protestants and Others in History and Culture*, ed. Beth Barton Schweiger and Donald G. Matthews (Chapel Hill: University of North Carolina Press, 2004), 115, quot-ing Paul Harvey, *Redeeming the South: Religious Cultures and Racial Identities among Southern Baptists, 1865–1925* (Chapel Hill: University of North Carolina Press, 1997), 17.

A "Biblical" Ideology of White Supremacy

Reconstruction did not pave the way for integration but only barely suppressed the forces of division. As soon as the US army withdrew in 1877, those forces reemerged and began tearing down the work of the Freedmen's Bureau and building up a wall of segregation in its place. The notion that white Europeans were superior to black Africans was entrenched from the time that the first slaves arrived in Jamestown, Virginia, in 1619. The culture of segregation rested on an ideology of white supremacy that was grounded in misreadings of the Bible.[34]

The biblical foundation of all white supremacist readings of the Bible was the story of the so-called curse of Ham in Genesis 9:20–27, quoted here from the King James Version:

> And Noah began to be an husbandman, and he planted a vineyard: And he drank of the wine, and was drunken; and he was uncovered within his tent. And Ham, the father of Canaan, saw the nakedness of his father, and told his two brethren without. And Shem and Japheth took a garment, and laid it upon both their shoulders, and went backward, and covered the nakedness of their father; and their faces were backward, and they saw not their father's nakedness. And Noah awoke from his wine, and knew what his younger son had done unto him.
>
> And he said, Cursed be Canaan; a servant of servants shall he be unto his brethren.
>
> And he said, Blessed be the Lord God of Shem; And Canaan shall be his servant. God shall enlarge Japheth, and he shall dwell in the tents of Shem; and Canaan shall be his servant.

White supremacists ignored the literary context of this passage, which anticipated a time when the Israelites would drive the Canaanites from their land (Gen. 10:15; 15:18–20; 17:8; Exod. 23:23, 28; Josh. 17:13; Judg. 1:28; etc.).

---

34. On the ideology of white supremacy, see Hale, *Making Whiteness*; Elizabeth Fox-Genovese and Eugene D. Genovese, *The Mind of the Master Class: History and Faith in the Southern Slaveholders' Worldview* (Cambridge: Cambridge University Press, 2005); Fox-Genovese and Genovese, "The Divine Sanction of Social Order: Religious Foundations of the Southern Slaveholder's World View," *Journal of the American Academy of Religion* 55, no. 2 (1987): 211–33; Paul Harvey, *Christianity and Race in the American South: A History*, Chicago History of American Religion (Chicago: University of Chicago Press, 2016).

Instead, they focused on a popular folk etymology of the name Ham, supposedly meaning "black," and, observing that Ham's children included Cush, Egypt, and Put (Gen. 10:6) and ignoring Ham's descendants in Asia (Gen. 10:7–14), they leaped to the conclusion that all of Ham's descendants were dark-skinned Africans. Further ignoring Japheth's descendants in Asia, they focused on those who represented Mediterranean islanders (e.g., Javan, Kittim; Gen. 10:2–5) and leaped to the conclusion that Shem, Ham, and Japheth, respectively, represented Asia, Africa, and Europe. They concluded that it was God's eternal plan for "black" Africans to be slaves to "red" Asians and "white" Europeans.

This white supremacist interpretation of Genesis 9–10 was not ancient.[35] The rabbinic commentary *Genesis Rabbah* 37 said that Ham was punished with black skin because he had copulated with a dog in the ark, but the same commentary also located Japheth in Africa. In the Middle Ages, as Islam united the tribes of North Africa and outlawed the enslavement of Muslims, Christians, and Jews living in Islamic lands, Muslims began bringing more slaves from sub-Saharan Africa, and they distinguished between higher-value light-skinned slaves and lower-value dark-skinned slaves, whom they called "sons of Ham."[36] But it was not until Portuguese slave traders began importing slaves from Guinea that European Christians began associating the curse of Ham with black-skinned sub-Saharan Africans, and Western art did not represent Ham with black skin until the nineteenth century.[37] It appears, then, that only after they developed an economic interest in black African slaves did Europeans begin to reimagine Genesis 9–10 so as to rationalize their rapacity as the will of God. Once established, the curse of Ham was taken as gospel truth and became the lens through which white supremacists read every other Bible reference to either African people or slaves.

The artificial categorization of people groups by continent of origin, a concept that had no meaning before the Age of Discovery, eventually evolved

35. For detailed critique of the numerous problems with the white supremacist reading of Gen. 9–10 and the history of alternate interpretations, see David M. Goldenberg, *The Curse of Ham: Race and Slavery in Early Judaism, Christianity, and Islam*, Jews, Christians, and Muslims from the Ancient to the Modern World (Princeton: Princeton University Press, 2003); Benjamin Braude, "The Sons of Noah and the Construction of Ethnic and Geographical Identities in the Medieval and Early Modern Periods," *William & Mary Quarterly* 54, no. 1 (1997): 103–42; Gene Rice, "The Curse That Never Was (Genesis 9:18–27)," *Journal of Religious Thought* 29, no. 1 (1972): 5–27.

36. William McKee Evans, "From the Land of Canaan to the Land of Guinea: The Strange Odyssey of the 'Sons of Ham,'" *American Historical Review* 85, no. 1 (1980): 28–31.

37. Evans, "From the Land of Canaan," 35–39; Braude, "The Sons of Noah," 120–21, 127.

into simplified categorization by color—"red and yellow, black and white," as the children's song goes. But the color labels were entirely arbitrary and malleable, and people argued vigorously about who should be classified into which group.[38] The power brokers worked hardest to define the privileged "white" category, into which immigrants from southern or eastern Europe struggled for admission. Those from other parts of the world were sometimes granted associate privileges. But people from Africa were always beaten back, because "whiteness" required a supposedly inferior "black" category in order to give meaning to its alleged superiority.

A minority alternative white supremacist theory pushed the inferiority of "blacks" to the extreme, denying that black people were descended from Ham and arguing instead that they were beasts without souls. As early as 1711, Francis Le Jau, a pioneering Anglican missionary in South Carolina, reported that a lady of his congregation asked him, "Is it Possible that any of my slaves could go to Heaven, & must I see them there?"[39] Apparently having heard from her priest the astonishing proposition that Negroes had souls, this Christian woman wanted assurance that heaven would at least be segregated. Consider also the observations of Thomas Jefferson:

> I advance it therefore as a suspicion only, that the blacks, whether originally a distinct race, or made distinct by time and circumstances, are inferior to the whites in the endowments both of body and mind. It is not against experience to suppose, that different species of the same genus, or varieties of the same species, may possess different qualifications. Will not a lover of natural history then, one who views the gradations in all the races of animals with the eye of philosophy, excuse an effort to keep those in the department of man as distinct as nature has formed them? . . . Among the Romans emancipation required but one effort. The slave, when made free, might mix with, without staining the blood of his master. But with us a second is necessary, unknown to history. When freed, he is to be removed beyond the reach of mixture.[40]

38. Matthew Frye Jacobson, *Whiteness of a Different Color: European Immigration and the Alchemy of Race* (Cambridge, MA: Harvard University Press, 1998).

39. Francis Le Jau, *Carolina Chronicle: 1706–1717*, ed. Frank J. Klingberg (Berkeley: University of California Press, 1956), 102, letter dated September 18, 1711.

40. Thomas Jefferson, *Notes on the State of Virginia* (Philadelphia: Richard & Hall, 1788), 153–54.

Jefferson was not certain whether Europeans and Africans were different species or, as he thought more likely, varieties of one species. Either way, he contemplated the "mixture" of the two groups as an experimental farmer would crossing varieties of peaches or sheep. Only he ignored the obvious point that farmers deliberately crossbreed in order to produce a hybrid that is superior to both of its progenitors. Instead, he thought the supposedly superior European bloodline would be "stained" by intermarriage with Africans, so it was best to keep the two groups "distinct as nature has formed them." Despite the logical fallacies, Jefferson's views seemed self-evident to American white supremacists, who searched for "biblical" authority and "scientific" evidence to support their ideology of racial superiority.

In the Reconstruction era, some Southerners took what had been popular speculation and began building a "biblical" case that black Africans were not human. A pamphlet by Nashville minister Buckner H. Payne (Methodist Episcopal Church South), writing under the pseudonym Ariel, argued that in the beginning God created, in this order: birds, fowl, creeping things, cattle, beasts, Adam and Eve.[41] According to Ariel, descendants of Adam, including Jesus, were white, while the Negroes were among the beasts, black skinned, but given the name "man" by Adam. He explained the flood as follows: "take one crime alone and by itself—one *only*, and that crime Adam's children, the sons of God, amalgamating, miscegenating, with the *negro—man—beast, without soul—without the endowment of immortality*, and you have the reason, *why* God repented and drowned the world, because of its commission."[42] Furthermore, the extermination of the Canaanites by Joshua was "simply because they were the progeny of amalgamation or miscegenation between Canaan, a son of Adam and Eve, and the negro, and were neither man nor beast." Again, "The seed of Adam, which is the seed of God, must be kept pure; it *shall be kept pure, is the fiat of the Almighty*. Man perils his existence, nations peril their existence and destruction, if they support, countenance, or permit [miscegenation]."[43]

In 1868, one "M.S." published a pamphlet refuting "the absurd doctrine of 'Ariel,' lately promulgated."[44] But then, having shown how badly Ariel

41. Ariel [Buckner H. Payne], *The Negro: What Is His Ethnological Status?* 2nd ed. (Cincinnati: n.p., 1867), 4.

42. Ariel, *The Negro*, 20.

43. Ariel, *The Negro*, 39.

44. M.S., *The Adamic Race: Reply to "Ariel," Drs. Young and Blackie, on the Negro* (New York: Russell Bros., 1868), 5. Cf. Robert A. Young, *The Negro: A Reply to Ariel* (Nashville: J. W. M'Ferrin, 1867), to which was appended "Dr. Blackie's Letter."

had twisted the Bible on that point, he concluded "that the negro is not a *beast*, but has a soul, but not created after the image of God; that he was created and placed upon the earth *anterior* to Adam, together with all the other inferior races, who were numerous in the valley of the Nile, as evidenced by the Mound Builders throughout Asia, and in both North and South America, when Adam and Eve were formed and placed in the garden of Eden, the last of all."[45]

In 1891, writing under the pseudonym Caucasian, the Reverend William H. Campbell found it necessary to refute Ariel at greater length with numerous insights from the emerging field of anthropology, also criticizing Darwin along the way.[46] But in the end, he concluded that, whether one viewed the Negro in Darwinian terms as a branch of the evolutionary tree "on a lower state of development" or in biblical terms as the descendant of Adam, "degraded by circumstances to the lowest grade of humanity," either way there was "but one species of man, and the law of a common brotherhood, with all it implies, must prevail."[47] Of course, what such "brotherhood" implied did not include marriage between blacks and whites. "Only men who give way to brutal passions cohabit with negresses, and nothing can be more shocking to a true woman, or more repulsive to her instincts, than the suggestion of marriage to a negro, Mongolian or Indian."[48] He went on to decry any efforts toward integration, as espoused during the Reconstruction era:

> It is unfortunately true that there are tendencies at work, and signs of the breaking down of racial barriers. The negroes and their friends are beginning boldly to claim social equality. Their education, as it is called, and the endeavors of religious fanatics to bring them into the church on a perfect equality with white people, putting them in civil offices over their superiors, the means resorted to by politicians to secure the negro vote, the instructions of teachers and preachers, all tend to bring the races nearer together and promote admixture. It is a further sign of the times and an evidence of the power of fanaticism to subordinate reason, common sense and Christian charity to stupid prejudice, that some Southern men, including a bishop of the Protes-

45. M.S., *The Adamic Race*, 67.

46. Caucasian [William H. Campbell], *Anthropology for the People: A Refutation of the Theory of the Adamic Origins of All Races* (Richmond, VA: Everett Waddey, 1891).

47. Caucasian, *Anthropology for the People*, 266.

48. Caucasian, *Anthropology for the People*, 270.

tant Episcopal Church, look forward to the amalgamation of all races of earth into one yellow mass as a desired consummation. . . . These men are . . . fighting against God.[49]

Campbell makes plain the logic of lynching and Jim Crow. The primary goal was to prevent interracial sex, expressed as protecting the sexual purity of white women from black men.[50] (Campbell is unusual in his concern about white men impregnating black women.) The means to that end was segregation, and in the interest of segregation Campbell denounced all efforts to integrate churches, to encourage black participation in politics, to establish education among African Americans, and to foster economic prosperity or even financial independence among African Americans.[51]

In 1901, Charles Carroll turned Ariel's 48-page argument into a 382-page book.[52] After lengthy, tortured explanations of Genesis and "scientific"

49. Caucasian, *Anthropology for the People*, 277–78.

50. See LeeAnn Whites, "Love, Hate, Rape, Lynching: Rebecca Latimer Felton and the Gender Politics of Racial Violence," in *Democracy Betrayed: The Wilmington Race Riot of 1898 and Its Legacy*, ed. David S. Cecelski and Timothy B. Tyson (Chapel Hill: University of North Carolina Press, 1998), 143–62.

51. On the political and economic motivations of mob violence against African Americans, see Michael Honey, "Class, Race, and Power in the New South: Racial Violence and the Delusions of White Supremacy," in Cecelski and Tyson, *Democracy Betrayed*, 163–84.

52. Charles Carroll, *The Negro a Beast, or in the Image of God* (Saint Louis: American Book and Bible House, 1900). Carroll's identity is unknown outside of his books. As anthropologists, both he and William Campbell were amateurs, and their arguments were preposterous. This chapter focuses on the biblical arguments, but secular writers would continue to search for scientific "proofs" of white supremacy that would eventually be adopted by the Nazis to justify their concentration camps. Notable were Madison Grant, *The Passing of the Great Race: Or the Racial Basis of European History*, rev. ed. (New York: Charles Scribner's Sons, 1918 [1st ed., 1916]), and Lothrop Stoddard, *The Rising Tide of Color against White World-Supremacy* (New York: Charles Scribner's Sons, 1920). Grant, a lawyer, and Stoddard, a historian, amassed irrelevant data and sorted it inconsistently to produce highly skewed and illogical classifications of people groups. Borrowing from Darwin's observations on biological natural selection in *Descent of Man* and applying those to sociological "evolution" of ethnic groups, Grant argued that "Man has a choice of two methods of race improvement. He can breed from the best or he can eliminate the worst by segregation or sterilization" (*Passing*, 51–52; cf. Stoddard, *Rising Tide*, 254–55). This solution, known as "eugenics," was popular in the United States and in Nazi Germany, even though it was based on studies that were obviously nonsense in comparison with the studies by qualified experts of the time, for example, sociologist W. E. B. Du Bois, in *The Souls of Black Folk* (Chicago: A. C. McClurg & Co., 1903); Du Bois, "Evolution of the Race Problem," in National Negro Conference, *Proceedings of the National Negro Conference, 1909: New York, May 31 and June 1* (New York, 1909), 142–58; and anthropologist M. F. A. Montagu,

evidence that Negroes were not human, Carroll argued for a white supremacist interpretation of Jesus Christ. "What the world wants," he wrote, "is
primitive Christianity,"[53] which he explained as follows:

> The drift of Bible history from the Creation to the birth of the Savior
> clearly indicates that he came to destroy man's social, political and
> religious equality with the Negro and mixed-bloods and the amal-
> gamation to which these crimes inevitably lead, and to rebuild the
> barriers which God erected in the Creation between man and the ape,
> and to reinstate man in his "dominion over every living thing that
> moveth upon the earth." The modern church, under the influence of
> atheism, has torn down the barriers which the Savior re-established
> between man and the ape, and has again degraded man to social,
> political and religious equality with the Negro and the mixed-bloods;
> has extinguished the light of the gospel; has hurled the Adamic fam-
> ily back into the darkness and gloom and hopelessness of atheism
> and into the cesspool of amalgamation.[54]

Carroll also did not go unchallenged. In 1903, W. S. Armistead published
a lengthy book in which he declared that Carroll's book was "the most wilful
attack upon the Bible ever made by living man! . . . a villainous assault upon
the Word of God," and proceeded to rebut his arguments point by point.[55] He
affirmed that "the Bible nowhere condemns race intermingling."[56] But in spite
of all this, Armistead accepted a racialized reading of Shem, Ham, and Japheth
as, respectively, red Asiatics, white Europeans, and black Africans, and he
accepted the common theory of the "curse of Canaan" as God's will that black
Africans should be perpetual slaves. He closed with the following disclaimer:

> I *object* to intermarriage of blacks and whites, for God Himself so
> objected. While it is true that God interposed no *scriptural* barrier
> based on *physical differences*, He having "made of *one blood* all the
> nations of men that dwell on earth" (Acts 17); yet, it is equally true

---

Man's Most Dangerous Myth: The Fallacy of Race, 5th ed. (New York: Harper and Bros., 1974
[1st ed., 1942]); etc. See also Jacobson, *Whiteness of a Different Color.*

53. Carroll, *Negro a Beast,* 266.

54. Carroll, *Negro a Beast,* 269–70.

55. W. S. Armistead, *The Negro Is a Man: A Reply to Professor Charles Carroll's Book "The
Negro Is a Beast, or in the Image of God"* (Tifton, GA: Armistead and Vickers, 1903), iv.

56. Armistead, *Negro Is a Man,* 77.

that God, "in scattering the race upon the face of the whole earth," and interposing *continental barriers*, signified, aye, expressed in no uncertain terms, His *willingness*, aye, His *imperative desire*, that *race intermingling* or *intermarriage, should not take place*. Else why separate the nations by such natural, and, withal, formidable barriers to such intermingling.[57]

Few Southern clergy embraced the theory that the Negro was a "beast," although the idea persisted in mocking references to apes. But for the most part, what settled the question of the black person's soul for average Christians was the first part of Acts 17:26: "[God] hath made of one blood all nations of men for to dwell on all the face of the earth" (KJV). If the Golden Rule had packed the greatest punch for abolitionists against slavery before the war,[58] the verse most frequently cited against the beast theory after the war was Acts 17:26. Nevertheless, segregationists liked to emphasize the second half of that verse, ". . . and hath determined the times before appointed, and the bounds of their habitation." In the popular mind, whether the Negro was man or beast amounted to a distinction without a difference.

Either way, miscegenation was *the* cardinal sin that justified segregation, as Churches of Christ minister Bryan Vinson from Houston made clear in a heated reaction to the *Brown* decision in 1954:

The question before us in this hour is not Segregation or Christianity, but rather it is Segregation or Miscegenation. Within a very few generations of non-segregation there shall be inevitably a widespread mixing and mongrelizing of the two races by intermarriage. The logic of the present Supreme Court's ruling would lead to the ruling that the law in Texas forbidding the marriage of a negro and a white person is unconstitutional. . . . The whole philosophy of this school of thought is identified with the "one world" idea of internationalism, and is playing into the hands of Communist propaganda and design. . . . While it is true that "what God has joined together let no man put asunder," equally true, in principle, is it that what God has separated let not man put together.[59]

57. Armistead, *Negro Is a Man*, 537.
58. Fox-Genovese and Genovese, *Mind of the Master Class*, 613–35.
59. Bryan Vinson, "Segregation or Christianity," *Gospel Guardian* 6, no. 25 (October 1954): 8–9.

Here is a segregationist stating plainly what all segregationists thought, and it was difficult for anyone to challenge segregation without a nod to the question of miscegenation.

If we consider that most Christians in the Jim Crow South never heard a preacher make a biblical case for integration, rarely heard a preacher speak against segregation or question a white supremacist twisting of a passage of Scripture, and fairly often did hear preachers express sentiments like those of Vinson, then we can understand the mentality of the Jim Crow culture. Segregation laws and customs were considered necessary obstacles to the horrific possibility that blacks and whites might procreate. In such a climate, lynching was a public spectacle for social control, intended to send a message that whites were in charge and blacks should stay in their place. We may also understand why lynching was so often rationalized by reference to rumors of rape.

Christianity against Jim Crow

Although a nonracialized reading of the "curse of Ham" passage was well known,[60] it is difficult to find any Southern church leaders who preached it in the Jim Crow era. Indeed, in the fraught atmosphere of the time, anyone who spoke in favor of integration could expect swift recriminations.[61] In the midst of a bout of lynching mania, even speaking against mob violence could be risky.[62]

Considering that the week before the Jesse Washington lynching Waco newspapers issued a barrage of headlines screaming "Murderer," "Fiendish

60. E.g., the pamphlet by Boston judge Samuel Sewall, *The Selling of Joseph: A Memorial* (Boston, 1700); the commentary by the British Methodist Adam Clark (1832); and Rev. I. N. Tarbox, "Fallacies about the Race of Ham," *Millennial Harbinger*, ser. 5, vol. 6 (1863), 163–65 (reprint from the *Congregationalist*).

61. E.g., Howard Kester, *Revolt among the Sharecroppers* (New York: Covici, Friede, 1936; reprint, Knoxville: University of Tennessee Press, 1997), provides a harrowing account of efforts to organize an integrated chapter of the Southern Tenant Farmers Union in Arkansas in 1934. Even a sermon preached in the First Presbyterian Church in Tyler, Texas, citing Acts 17:26 in support of foreign missions seemed edgy: Rev. Robert Hill, "Of One Blood," in *In the Swelling of the Jordan: Sermons by Texas Presbyterian Preachers*, ed. C. T. Caldwell (Grand Rapids: Zondervan, 1940).

62. Will Willimon, *Who Lynched Willie Earle? Preaching to Confront Racism* (Nashville: Abingdon, 2017), on a sermon by Methodist minister Hawley Lynn in response to a lynching near Greenville, South Carolina, in 1947.

Brutality," "Black Brute," and "Fiendish Crime," we may appreciate three public statements denouncing the lynching. First, Rev. C. T. Caldwell, pastor of
First Presbyterian Church of Waco, denounced mob violence in his sermon
the Sunday after the lynching, and his congregation adopted a resolution in
"protest against the fearful, lawless occurrences of last Monday" and implor-
ing God not to deal with the whole community after the sins of the few.[63] Second, the Waco Baptist Pastors Association published a resolution of "intensest
denunciation of this criminal violence on the part of persons composing a
mob manifestly made up of the lowest order of society, collected from various communities."[64] Third, the faculty of Baylor University, led by Dean J. L.
Kesler, adopted a resolution declaring, "we abhor and deplore the violent acts
of the mob," and "we express our disapproval of every form of mob violence."[65]
These resolutions reflected an urge to minimize the size of the mob and distance decent Waco society from the perpetrators. But none of these resolutions questioned Washington's guilt, the fairness of his trial, or the justice of
his death sentence. And they certainly did not challenge the social structures
of segregation that created the climate for lynching in the first place. Still,
when all around is darkness, even a dimly burning wick may offer hope.

In the dark days of Jim Crow, good candles were few and far between.
One bright light was the Fellowship of Southern Churchmen (FSC), who
worked on issues of rural poverty, worker's rights, and racism and published
a journal called *Prophetic Religion* (1938–1955). Beginning in 1934 as an ecumenical network of ministers, most of whom had been influenced directly
or indirectly by Reinhold Niebuhr of Union Theological Seminary, New
York, the fellowship was committed to "the life and teachings of Jesus" as "a
revelation of the nature of reality, of God, obedience to whose will is peace,
and disobedience, suffering and death."[66] Cofounder Thomas B. Cowan, pastor of Third Presbyterian Church in Chattanooga, wrote in 1938:

> Surely there is something wrong with a society that can find noth-
> ing to do with the Son of Man but to crucify him. There must be

63. "Waco Pastors Will Take a Stand Denouncing Lynching," *Waco Morning News*, May
29, 1916, 3. The story reported that Dr. F. C. Culver of Austin Ave. Methodist Church planned
to preach against "lawlessness" the following Sunday.

64. "Baptist Pastors of Waco Denounce Mob Spirit," *Waco Morning News*, May 31, 1916, 10.

65. Minutes of the Baylor University Faculty Senate meeting on May 27, 1916 (Baylor
University archives, box 3E163). Thanks to archivist Paul Fisher for locating this record.

66. Eugene Smathers, "The Land, Democracy, and Religion," *Prophetic Religion* 5, no. 1
(February-March 1941): 7. Thanks to Don Haymes for a transcription of this text.

something corrupt politically, economically, socially, religiously in a social order which cannot find room for God. And the things incompatible with God's dwelling among men are the unspiritual gods of violence, nationalism before justice, economic interests before human values, religious traditionalism before the body-soul redemption of men, the cannibalistic struggle for power, and man's defiant deification of himself. I make this brief excursion into theology because it is my growing conviction, still inadequately expressed, that Christian Propheticism will never recover its fire, its penetration, its God-like love and indignation (swapped for simulated pulpit anger) until we are possessed with the Divine Madness of the Cross.[67]

Cowan did not name segregation explicitly, but he and the FSC were striking at the social structures that kept it in place.

More explicit was Episcopal priest Quincy Ewing, who served churches in New Orleans and Greenville, Mississippi. In 1909 he declared plainly that the "race problem" in the South was, "How to maintain the social, industrial, and civic inferiority of the descendants of chattel slaves."[68] That, in essence, was the aim of the lynching culture.

So, there were a few who preached against segregation. But not until after the *Brown* decision, when the civil rights movement was well under way, do we find a significant book from the Southern Baptist pastor and professor Thomas Buford Maston, who not only dismantled racist readings of Genesis and other Bible passages but also offered a positive case for racial integration based on the Bible.[69] Yet, even he included the obligatory paragraph at the end disclaiming any endorsement of intermarriage between blacks and whites.

Meanwhile, others tried to push back the darkness not by writing arguments but simply by practicing integration. Intriguing was the Manasseh Society of Chicago. Organized in 1892, it consisted of men of color who had white wives.[70] But our interest is especially in groups that practiced integration on avowedly Christian principles, of which we may consider two examples.

67. Thomas B. Cowan, "The Need for Prophets," *Prophetic Religion* 1, no. 7 (December 1938): 6.

68. Quincy Ewing, "The Heart of the Race Problem," *Atlantic Monthly* 103, no. 3 (March 1909): 389. Cf. Ewing, "The Beginning of the End," *Colored American Magazine* 3, no. 6 (October 1901): 471-77.

69. T. B. Maston, *The Bible and Race* (Nashville: Broadman, 1959).

70. *Piqua (OH) Daily Call*, March 8, 1892, 8.

The first example was the vision of Presbyterian minister John G. Fee, who, along with Cassius M. Clay and the support of the American Missionary Society, founded the fully integrated town of Berea, Kentucky, in 1854. Fee had planned to start a school, but local citizens drove him out of the state in 1859. He returned to Kentucky, however, in 1865 and launched Berea College in 1866. Despite violent opposition from the KKK, Berea College began as the first college in the nation to be both racially integrated and coeducational, and officially allowed interracial dating beginning in 1874.[71]

The second example was the vision of two young Southern Baptist ministers, Martin England and Clarence Jordan.[72] England was a missionary, and Jordan, with a PhD in Greek from Southern Baptist Theological Seminary, was a teacher at Simmons University, an African American school in Louisville. In 1941, the two pooled their meager resources and, with the providential help of a donor, bought land in Americus, Georgia, where they launched an integrated cooperative called Koinonia Farm. Over the years, especially as the civil rights movement heated up, the Koinonia members were shot at, bombed, and thrown out of the local Baptist church, but the families endured on the farm. Koinonia would become the incubator for Habitat for Humanity, and Jordan's popular *Cotton Patch Version* of the New Testament would help a generation of younger Christians see more clearly how Jesus's message applied to the segregated South. More than anything else, Koinonia demonstrated what it meant to live the teachings of Jesus every day, and not just to read about him.

By far the clearest and strongest critiques of white supremacist ideology and demonstrations of authentic Christianity in the Jim Crow era were in the black churches. The black churches were places of consolation and encouragement, moral and social uplift, education, leadership development, and truth telling.[73] One way of telling the truth was to challenge the prevailing white narrative directly with an alternative narrative.[74]

71. Richard D. Sears, *"A Practical Recognition of the Brotherhood of Man": John G. Fee and the Camp Nelson Experience* (Berea, KY: Berea College Press, 1986).

72. *Clarence Jordan: Essential Writings*, ed. Joyce Hollyday, Modern Spiritual Masters (Maryknoll, NY: Orbis, 2003).

73. William E. Montgomery, *Under Their Own Vine and Fig Tree: The African-American Church in the South, 1865–1900* (Baton Rouge: Louisiana State University Press, 1993).

74. E.g., the 1930 sociological study by Benjamin E. Mays (Baptist) and Joseph W. Nicholson (Christian Methodist Episcopal), "The Genius of the Negro Church," in Sernett, *African American Religious History*, 423–34; Rev. Reverdy Ransom (African Methodist Episcopal),

That was the strategy of Churches of Christ evangelist and educator Samuel Robert Cassius. In his book *Third Birth of a Nation*,[75] Cassius directly challenged Charles Carroll's *The Negro a Beast*, Thomas Dixon's novels, and D. W. Griffith's film *Birth of a Nation*.[76] He refuted the notion that the Negro was a beast with accounts of achievements and contributions to civilization by Africans both ancient and modern. He challenged white supremacist portrayals of the "licentious brute" as an invention of Southern white men "to poison the minds of Northern and Western white men against the negro," specifically because "He fears that the black man will supplant him in the matters of trade, business, and profession."[77] He called out whites' rhetoric about protecting the purity of white women: "Many white men of the South, in their efforts to discredit the negro in the eyes of the world, did not hesitate to use their own sisters, daughters, wives and mothers as a means for an excuse to work their spite on the negro because he had made good."[78]

As for miscegenation, Cassius rejected it unequivocally. At first glance, he appeared to adopt the arguments of white supremacists in affirming God's will that the various ethnic groups remain separate. But on closer inspection, he was actually standing the white argument on its head. Where whites from Thomas Jefferson down to his own day worried about weakening the white race and tainting it by admixture of black blood, Cassius asserted the opposite. He argued that the American nation had set out deliberately "to degrade its former slaves in the eyes of the world."[79] For Cassius, generations

"The Race Problem in a Christian State, 1906," in Sernett, *African American Religious History*, 337–46.

75. S. R. Cassius, *Third Birth of a Nation*, rev. ed. (Cincinnati: F. L. Rowe, 1925). The full text is available online at Digital Commons @ ACU, accessed December 4, 2017, https:// digitalcommons.acu.edu/crs_books/94, and also reset in *To Lift Up My Race: The Essential Writings of Samuel Robert Cassius*, ed. Edward J. Robinson (Knoxville: University of Tennessee Press, 2008), 85–159.

76. Cassius, *Third Birth*, 46.

77. Cassius, *Third Birth*, 38. For a similar argument, see Christian Methodist Episcopal Church bishop L. H. Holsey, "Race Segregation," *A.M.E. Church Review* 26 (October 1909): 109–23, discussed in Paul Harvey, *Freedom's Coming: Religious Culture and the Shaping of the South from the Civil War through the Civil Rights Era* (Chapel Hill: University of North Carolina Press, 2005), 14. Holsey argued that the segregation laws were designed to prove that blacks were incapable of "rising to the dignity of a full-fledged common citizenship" (111), that white people were jealous of the "prosperous Negro" (115) so that education and attainment "endanger his life and property" (116).

78. Cassius, *Third Birth*, 35.

79. Cassius, *Third Birth*, 42. For another example of turning the white supremacist nar-

of white men raping black women had "degraded" the black bloodline and weakened it, or in Jefferson's words, "stained" it. The irony was that Cassius himself was born in slavery to a black slave mother who was raped by her drunken white owner.[80] We might read his argument against miscegenation as an exercise in self-loathing, or as the obligatory disclaimer in his otherwise incendiary book that kept him from becoming another victim of lynching, or, as he probably intended it, as an expression of black separatism. In any case, according to Cassius, whites had created the race problem in that "Two hundred and forty years of degradation and slavery put into the heart of the slave a hatred against the slaveholder," while, "on the other hand, the white man has been taught by generations of learned men that the negro is an inferior."[81] In other words, fear and hatred were learned traditions, not natural human interactions.

Cassius's solution was a plea for embracing simple Christianity: "I contend that there would be no race problem to solve if the so-called Christian people of America would take the word of God as the man of their counsel and its teachings as their rule of faith and practice. . . . Our children would go to the same schools, learn the same lessons. . . . Christians would not be afraid of social equality injuring their home, because the grace of God would cast out all fear . . . we would live together and be happy."[82] Cassius believed a restoration of simple, New Testament Christianity would dismantle the ideology of segregation.[83]

Apart from challenging the white narrative directly, black Christians worked out their own theological responses to segregation in the contexts of their own churches. Black churches were places where black Christians could read the Bible and see for themselves that God was always on the side of the oppressed. God was on the side of Joseph, on the side of the destitute widow of Sidon, on the side of exiles in Babylonia, on the side of the beggar Lazarus, on the side of Stephen when he was stoned, and on the side of Paul

---

rative on its head, see Mary White Ovington's short story "The White Brute," *Masses* 8, no. 1 (October-November 1915): 17–18; and Ovington's letter to the editor, *Masses* 8, no. 3 (January 1916): 20.

80. Edward J. Robinson, *To Save My Race from Abuse: The Life of Samuel Robert Cassius*, Religion and American Culture (Tuscaloosa: University of Alabama Press, 2007), 11–12.

81. Cassius, *Third Birth*, 89.

82. Cassius, *Third Birth*, 83.

83. For a less confrontational challenge to the white narrative, see African Methodist Episcopal bishop George W. Clinton, "What Can the Church Do to Promote Good Will between the Races?," in McCulloch, *Democracy in Earnest*, 366–77.

and Silas in jail. And, of course, the premier example is that God was on the side of Israelite slaves in Egypt.[84]

The black experience resonated with the teachings of Jesus in ways that the experience of most whites did not: "Blessed are those who mourn" (Matt. 5:4).[85] "Blessed are the meek" (5:5). "Blessed are those who hunger and thirst for righteousness" (5:6). "Blessed are you when people revile you and persecute you and utter all kinds of evil against you falsely on my account" (5:11). In black churches the prayer of Jesus rang out: "Give us this day our daily bread" (6:11). "Rescue us from evil" (6:13). Here the teachings of Jesus made sense: "If anyone strikes you on the right cheek, turn the other also" (5:39). "Love your enemies" (5:44). "Everyone then who hears these words of mine and acts on them will be like a wise man who built his house on rock" (7:24).

God's prophets in the Old Testament hammered the wealthy and powerful who "trample on the poor" and "push aside the needy" (Amos 5:11, 12). They railed against rulers who "abhor justice and pervert all equity, who build Zion with blood" (Mic. 3:9–10). They mourned for "lost sheep" whose "shepherds have led them astray" (Jer. 50:6). God's prophets told the truth. And black churches rang with prophetic preaching. In his study of sermons from the Jim Crow era, Kenyatta Gilbert observes that "African American prophetic preaching interprets *to evangelion* ('the gospel') with regard to justice ideals and the active pursuit of hope for emancipatory ends . . . corresponding with the Old Testament prophet's vision and message of justice and hope."[86] He describes African American prophetic preaching as preaching that "(1) unmasks systemic evil and opposes self-serving, deceptive human practices, (2) remains interminably hopeful when confronted with human tragedy and communal despair, (3) connects the speech-act with just actions and concrete praxis to help people freely participate in naming their reality, and (4) carries an impulse for beauty in its use of language and culture."[87] Listen, for example, to what Bishop Reverdy Ransom preached to the AME General Conference in New York City in 1936, in a sermon titled "The Church That Shall Survive." Hear the reality check, the hope, the call to action, and the lyricism in this charge to fellow shepherds of the flock:

84. On exodus imagery in black preaching, see Rhondda Robinson Thomas, *Claiming Exodus: A Cultural History of Afro-Atlantic Identity, 1774–1903* (Waco: Baylor University Press, 2013).

85. Bible quotations in this chapter are from the NRSV unless otherwise indicated.

86. Kenyatta R. Gilbert, *A Pursued Justice: Black Preaching from the Great Migration to Civil Rights* (Waco: Baylor University Press, 2016), 61.

87. Gilbert, *A Pursued Justice*, 68.

The bishops and ministers that lead this church must have their call and commission from God, and the geniuses of the credentials and the divine authority with which they are clothed must be witnessed by the power and faith to proclaim and uphold the gospel message in an evil time. It must be a prophetic church, not only beholding the Lord and lifting up, while the cherubim cry "Holy, Holy, Holy" round the throne; but while the church is marching through the wilderness, they must point to the realm of hope and promise that lies just beyond. They must proclaim liberty to the captives—those that are socially, economically, and politically disinherited—with authority of a divine justice that will not rest until every fetter of injustice and oppression is broken.[88]

And, above all, God was in Jesus. In 1949 Howard Thurman wrote a Christian manifesto for integration titled *Jesus and the Disinherited* that would help give Christian direction and focus to the civil rights movement.[89] Thurman pointed out that Jesus was a Jew, poor, and a member of a minority group in a country controlled by a larger, dominant group. He showed how Jesus addressed the problems of fear, deception, and hate in his own time and how he taught an alternative way of love. Furthermore, as James Cone has pointed out in *The Cross and the Lynching Tree*, God was present when Jesus Messiah was arrested on trumped-up charges, tried in a kangaroo court, and lynched while the crowd looked on and mocked. Whites have been oblivious to the truth that blacks knew all along: Jesus was lynched.[90]

So, how was it that fifteen thousand citizens of Waco, most of whom were Christians, were able to participate in the lynching of Jesse Washington, or watch without intervening, and then go back to church the next Sunday as if nothing had happened? Sure, they worried about their city getting bad press, but why was there no moral outrage on behalf of Jesse

88. Gilbert, *A Pursued Justice*, 82. For another example, see African Methodist Episcopal Zion bishop James Walker Hood (1835–1918), "The Streams Which Gladden God's City," in *Sermons and Addresses Written and Compiled by James Walker Hood, Bishop* (Washington, DC: AME Zion Bicentennial Historical Commission, 1995), 178–89.

89. Howard Thurman, *Jesus and the Disinherited* (Nashville: Abingdon, 1949; reprint, Boston: Beacon, 1996). On a classic sermon from African Methodist Episcopal bishop Henry McNeil Turner a generation before Thurman, see Andre E. Johnson, "God Is a Negro: The (Rhetorical) Black Theology of Henry McNeil Turner," *Black Theology* 13, no. 1 (2015): 29–40.

90. James Cone, *The Cross and the Lynching Tree* (Maryknoll, NY: Orbis, 2011).

Washington? The answer is that they had been breathing polluted air for so long that they forgot what fresh air smelled like. Two and a half centuries of living in a slave-based economy had taught them to rationalize slavery as both natural and the will of God. They invented scientific "proofs" that Africans were "inferior" to Europeans. They ignored the central message of the Bible, instead twisting select verses out of context. When the slaves were freed and the economy collapsed, Southerners resented the losses, and they resented the idea that former slaves should be considered their equals.

Over the centuries, Americans in general embraced an artificial, color-coded idea of "race." Because the self-styled "whites" viewed interracial sex as a threat to the imagined "purity" of their "breed," they imposed strict segregation rules. Those rules were pervasive in America but more rigid in the South. Americans everywhere, and especially in the South, impeded educational, political, and commercial opportunities for blacks to improve themselves, because the mere existence of an educated and successful black gentleman put the lie to the whole theory of racial superiority and inferiority. For a few agonizing decades in America, especially but not only in the South, lynchings and race riots served to reinforce a message that blacks were uncivilized and could be controlled only with brute force—and to warn black Americans not to challenge white privilege.

But a few whites and most blacks saw through the smog. They smashed down barriers and allowed the witness of Scripture to freshen the air: "Love your enemies" (Matt. 5:44). "In everything do to others as you would have them do to you" (7:12). "Love your neighbor as yourself" (22:39). "Just as you did it to one of the least of these who are members of my family, you did it to me" (25:40). "From one blood he made all nations to inhabit the whole earth" (Acts 17:26). They caught the vision of God's glorious future: "I looked, and there was a great multitude that no one could count, from every nation, from all tribes and peoples and languages, standing before the throne and before the Lamb, robed in white, with palm branches in their hands. They cried out in a loud voice, saying, 'Salvation belongs to our God who is seated on the throne, and to the Lamb!'" (Rev. 7:9–10).

Lynching is usually discussed as a social or political problem, but it is one of the essential stories of Christianity in America, and all Christians need to understand what happened and why, because white supremacy is making a comeback in the twenty-first century. Christians today will be better able to recognize and address the problem if they understand what it looked like and how faithful Christians addressed it in the past. Throughout the chapter, I have tried to identify the denominational affiliations of people as much as possible, so it should be clear that no denomination has completely pure hands, but at the same time in every denomination there were a few heroes trying to clean the air. Your task is to find additional stories of lynchings and champions of segregation in your county and your religious tradition. And you should find and tell the story of at least one hero in your county or religious tradition who took a risk to stand against the racism of the time. Then go and do likewise.

Civil Rights and the Religious Right— Christian Roots but "One in Christ"?

Kathy Pulley

A postracial United States is still beyond the nation's grasp. Historian Ibram X. Kendi succinctly makes this point: "There will come a time when Americans will realize that the only thing wrong with Black people is that they think something is wrong with Black people."[1] The relationship among race, religion, and politics in America is complicated. This essay will explore one intersecting point: how the Religious Right and the civil rights movements, though not completely contemporaneous, could have worked toward racial unity. They did not. There were many missed opportunities. For a variety of reasons, injustices based on race remain a problem.[2]

Racial unity has not been achieved in American society, including in our religious institutions. Before delving into the question of how two mid-to-late twentieth-century movements (civil rights and the Religious Right) interacted with the issue of racial unity, it is important to provide some context for understanding what we call the Religious Right.

The Religious Right is a branch of evangelicalism but not the same as evangelicalism. Evangelicalism has a much longer history that may be traced back to an interpretation of the *sola Scriptura* and pietism themes of the Reformation era. In the United States, however, evangelicalism has

---

1. Ibram X. Kendi, *Stamped from the Beginning: The Definitive History of Racist Ideas in America* (New York: Nation Books, 2017), 511.

2. The methodology used in this chapter is historical analysis. The chapter provides an overview of two specific movements, and how the primary leaders and events of those movements dealt with racial unity. A more complete understanding of this topic could be done by studying the grass roots—what were ordinary people doing and thinking behind the public discourse and events? For example, the voices and work of black and white women were seldom a part of the public discourse. Furthermore, the black churches were powerful facilitators of the civil rights movement. Successful mobilization efforts do not happen without a lot of "boots on the ground." Those stories are also important to hear but fall outside the focus of this chapter.

been and remains an important part of the religious landscape, but it is not easy to define.[3] For purposes of this chapter, "evangelicalism" functions as an umbrella term, applicable to theologically conservative Protestants who are transdenominational, who believe the Bible to be authoritative, and who claim that an individual's life may be spiritually transformed by his or her God. Though evangelicals can be said to be somewhat united in their claims about the authority of Scripture, there is also much confusion, and often disagreement, about how those Scriptures are interpreted. Thus, no one definition fits all who might call themselves evangelicals. For example, those who call themselves Baptist or Pentecostal are usually recognized as part of the larger "evangelical" group even though they differ in theology. Evangelicals may also hold diverse political viewpoints.

In the United States, evangelicalism thrived during the great revivals. Sociologist William Martin claims that the Great Awakening "turned the American South into perhaps the most distinctively and self-consciously religious region in Christendom."[4] However, by the late 1800s and early 1900s, evangelicalism was challenged by a number of theological and cultural factors. At the turn of the century came the modernist-fundamentalist controversies. In the early twentieth century, the term "fundamentalist" was the most identifiable descriptor of conservative Protestants, though it did not encompass all conservative Protestants. Among other things, fundamentalism embraced an inerrantist interpretation of Scripture and an ardent commitment to nationalism, and fundamentalists staked a strong claim against such ideas as Darwinism but supported the ideas behind dispensationalism.[5] Fundamentalists also resisted what their leaders perceived as sinful personal habits, such as drinking and gambling, which were increasing in popularity as the culture became more urban and industrialized.

When the civil rights movement began in the mid-1950s, two significant groups of conservative Protestants existed: the stricter and more conservative fundamentalist group and the more inclusive evangelical group.

3. George M. Marsden, *Understanding Fundamentalism and Evangelicalism* (Grand Rapids: Eerdmans, 1991). For a more complete understanding of the challenges of late twentieth-century evangelicalism in America, see Mark A. Noll, *The Scandal of the Evangelical Mind* (Grand Rapids: Eerdmans, 1994).

4. William C. Martin, *With God on Our Side: The Rise of the Religious Right in America* (New York: Broadway Books, 2005), 4.

5. Charles C. Ryrie, *Dispensationalism*, rev. ed. (Chicago: Moody Publishers, 2007).

As the movement was coming to an end in the mid-to-late 1960s, both fundamentalists and evangelicals wanted to unify around both a conservative political agenda and a conservative religious agenda in order to make the United States a godlier nation. Many in both groups believed that Christians were in a fight against secularism and decaying moral values in America. They believed that if they became politically active, they could change national politics. And they did. "They" are often referred to as the "Religious Right" or the "Christian Right."

Historically, it is not unusual for religious groups to take a stand on social and political issues, as was clearly evident during Prohibition. According to historian Daniel Williams, however, what was unique about the Religious Right, by the end of the 1970s, was the development of their strong and singular commitment to a specific political party: the Republican Party.[6]

Numerous factors led to the alignment of the Religious Right with the Republican Party; however, Williams claims it was the end of the civil rights movement that "facilitated the formation of a new white Christian political coalition, because it enabled fundamentalists and evangelicals who had disagreed over racial integration to come together."[7] But this alliance did not come together to promote racial unity. In fact, black evangelicals were usually not included.[8] The primarily white Religious Right was a strong influential group at least through the end of the twentieth century, when questions began to arise about the success of the movement.

In the second half of the twentieth century, the Religious Right galvanized certain clusters of evangelicals toward political activism specifically aligned with the Republican Party.[9]

---

6. Daniel K. Williams, *God's Own Party: The Making of the Christian Right* (New York: Oxford University Press, 2012), 2.

7. Williams, *God's Own Party*, 6.

8. Molly Worthen, *Apostles of Reason: The Crisis of Authority in American Evangelicalism* (New York: Oxford University Press, 2014), 5.

9. Donald W. Dayton, "Some Doubts about the Usefulness of the Category 'Evangelical,'" in *The Variety of American Evangelicalism*, ed. Donald W. Dayton and Robert Johnston (Eugene, OR: Wipf and Stock, 1997), 250. Dayton argues that the diverse uses of the term "evangelical" are so great that it is a somewhat useless term. Rather than theological and historical clusters, he suggests that perhaps the greatest commonality among the various clusters is their desire to stake out significant power.

The Rise of the Civil Rights Movement

The specific catalysts behind the civil rights movement were the murder of a black man, Emmett Till, and the refusal of a black woman, Rosa Parks, to give up her seat on a bus.

The murder took place in late August 1955, in Money, Mississippi. By some estimates, fifty thousand people attended the open-casket funeral of fourteen-year-old African American Emmett Till at the Roberts Temple Church of God in Chicago. Till was murdered for whistling at a white woman; her husband and his half brother killed him. A picture of his disfigured body was published for the world to see. His mother's description of Emmett's face illustrated the gruesome death: "his tongue was choked out. The right eye was lying midway of his chest. His nose had been broken like someone took a meat chopper. . . . I saw a hole, which I presumed was a bullet hole."[10] The men who killed Emmett Till and threw him into the Tallahatchie River with a seventy-five-pound cotton gin fan attached to his neck were acquitted of all charges; later, they acknowledged that they had killed Till. His death was a defining moment for the civil rights movement. He was not the only black person unjustly killed, or the only one who had died under suspicious circumstances, but the flagrant injustice was clear, and his mother's decision to let the world see Emmett's body fueled the activism.

In early December 1955, less than four months after Till's death, Rosa Parks, in Montgomery, Alabama, courageously decided to keep her seat on the bus rather than give it up to a white man, as was the norm. Her action served as the beginning of the nonviolent Montgomery bus boycott, intended to integrate public facilities. Martin Luther King Jr., a new minister at the Holt Street Baptist Church, was chosen to lead the boycott. Traditionally, the Montgomery bus boycott, which involved hundreds and lasted over a year, is understood as the starting point for the civil rights movement; however, the murder of the innocent Emmett Till cast a huge shadow over the boycott.[11] Both events were defining moments in the African Americans' quest to live free from racial injustices.

Till's death and the Montgomery bus boycott symbolized the lack of civil rights for black people in all areas of life. In 1954 the Supreme Court ruled for

10. Keith A. Beauchamp, "The Murder of Emmett Louis Till: The Spark That Started the Civil Rights Movement," *Black Collegian* 35, no. 2 (February 2005): 88–91.

11. See Martin Luther King Jr. and Clayborne Carson, *Stride toward Freedom: The Montgomery Story*, King Legacy Series (Boston: Beacon, 2010); Jo Ann Gibson Robinson and David J. Garrow, *The Montgomery Bus Boycott and the Women Who Started It: The Memoir of Jo Ann Gibson Robinson* (Knoxville: University of Tennessee Press, 1987).

integration of schools in the case of *Brown v. Board of Education of Topeka, Kansas,* and there was resistance to implementing that ruling. The issue came to a head when President Eisenhower sent a thousand federal troops to Arkansas in 1957 to force integration at Central High School in Little Rock.[12] Central High was integrated, but desegregating all the public schools in the South took another decade.[13]

By the early 1960s, Martin Luther King Jr. had emerged as the charismatic leader for civil rights.[14] A Baptist preacher and the son of a Baptist preacher, he was influenced by his liberal Protestant education, but in his sermons and writings he expressed a belief in a personal and relational God.[15] He quoted the Bible often, especially Jesus's Sermon on the Mount. Theologian Peter Heltzel stops short of calling King an evangelical, but he makes a strong case for King's theology being a blend of the black church, evangelical theology, and liberal theology.[16]

The "beloved community" was heralded by King as a way to advocate for reconciliation of the whole human race.[17] King spoke of the "creation of a society where all men can live together as brothers, where every man will respect the dignity and worth of human personality."[18] In such a society, the nation and its religious institutions would work and live together peacefully and as one. King's "beloved community" represented the heart of the Christian gospel: to proclaim the good news of Jesus to all humanity. The idea of reconciliation *of all* through Christ was and is a cornerstone in the Christian tradition; yet, racial reconciliation was not a part of the Christian mission among the white evangelicals and fundamentalists.

King, like Gandhi, like Jesus, unequivocally emphasized that the method for change must come through nonviolence. In one of his early speeches in Montgomery, King said,

12. Erin Krutko Devlin, *Remember Little Rock* (Amherst: University of Massachusetts Press, 2017).

13. Williams, *God's Own Party,* 6.

14. Taylor Branch, *Parting the Waters: America in the King Years, 1954–63* (New York: Simon and Schuster, 1988).

15. See King and Carson, *Stride toward Freedom,* 124–25.

16. Peter Heltzel, *Jesus and Justice: Evangelicals, Race, and American Politics* (New Haven: Yale University Press, 2009), 46.

17. See Charles Marsh, *The Beloved Community: How Faith Shapes Social Justice, from the Civil Rights Movement to Today* (New York: Basic Books, 2005), 1.

18. Martin Luther King Jr., "The American Dream," in *A Testament of Hope: The Essential Writings of Martin Luther King, Jr.,* ed. James Melvin Washington (San Francisco: Harper and Row, 1986), 215.

> Violence never solves problems. It only creates new and more complicated ones. If we succumb to the temptation of using violence in our struggle for justice, unborn generations will be the recipients of a long and desolate night of bitterness. . . . We have before us the glorious opportunity to inject a new dimension of love into the veins of our civilization. There is still a voice crying out in terms that echo across the generations, saying; Love your enemies, bless them that curse you, pray for them that despitefully use you, that you may be the children of your Father which is in heaven. [19]

King was a visionary and a compelling orator who often used Scriptures from both Old and New Testaments to make his case for racial reconciliation.

In 1963, King was in Birmingham, Alabama, marching for freedom when he was arrested along with many others. While incarcerated, King wrote his "Letter from Birmingham City Jail." The letter intended to make a case for civil disobedience when a law was unjust. It was written in response to eight white clergy who had published a letter urging the civil rights movement to be more patient. In his response, King called out these white moderates and said, "Lukewarm acceptance is much more bewildering than outright rejection."[20] In part, his prophetic message to white churches was this:

> So often the contemporary church is a weak, ineffectual voice with an uncertain sound. . . . But the judgment of God is upon the church as never before. If the church does not recapture the sacrificial spirit of the early church, it will lose its authenticity, forfeit the loyalty of millions, and be dismissed as an irrelevant social club with no meaning for the twentieth century. . . . I am thankful to God that some noble souls from the ranks of organized religion have broken loose from the paralyzing chains of conformity and joined us as active partners in the struggle for freedom. [21]

It is difficult to read King's writings and not realize how much he saw himself, black churches, and the civil rights movement as a "partner" with

19. Martin Luther King Jr., "Facing the Challenge of a New Age," in Washington, *A Testament of Hope*, 139.

20. Martin Luther King Jr., *Why We Can't Wait*, King Legacy Series (Boston: Beacon, 2010), 96.

21. King, *Why We Can't Wait*, 105–6.

white Christians in the struggle for freedom for all. Large numbers of black and white Christians supported civil rights and racial unity. Many white southern evangelical and fundamentalist churches failed to support racial integration.

Billy Graham is an example of an influential leader who leaned toward supporting integration but withheld his full endorsement of King and the civil rights movement. Graham's career was taking off in the 1950s, due in part to his weaving of anticommunist rhetoric into his revivals. As Daniel Williams notes, Graham was not only calling individual sinners to repent and be born again, but he was also calling the nation to repentance, because America was a chosen nation; however, America was also a nation that was morally flawed.[22] Through repentance, America's fears could be diminished and the nation could be victorious over godless communism.

Graham's views on the civil rights movement were filtered through his strong anticommunist sentiments. Graham believed the Russians were using the racial tensions in America as propaganda against the nation; thus, Graham could not support King's calls for civil disobedience.[23] This may partially account for his moderate approach toward civil rights. While Graham's revivals were integrated, he did not endorse the Civil Rights Act of 1964 or the Voting Rights Act of 1965 until after they had passed.[24] He spoke against racism, yet he and other southern white evangelicals did not join the civil rights marches or fully embrace the activities of the civil rights movement.[25]

Evangelicals and fundamentalists of this period were comfortable speaking out against communism; however, they were not as comfortable speaking out against segregation and racial prejudice. In the late 1940s, Carl Henry, a respected leader among both evangelicals and fundamentalists, wrote that he advocated for engagement in the world, and set himself and evangelicalism apart from those within fundamentalism who advocated against any involvement in changing the world: "The picture is clear when one brings into focus such admitted social evils as aggressive warfare, racial hatred and intolerance, the liquor traffic, and exploitation of labor or management. . . . The social reform movements dedicated to the elimination of such evils do not have the active, let alone vigorous, cooperation of large

22. Williams, *God's Own Party*, 23.
23. Williams, *God's Own Party*, 29.
24. Frances FitzGerald, *The Evangelicals: The Struggle to Shape America* (New York: Simon and Schuster, 2017), 205.
25. FitzGerald, *The Evangelicals*, 204–7.

segments of evangelical Christianity. In fact, Fundamentalist churches increasingly have repudiated the very movements whose most energetic efforts have gone into an attack on such social ills."[26] Henry's writings influenced many through the years, yet he and his allies were never able to pull together a "coherent social and intellectual framework" to lead the kind of social reform movements of which he spoke.[27]

Fundamentalist southern leaders mostly opposed integration, citing Scripture to defend the status quo. One example comes from fundamentalist Bob Jones Sr., the founder of Bob Jones University in Greenville, South Carolina. On Easter Sunday, April 17, 1960, on WMUU, the Bob Jones University radio station, Jones delivered a sermon entitled "Is Segregation Scriptural?"[28] He based his sermon on the premise that what the Bible says is from God and must be followed, using Acts 17:26: "And hath made of one blood all nations of men for to dwell on all the face of the earth, and hath determined the times before appointed, and the bounds of their habitation" (KJV). The gist of his message was, God never intended to have one race; thus, God "fixed the bounds of their habitation," which meant, as he explained it, that all races needed to remain within their national boundaries. He specifically addressed the "sinfulness" of interracial dating, which Bob Jones University forbade at that time. A concise statement about his views toward white superiority may be seen in his closing prayer on that Easter: "We thank Thee for the ties that have bound these Christian white people and Christian colored people together through the years, and we thank thee that white people who had a little more money helped them build their churches and stood by them and when they got sick, they helped them. No nation has ever prospered or been blessed like the colored people in the South."[29]

A black man was lynched in Bob Jones's South Carolina just thirteen years earlier.[30] Sadly, scholars generally conclude that there was support by white

---

26. Carl F. H. Henry, *The Uneasy Conscience of Modern Fundamentalism* (Grand Rapids: Eerdmans, 2003), 3.

27. FitzGerald, *The Evangelicals*, 257.

28. Bob Jones Sr., *Is Segregation Scriptural?*, ed. Nathanael Strickland (n.p.: CrossReach Publications, 2017).

29. Justin Taylor, "Is Segregation Scriptural? A Radio Address from Bob Jones on Easter of 1960," The Gospel Coalition, July 26, 2016, https://www.thegospelcoalition.org/blogs/evangelical-history/is-segregation-scriptural-a-radio-address-from-bob-jones-on-easter-of-1960.

30. Rebecca West, "Opera in Greenville," *New Yorker*, June 14, 1947, https://www.newyorker.com/magazine/1947/06/14/opera-in-greenville. See also William H. Willimon, *Who Lynched Willie Earle? Preaching to Confront Racism* (Nashville: Abingdon, 2017). These

conservative Christians for segregation.[31] Jones is an example of a preacher who used the Bible to spread his prejudice against integration both on his campus and on the airwaves. His Easter sermon was preached six years after the *Brown v. Board of Education* decision ordering integration, which shows that he and his followers had not given up the fight to maintain segregationist attitudes, and were willing to use their Bible and their God as the endorser of their prejudice.

Another white southern fundamentalist and segregationist voice of the 1950s was Jerry Falwell, who later led the Moral Majority. His initial platform was Thomas Road Baptist Church in Lynchburg, Virginia, which he founded in 1956. In 1958, in a sermon entitled "Segregation or Integration—Which?" he noted that a battle between God and the devil was going on, and "the true negro does not want integration." He told his congregation where the real blame lay: "Who then is propagating this terrible thing? . . . We see the hand of Moscow in the background."[32] Once again, evil Russian communism was being tied to King's civil rights movement. In the 1950s the United States feared nothing more than communism. Russia could use the protests and demonstrations of the civil rights movement as a sign of the failings of Western democracy and capitalism. When the civil rights movement is coupled with communism, and a biblical endorsement of segregation is added to the mix, it is difficult to imagine how King's "beloved community" could possibly have been birthed.

Theologically, Falwell and others argued against integration by claiming that Christians were to stay out of worldly matters and focus on individual sin, not systemic sin; thus, the best way to change the world was through changing the sinful hearts of individuals. In another sermon in the mid-1960s, Falwell said, "Preachers are not called to be politicians, but soul winners."[33] Graham and other evangelicals and fundamentalists preached a message similar to Falwell's.

Falwell was also a premillennialist, which meant, among other things, that he believed the end of the world was coming soon.[34] Premillennial-

---

accounts of twenty-eight men who were tried and acquitted in the lynching of Willie Earle provide an important lens into the culture of Greenville, South Carolina.

31. Joseph Kip Kosek, *American Religion, American Politics: An Anthology* (New Haven: Yale University Press, 2017), 170.

32. Jerry Falwell, "Segregation or Integration—Which?," quoted in Williams, *God's Own Party*, 33.

33. Jerry Falwell, "Ministers and Marchers," quoted in Max Blumenthal, "Agent of Intolerance," *Nation*, May 16, 2007, https://www.thenation.com/article/agent-intolerance. For more discussion of this sermon, see FitzGerald, *The Evangelicals*, 284–86.

34. For a short definition of premillennialism, see FitzGerald, *The Evangelicals*, 639. For

ism was promoted by many evangelicals and fundamentalists. American religious historian Randall Balmer claims that such an apocalyptic view "absolved evangelicals of social responsibility. . . . This world, after all, was doomed and transitory."[35] There was less incentive to be concerned about social and political issues if God was going to return and bring in God's kingdom to rule the earth. Racial unity was not the focus.

Calls for creating a "beloved community" were not heard by many white churches; reconciliation was missed. Evangelical historian Mark Noll summarizes this period well:

> The Civil Rights Movement of this period had less of an immediate effect on white evangelicals than one might expect, given the substantial contribution to that movement of biblical and evangelical themes. The cultural distance between black activists and white evangelicals North and South was simply too great for the whites to recognize how much revivalist evangelicalism contributed to the Civil Rights Movement. . . . For most evangelicals, the movement remained extrinsic to their most basic concerns, but it did provide a rallying point for a few young evangelicals, and in only a few years' time it became a model for political engagement by evangelicals eager to agitate on behalf of other causes.[36]

The Post-Civil Rights Era

The civil rights movement could claim major victories when President Lyndon Johnson signed the monumental Civil Rights Act of 1964 (outlawing discrimination based on race, color, religion, sex, or national origin), and when the Voting Rights Act passed the following year, allowing increased numbers of blacks to register to vote.

When King was assassinated in 1968, the primary leader of the civil rights movement, as well as the leader of the black churches that were the backbone of that movement, was gone. In this vacuum, other organizations were born. The black power movement achieved national fame between

---

a more exhaustive understanding of dispensationalism and premillennialism, see Ernest R. Sandeen, *The Roots of Fundamentalism: British and American Millenarianism, 1800–1930* (Chicago: University of Chicago Press, 2008).

35. Randall Balmer, *Redeemer: The Life of Jimmy Carter* (New York: Basic Books, 2014).

36. Noll, *The Scandal of the Evangelical Mind*, 170.

1966 and 1975.[37] There was impatience because some thought the civil rights movement had not gone far enough. Race riots and radical calls for self-determination stirred fears among some. Nonviolence, unity, and the "beloved community" that King, and others in the movement, had so passionately embraced as the foundation for the movement were no longer the only path toward racial equality. The civil rights movement fragmented. Nonetheless, many black churches served as sources of leadership and as centers for social services and the planning of rallies and other events. Black churches continued to preach King's biblically prophetic message about the need to liberate the poor and oppressed, and that prophetic message tended to be located in political liberalism; thus, black churches became aligned with the Democratic Party.[38] Whether at the local level or the national level, the black churches were, and still are, centers for both religious and political activism.

Some evangelical churches and leaders, both black and white, worked to create racial unity, but most did not. The evangelical minority that sought racial unity was made up of theologically conservative white and black Christians committed to social activism. They were known as "progressive evangelicals" or "the evangelical Left." President Jimmy Carter is the most well-known of early progressive evangelicals. Justice was one of Carter's themes; he was familiar with the writings of both Reinhold Niebuhr and King. Carter once remarked that he admired King's optimism about the importance of continuing to pursue justice, despite the difficulties presented by society's imperfections.[39]

Progressive evangelicals represented a voice for racial unity, along with other social issues of national concern, including women's rights and fighting against poverty and hunger.[40] Though not a united group, they shared a common concern regarding racism. Racial reconciliation could come only

---

37. Joseph E. Peniel, "Rethinking the Black Power Era," *Journal of Southern History* 75, no. 3 (2009): 711.

38. Robert Booth Fowler, *Religion and Politics in America: Faith, Culture, and Strategic Choices*, 4th ed. (Boulder, CO: Westview Press, 2010), 282.

39. E. Brooks Holifield, "The Three Strands of Jimmy Carter's Religion," *New Republic* 174, no. 23 (June 5, 1976): 17.

40. David R. Swartz, *Moral Minority: The Evangelical Left in an Age of Conservatism* (Philadelphia: University of Pennsylvania Press, 2014). In addition to his analysis of the evangelical Left, Swartz also provides an in-depth look at some of the specific leaders in the group, including Carl Henry, John Alexander, Jim Wallis, Sharon Gallagher, Mark Hatfield, Samuel Escobar, Richard Mouw, and Ron Sider.

through Christ, and in their publications and speeches it was clear that their strong Christian message was directed first toward the Christian community.[41] In 1970, Tom Skinner, a former Harlem gang leader, writer, and evangelical preacher, delivered a powerful message at the InterVarsity Christian Fellowship convention on the University of Illinois–Urbana campus. Among other statements about a Christian's relationship to politics, Skinner said, "I as a black Christian have to renounce Americanism. . . . I disassociate myself from any argument that says a vote for America is a vote for God. . . . The thing you must recognize is that Jesus Christ is no more a capitalist than he is a socialist or a communist. He is no more a Democrat than he is a Republican."[42] Skinner was an advocate for change and confronted his fellow evangelicals, saying, "The evangelical, bible-believing, fundamental, orthodox, conservative church in this country was strangely silent. . . . The evangelical church in America supported slavery; it supported segregation." He finished by proclaiming that God's righteousness would prevail, and those listening should "go into the world and tell men who are bound mentally, spiritually, and physically, 'The liberator has come.'"[43] Skinner and others, including the young Jim Wallis, who went on to found the present-day evangelical social justice magazine *Sojourners*, were strong advocates for challenging the injustices in American society.

Historian David Swartz believes that the message of the evangelical Left eventually helped to move many evangelicals toward engagement in sociopolitical issues, because it provided a shift away from a theology emphasizing only one's personal sins and individual obligations.[44] That is, from Swartz's vantage point, conservative Christians came to believe that Jesus called disciples to be engaged in both personal and social transformation. Jesus's prophetic message was not based on a specific political party, and the prophetic message of the evangelical Left served as an example of the gospel message. Unfortunately, in the years following the civil rights movement, as the Religious Right was building its movement, another opportunity for racial reconciliation was lost because the Religious Right did not promote racial reconciliation as part of its message.

41. Antony W. Alumkal, "American Evangelicalism in the Post Civil Rights Era: A Racial Formation Theory Analysis," *Sociology of Religion* 65, no. 3 (2004): 198.
42. Tom Skinner, "The U.S. Racial Crisis and World Evangelism," Urbana, accessed November 25, 2017, https://urbana.org/message/us-racial-crisis-and-world-evangelism.
43. Skinner, "The U.S. Racial Crisis and World Evangelism."
44. Swartz, *Moral Minority*, 266.

Catalysts, Events, and Leaders of the Religious Right

Jerry Falwell is one example of change in the Religious Right. He shifted away from a hard-segregationist position and toward the acceptance of integration when the civil rights legislation became the law of the land. Falwell declared that he had been misguided by culture in the days when he supported segregation, and it was "God's voice in my heart that was the real instrument of change and growth."[45] His shift, away from promoting segregation, allowed for an alliance between two conservative Protestant groups: fundamentalists and evangelicals. This union eased the way for what became the politically active Religious Right movement, affiliated with the Republican Party.

The catalyst for the Religious Right is often identified as the Supreme Court's *Roe v. Wade* abortion decision in 1973. According to Balmer and others, however, the first spark was the perceived government intrusion into Christian schools' policies.[46] In a 1971 lower court case, *Green v. Connally*, concerning a segregated school in Mississippi, the government ruled that it would no longer provide tax exemption to private schools that had racial discrimination policies. This threat escalated fears throughout evangelical and fundamentalist private Christian schools because they believed their schools would go bankrupt without tax exemption. Balmer says these groups "chose to interpret the IRS ruling against their private schools as an assault on the integrity and the sanctity of the Evangelical subculture."[47]

The case that became the most well-known was not against a Christian K-12 school but against Bob Jones University. The university refused to admit black students until 1971, and interracial dating was forbidden until 2000. The question was whether the school could remain a beneficiary of tax exemption if the policy remained in place. The case seemed to pit the liberty to practice one's religious beliefs against the government mandate to eliminate racial discrimination in the schools. By 1975, the IRS notified the university that it was pulling its tax-exempt status, retroactive to 1971. This set off intense reactions from conservatives. It is estimated that the IRS received 125,000 letters of protest, and Falwell was quoted as saying, "In some states it's easier to open a massage parlor than to open the doors of a

---

45. Susan Friend Harding, *The Book of Jerry Falwell: Fundamentalist Language and Politics* (Princeton: Princeton University Press, 2001), 25.

46. Balmer, *Redeemer*, 102-8.

47. Randall Balmer, *The Making of Evangelicalism: From Revivalism to Politics, and Beyond* (Waco: Baylor University Press, 2010), 64.

Christian school."[48] The case was not resolved until it reached the Supreme Court in 1983; the Court ruled against Bob Jones University. Although the university eliminated its policy against interracial dating in 2000, its tax-exempt status was not restored until early 2017.[49]

Gallup polling indicated that in 1978 only 36 percent of those polled approved of interracial dating, and it was not until 1997 that the American public showed majority support (64 percent).[50] Clearly, many conservative Christians were obstructionists when it came to racial integration; nonetheless, the Gallup figures indicate that racial bias was not limited to a religious subculture in the United States—the nation did not look so different from the subculture. In the years between 1978 and 1997, the Religious Right might have embraced the prophetic racial justice messages well articulated by the evangelical Left. The Religious Right might have provided such leadership to schools as well as the nation, but it did not. Another opportunity to lead and work for racial integration and the "beloved community" was lost.

The Religious Right played a significant role in the presidential election of 1976. In the mid-1970s, Jimmy Carter, a progressive evangelical and an advocate for racial justice, was strongly supported by the conservative evangelicals and fundamentalists in his bid for the presidency. Carter, however, did not have their support in the 1980 campaign when they chose to back Ronald Reagan. Although many political issues were working against Carter's winning a second term, Balmer makes the case that Carter was at least partially rejected by religious conservatives because of his seeming support for the government in the case against Bob Jones University, even though that ruling was passed shortly before Carter took office.[51] By the 1980 presidential campaign, the evangelicals and fundamentalists solidly aligned behind the Republican Party. They no longer believed Jimmy Carter represented their agenda.

In the late 1970s, Republican strategist Paul Weyrich became the chief architect of the Religious Right movement, a coalition that would serve as a

48. Balmer, *Redeemer*, 105–6.

49. Nathaniel Cary, "Bob Jones University Regains Nonprofit Status 17 Years after It Dropped Discriminatory Policy," *Greenville News*, February 21, 2017, http://www.greenville online.com/story/news/education/2017/02/16/bju-regains-nonprofit-status-17-years-after -dropped-discriminatory-policy/98009170.

50. Lydia Saad, "Gallup Vault: Americans Slow to Back Interracial Marriage," Gallup, June 21, 2017, http://news.gallup.com/vault/212717/gallup-vault-americans-slow-back-inter racial-marriage.aspx.

51. Balmer, *Redeemer*, 93–118.

dominant voting bloc for conservative issues.[52] The Moral Majority, founded by Jerry Falwell in 1979, was a large organization intended to mobilize voters into a political force to fight secularism and immorality in the nation; thus, the Moral Majority represented the first large effort of the Religious Right. This mobilization effort went beyond evangelical and fundamentalist groups and included Catholics, Jews, and Mormons. Falwell was one of many who passionately argued that the government had overstepped its boundaries and violated the First Amendment in regard to religious liberty. He also articulated fears about the state of society. For a decade, the Moral Majority mobilized its members, with an estimated three or four million people involved. They focused primarily on educational, family, and sexual issues; however, they also endorsed the Republican candidates and their issues. The Religious Right argued for a "Christian" nation rather than an "ungodly" secular nation. They argued for America to get back to traditional values. However, by the end of the 1980s, Falwell announced the closing of the Moral Majority because of financial difficulties. The sexual scandals of televangelists also negatively affected the organization. But their lobbying efforts were not in vain. Among its successes, the Moral Majority helped to elect Republican candidates nationwide—one of whom was Ronald Reagan.[53]

Missing from the 1970s' mobilizations around Republican Party politics for the Religious Right was any attention to racial justice. Political scientist Nancy D. Wadsworth describes this period: "In the 1970s and 1980s, organized white evangelicals turned their attention to threats to their traditional value system . . . while race issues stayed 'off the table.' The declension of attention to racial issues reflected national trends."[54]

The late 1970s and the 1980s ushered in various parachurch organizations that emerged to support the values of the Religious Right. These included Concerned Women for America (CWA), Focus on the Family, and Family Research Council. There were others, but the goal of each was basically the same: to return to America's traditional values by being political activists.[55] Racial issues were not a priority of these organizations in this period.

52. Balmer, *Redeemer*, 101.

53. Peter Steinfels, "Moral Majority to Dissolve; Says Mission Accomplished," *New York Times*, June 12, 1989, http://www.nytimes.com/1989/06/12/us/moral-majority-to-dissolve -says-mission-accomplished.html.

54. Nancy D. Wadsworth, *Ambivalent Miracles: Evangelicals and the Politics of Racial Healing*, Race, Ethnicity, and Politics (Charlottesville: University of Virginia Press, 2014), 52.

55. David P. Gushee, *The Future of Faith in American Politics: The Public Witness of the Evangelical Center* (Waco: Baylor University Press, 2008), 26–27.

Falwell and the Religious Right often took credit for Reagan's election in 1980. Reagan offered the Religious Right religious rhetoric and declared 1983 the "Year of the Bible." The Religious Right, however, gained nothing. Prayer was not returned to the classroom, and *Roe v. Wade* was not overturned. Reagan's presidency has been characterized as one of racial polarization, which may be seen in his opposition to busing as a means of integrating schools, and in his efforts to regain tax-exempt status for Bob Jones University.[56]

Two charismatic religious leaders ran for president in 1988. The white Republican Baptist preacher and highly successful televangelist Pat Robertson was a representative of the Religious Right who criticized the secular teachings in the schools and the lack of moral leadership, and he wanted to restore America to its biblical roots.[57] Again, racial issues were not part of the agenda. Democrat Jesse Jackson was a black Baptist preacher, civil rights activist, and politician. He spoke prophetically of America's need to lift up the downtrodden and address the injustices of all, whether those were social or economic.[58]

Neither candidate captured his party's nomination, but both candidates left behind organizations that continued their work. Robertson created the Christian Coalition, and Jackson created the National Rainbow Coalition. They both ran as populist outsiders who were "continuing populist protests by Christian communities against perceived corrosive or exploitive individualism in economics and culture."[59] Jackson lost in the primaries, both in 1984 and in 1988. Despite the losses, his campaigns manifested what some have called a "black revolution in consciousness."[60] The importance of the black voice was being recognized, and though it is difficult to measure, that voice undoubtedly served as an undercurrent for the return of racial issues to national attention in the 1990s.

Robertson founded the Christian Coalition in 1989, shortly after Falwell disbanded the Moral Majority, and soon after the end of Robertson's cam-

56. Juan Williams, "Reagan, the South and Civil Rights," *National Public Radio*, June 10, 2004, https://www.npr.org/templates/story/story.php?storyId=1953700.

57. Allen D. Hertzke, *Echoes of Discontent: Jesse Jackson, Pat Robertson, and the Resurgence of Populism* (Washington, DC: CQ Press, 1993), 27.

58. Jesse Jackson, "Address before the Democratic National Convention," *Frontline*, Public Broadcasting System, July 18, 1984, https://www.pbs.org/wgbh/pages/frontline/jesse /speeches/jesse84speech.html.

59. Hertzke, *Echoes of Discontent*, xiii.

60. C. Eric Lincoln and Lawrence H. Mamiya, *The Black Church in the African American Experience* (Durham, NC: Duke University Press, 1990), 166–67.

paign for the presidency.[61] Robertson appointed Ralph Reed as the director. The goal of the organization was to mobilize voters who embraced the Religious Right's values and get them to the polls. Initially, racial issues were not included. Under Reed's leadership, the organization opened chapters in forty states.

The 1990s: The Declining Religious Right and the Increasing Discourse on Race

The Christian Coalition languished during Bill Clinton's years as president. The political power of the Religious Right to influence elections and create the changes they worked for was diminishing by the end of the 1990s. Most of the significant national organizations were either weak or closed. Although there continued to be Christian leaders and organizations that mobilized around a given issue, the main goals of the Religious Right were unmet. It was one of the most successful movements in the twentieth century in influencing political elections, yet it did not win the cultural battles for its own values.[62] It was somewhat shocking that Weyrich concluded in the late 1990s that the Religious Right was finished, and members should separate themselves from the hostile culture rather than continuing with political mobilization efforts.[63] They were successful at getting candidates elected, but a political win did not result in the policy changes they desired. Weyrich believed battles would still be fought, but that the Religious Right had probably lost the war. "We are not in the dawn of a new civilization, but the twilight of an old one. We will be lucky if we escape with any remnants of the great Judeo-Christian civilization that we have known through the ages."[64]

As the role of the Religious Right declined, racial issues returned to America's public discourse in the 1990s. Police brutality became part of that conversation, as was evident with the Rodney King beating and the subse-

---

61. Robertson was also the founder of Regents University, the Christian Broadcasting Network, and the Family Channel. For more information about Robertson's life and career, see David Edwin Harrell Jr., *Pat Robertson: A Life and Legacy* (Grand Rapids: Eerdmans, 2010).

62. Fowler, *Religion and Politics*, 143.

63. Paul Weyrich, "The Moral Minority," *Christianity Today*, September 6, 1999, http://www.christianitytoday.com/ct/1999/september6/9ta044.html.

64. Weyrich, "The Moral Minority."

quent Los Angeles riots.[65] In 1991, Clarence Thomas became America's second African American Supreme Court justice, but not without the televised testimony of Anita Hill, who accused him of sexual harassment.[66] There were other events, such as the O. J. Simpson trial, and over six hundred burnings of black churches also caught the nation's attention.[67] Social and political factors pointed more attention to race. Race was also reemerging as a topic within religious communities.

In the mid-1990s, still under the leadership of Ralph Reed, the Christian Coalition began to promote racial unity, even though both Reed and the Christian Coalition were weaker and Reed's motivations were suspected of being hypocritical.[68] In the mid-1990s Reed repudiated racism and considered the racial history of the white evangelical church a "shameful legacy."[69] Despite his politically progressive words strongly supporting racial unity, Reed was still part of the Religious Right. This was clear in his critical remarks about some of the radical steps taken by activists in the civil rights movement. Basically, he did not believe society's ills could be alleviated through government, which was completely contrary to the very reasons for the existence of the Religious Right.[70]

In addition, major conservative denominations, including the Southern Baptist Convention, publicly confessed their racial sins and used the language of reconciliation found in the Bible to promote their desire for racial unity. At their 1995 meeting, the Southern Baptist Convention passed a resolution on racial reconciliation, saying they "unwaveringly denounce racism in all its forms," asking for forgiveness, and committing to "eradicate racism

65. Los Angeles Times Staff, "The L.A. Riots: 25 Years Later," *Los Angeles Times*, April 26, 2017, http://timelines.latimes.com/los-angeles-riots.

66. Jill Smolowe, "Sex, Lies and Politics: He Said, She Said," *Time*, October 21, 1991, http://content.time.com/time/magazine/article/0,9171,974096,00.html.

67. Janell Ross, "Two Decades Later, Black and White Americans Finally Agree on O. J. Simpson's Guilt," *Washington Post*, March 4, 2016, https://www.washingtonpost.com/news/the-fix/wp/2015/09/25/black-and-white-americans-can-now-agree-o-j-was-guilty. Sarah Kaplan and Justin Wm. Moyer, "Why Racists Target Black Churches," *Washington Post*, July 1, 2015, https://www.washingtonpost.com/news/morning-mix/wp/2015/07/01/why-racists-burn-black-churches.

68. Ann Monroe, "Race to the Right," *Mother Jones*, May/June 1997, http://www.motherjones.com/politics/1997/05/race-right.

69. Jason Deparle, "The Christian Right Confesses Sins of Racism," *New York Times*, August 4, 1996, http://www.nytimes.com/1996/08/04/weekinreview/the-christian-right-confesses-sins-of-racism.html.

70. Wadsworth, *Ambivalent Miracles*, 109.

in all its forms."[71] Billy Graham was present and endorsed the resolution. The tide had turned from the days of the civil rights movement.

Among the religiously conservative, interracial relationship building was seen as the way to bring reconciliation. Some from the evangelical Left, such as John Perkins, Tom Skinner, and Jim Wallis, believed a genuine interest in racial reconciliation had to include policies that would eliminate racial injustices.[72] Black Christians wanted white Christians to understand the systemic racial inequalities that continued to exist. They too were hopeful, even though African Americans saw the racial reconciliation efforts as only a first step.[73] By the end of the twentieth century, race was a part of the public discourse and racial reconciliation was a part of the conversation among a broad swath of evangelicals. There was reason for cautious optimism.

Racial Unity—a Dream Worthy of Our Best Efforts

In the larger context of the twentieth century, racial unity was not achieved. Despite the far-reaching influence of the civil rights movement in the second half of the twentieth century, the Religious Right did not make racial unity a part of its agenda of saving the nation for God. Overall, the story of race and the Religious Right is primarily one of missed opportunities for unity. Cultural and religious change was slow. Even in the 1990s, racial reconciliation focused on relationship building rather than recognizing that racial justice was also necessary, and that it required intentional action against injustices.

Racial reconciliation was a vital part of King's message. His vision of the "beloved community" was not limited to cultivating personal relationships across racial lines. Reconciliation was also about actively and intentionally joining forces to expunge systemic economic disparities and social inequities that kept the races divided. For King, the work of racial reconciliation could not be separated from the work of racial justice; the "beloved community" required both from both whites and blacks. In a presentation delivered at

71. "Resolution on Racial Reconciliation on the 150th Anniversary of the Southern Baptist Convention," Southern Baptist Convention, accessed December 2, 2017, http://www.sbc .net/resolutions/899/resolution-on-racial-reconciliation-on-the-150th-anniversary-of-the -southern-baptist-convention.

72. Wadsworth, *Ambivalent Miracles*, 159.

73. Wadsworth, *Ambivalent Miracles*, 114.

Riverside Church in New York in April 1967, a year before his death, he spoke of the Good Samaritan and the need to change hearts as well as societal structures:

> A true revolution of values will soon cause us to question the fairness and justice of many of our past and present policies. On the other hand, we are called to play the good Samaritan on life's roadside; but that will be only an initial act. One day we must come to see that the whole Jericho road must be transformed so that men and women will not be constantly beaten and robbed as they make their journey on life's highway. True compassion is more than flinging a coin to a beggar; it is not haphazard and superficial. It comes to see that an edifice which produces beggars needs restructuring.[74]

Religious faith is in transition. The struggle for racial unity within the Christian tradition has not been achieved; however, at the end of the twentieth century, signs of hope could be seen in the reconciliation efforts made by churches and organizations—first steps were taken. Perhaps racial unity was in the process of becoming a priority. King's prophetic message of reconciliation and justice and the transformation of social structures was a holistic message. It continues to be a dream worthy of our best efforts. Perhaps in the twenty-first century the dream will be realized!

74. Martin Luther King Jr., "A Time to Break Silence," in Washington, *A Testament of Hope*, 240–41.

White Christianity and Resistance to Civil Rights for Racial Minorities in Twenty-First-Century America

Joel A. Brown

Mark Twain once said that history does not repeat itself, but it rhymes. Following the campaign and election to the presidency of Donald Trump in 2016, many of those familiar with the histories of race and racism in America have new reason to believe Twain's seasoned adage. This moment in American history has all the feel of the era of redemption that Paul Harvey outlines:

> A tense, volatile electoral season, accusations of "voter fraud," and real instances of thuggery on the campaign trail. Documented instances of real voter suppression due to newly instituted state policies attempting to restrict voting disproportionately by race. Real or implicit threats of violence against minority voters. Surging anti-immigrant and exclusionist sentiment, particularly against relative newcomers who practiced seemingly strange religions. And a beleaguered set of progressive civil rights and church leaders, who looked to the recent past when the signs seemed so much more hopeful. Some might describe the recent [2016] electoral campaign that way, but I have in mind the election campaign of 1876. . . . In subsequent decades, newly "redeemed" state governments ("redeemed" from Reconstruction), under white Democratic control, instituted far-reaching measures of voter suppression that destroyed the effective intent of the 14th and 15th Amendments to ensure equality for emancipated slaves. The era that contemporaries trumpeted as "Redemption," was unfortunately marked by a cleansing of the nation's soul from the "alleged sins" of Reconstruction. Surging sentiments of white nationalism, xenophobia, and mistrust of government intervention towards those perceived as less worthy fueled growing tides of racist sentiment expressed politically and culturally.[1]

1. Paul Harvey, "Religion and the Second Redemption," *OUPblog*, December 21, 2016, https://blog.oup.com/2016/12/religion-second-redemption/.

The campaigns of 1876 and 2016 bear many similarities, but the most important one is that both elections ignited powerful counterreactions to advances in civil rights for racial minorities, including in both instances the rise of reactionary, violent white nationalist groups in the political and cultural mainstream. During the period of Reconstruction (1865–1877), African Americans, many of whom had been formerly enslaved, won significant advances and political opportunities, particularly following the Reconstruction Act of 1867. Black leaders, most of them church leaders, seized on these newly won freedoms and began to pave a way for black Americans toward full participation in American life. However, by way of an insidious strategy, which included targeted voter suppression, political skulduggery, and racial terrorism and intimidation, white Americans effectively reversed many of the civil rights gains made by black Americans during Reconstruction. This "redemption" of white America left black Americans disenfranchised and with little hope for advancement. Notably, the experience of black Americans a century later, bookended on both ends by the era of Jim Crow, may have been different in form, but it certainly had a clear rhyme to it.[2]

During the second reconstruction, that is, the period beginning with the civil rights movement of the 1950s and '60s, black Americans again won legislative and legal battles to reinstitute enforcement mechanisms to prevent the possibility of a second redemption, victories achieved largely as a result of the oft-costly actions of black freedom fighters and white allies. For a period following the civil rights era, black Americans increasingly carved out new space for themselves in the life and identity of America, operating on the tenuous assumption that the federal government would not abandon their rights this time around. However, they were again betrayed. Beginning in the 1980s, a second counterreaction to the advancement of civil rights for racial minorities rolled back hard-won civil rights yet again.

Thus we are now living in the midst of a second redemption, an era in which the legal and legislative victories of the civil rights movement (i.e., mechanisms designed specifically to prevent racial segregation and oppression) are being challenged and often undone. And, perhaps to the surprise of some, white Christianity is complicit in this project of resistance. This chapter explores the nature of this resistance and the role of Christianity

---

2. Harvey, "Religion and the Second Redemption." For a detailed analysis of the religious experience of black Americans in the era following redemption, see John M. Giggie, *After Redemption: Jim Crow and the Transformation of African American Religion in the Delta, 1875–1915* (Oxford: Oxford University Press, 2008).

in it. In particular, it argues that a certain impulse—to preserve and protect whiteness (i.e., white values and cultural norms)—motivated white resistance to civil rights throughout much of the twentieth century, and this impulse continues to undergird the activity and rhetoric of white Christians in the twenty-first century, including many well-meaning white Christians who otherwise believe themselves not to be racist. A religiously inflected "racial protectionism" motivates white resistance to civil rights for racial minorities, which manifests both in an explicitly racist white nationalism and in a subtler but no less sinister form of racism that I am calling "white Christian color blindness," presuming an antiracist posture and rhetoric while at the same time acceding to and often actively promoting systems of structural racism that function precisely to inhibit the progress of civil rights for racial minorities.[3] This chapter examines both of these phenomena: the religious nature of white nationalist racism as well as a broader Protestant participation in structural racism. A final section will move in the direction of "explaining" white Christian resistance to civil rights for racial minorities in the United States.

White Nationalism and the Religion of Racial Protectionism

Over the last several decades, white nationalists have been the most vocal and least abashed opponents of progress for racial minorities in the United States. Composed of several different groups (e.g., the alt-right, neo-Confederatism, neo-Nazism), white nationalists are united by a shared racial ideology that embraces the impulse to protect white cultural and political dominance and is obsessed with racial survival.[4] White nationalists

3. I am here adopting Damon T. Berry's concept of "racial protectionism" from his book, *Blood and Faith: Christianity in American White Nationalism*, Religion and Politics (Syracuse, NY: Syracuse University Press, 2017). He defines racial protectionism as an obsession with white racial survival (3). However, whereas Berry identifies "racial protectionism" as an "ideological orientation" exclusive to white nationalists, I am arguing that "racial protectionism" functions not only as an explicit ideology but also as an impulse shared by many white Americans, including well-meaning Christians who believe themselves not to be racist.

4. I use "white nationalism" to refer to the kind of explicitly racist ideology that actively promotes a white supremacist agenda in America. Due to limits of space, neo-Confederatism will not receive the same in-depth treatment in this chapter. The neo-Confederate movement has existed since the days of Reconstruction. Ostensibly their aim has been to commemorate and glorify the history of the Southern Confederacy, but what they really are about is white supremacy, that is, white nationalism. They use the Confederacy (especially the Confederate

share the fundamental belief that the white race is imperiled and that members of the white race have a duty to protect it from the forces of multiculturalism, integration, and immigration.[5] Damon T. Berry, a scholar of white nationalism and the racist Right, terms this shared ideological orientation *racial protectionism*.[6]

There are two distinct yet related ways in which we should think about white nationalism in terms of "religion." First, and perhaps less obvious, is the need to think about it *as* a religious phenomenon. In other words, white nationalist racial ideology and its commitment to whiteness and racial protectionism as an object of "ultimate concern" are elevated to a kind of transcendent mode of being that one might otherwise recognize as religious, particularly in terms of values, rituals, communal identity, and morality.

The religious nature of white nationalism is especially notable for its world-making or mythological (i.e., sacred narrative) power and its community-building role in creating and legitimating a particular "imagined community" bounded by race.[7] On mythology, the language of racial protectionism creates a world in the minds of white nationalists that marshals the historical power of whiteness and combines it with a vision for a nation-state determined by racial and ethnic lines.[8] This world is at once "real" for white nationalists and "not yet." Their racist language is descriptive of the way things really are while at the same time it is prescriptive or aspirational, imagining a future society governed by a certain racial code and

flag) as a symbol of white supremacy. See Eric Foner, *America's Reconstruction: People and Politics after the Civil War*, New American Nation Series (Baton Rouge: Louisiana State University Press, 1997).

5. For an overview of white nationalism, see Michael O'Meara, "Toward the White Republic," in *Toward the White Republic, and Other Essays*, ed. Greg Johnson (San Francisco: Counter-Currents, 2010), 1; Carol Swain, *The New White Nationalism in America: Its Challenge to Integration* (New York: Cambridge University Press, 2002), 1, 3.

6. Berry, *Blood and Faith*, 3.

7. I am indebted to Berry for this reading of white nationalism as religious, together with Benedict Anderson's notion of "imagined community." See Berry, *Blood and Faith*, 11–12; Benedict Anderson, *Imagined Communities: Reflections on the Origins and Spread of Nationalism*, rev. ed. (New York: Verso, 1991), 6–7.

8. Bruce Lincoln provides a helpful framework for interpreting the racist language of white nationalism as mythology, reading such hate speech as a type of discourse that "is not just a coding device in which important information is conveyed, on the basis of which actors can then construct society" but as "a discursive act through which actors evoke the sentiments out of which society is then actively constructed." Lincoln, *Discourse and the Construction of Society: Comparative Studies of Myth, Ritual, and Classification* (New York: Oxford University Press, 1989), 25.

hierarchy. White nationalist racist language thus takes on a mythological character (i.e., sacred storytelling) that creates and conveys their deepest beliefs, anxieties, hopes, and commitments. In this way, white nationalists weave a sacred narrative that imagines the "world as the stage for enacting racial survival."[9]

On the community-building role, the religious function of the racist rhetoric and activity of groups like white nationalists reveals the extent to which their racism is largely a social phenomenon, rather than merely a human choice or an individualized pathology, as it is often treated in the media. This is particularly evident in the extent to which white nationalist sacred storytelling (i.e., its "social mythology") is invested in the production, maintenance, and empowerment of a particular "imagined community" bounded by race.[10] An important, if oft-overlooked, implication of this imagined racial community is its grounding in the virtue of love. Admittedly, this seems counterintuitive: What could racism possibly have to do with love? And yet, an analysis that tends to the "religious" in white nationalism reveals that "loving attachment to the imagined racial community" contributes to the production of racial hatred.[11] Love of race, and a particular commitment to protect an imagined community bounded by race, is at the root of racial hatred and violence in white nationalism.[12] To summarize: by analyzing white nationalist racist rhetoric and activity *as religious*, we observe that the white nationalist worldview can be described in terms of a social mythology that constructs their imagined racial community, which in turn informs the white nationalist ethic of racial protectionism grounded in love for that imagined community.

The second instance in which "religion" should be considered in regard to white nationalism is in its relationship to established religious traditions and to Christianity in particular, a relationship that is at once foundational for white nationalism and problematic. Christianity has served as an organizing framework for white racist movements in America and, more recently, has come to pose a "problem" for white nationalists. Either way,

---

9. Berry, *Blood and Faith*, 12.

10. Berry offers a compelling argument for treating white nationalist mythology vis-à-vis Benedict Anderson's notion of "imagined community" (Berry, *Blood and Faith*, 12–13; Anderson, *Imagined Communities*, 6–7).

11. Berry, *Blood and Faith*, 14.

12. Berry, *Blood and Faith*, 12–13. See Henry Bergson, *Two Sources of Morality and Religion*, trans. Ashley Audra and Cloudesley Brereton, with W. Horsfall Carter (Garden City, NY: Doubleday Anchor, 1935), 15.

religion—and particularly Christianity—has played a significant role in the formation of white nationalist identity and in the production of racialized hatred in America.[13]

White nationalism, arguably the most prominent and influential white racist movement in America, should not be confused with earlier forms of white racist activism in the United States (e.g., the Ku Klux Klan). White nationalism's divergence from its racist predecessors is perhaps nowhere more obvious than in its relationship to Christianity. Whereas earlier forms of racist organization to oppose the advancement of civil rights for racial and ethnic groups not deemed "white" relied on the framework and symbols of Protestant Christianity, today's American racist Right (and especially white nationalism) finds itself in a much more precarious relationship to Christianity.[14] In fact, it would not be too bold to posit that Christianity exists as a problem for most white nationalists in the twenty-first century.

The problematics are threefold: First, a growing group of white nationalist "intellectuals" and leaders consider Christianity an inherently dangerous ideology, and they denounce it specifically for being too "Jewish" and therefore an insidious existential threat to the survival of the white race. However, in the second instance, many white nationalists anxious about the unity of their movement worry that a categorical rejection of Christianity will alienate some who ascribe to their racist ideology and thus limit their cultural relevance and power. Third, and related to the above-mentioned problems, Christianity poses a problem for white nationalist groups in the sense that white nationalist leaders, the majority of whom reject Christianity, must navigate a seeming minefield in their attempts to access and enter the "mainstream" of the conservative movement, which is staunchly Christian.[15]

The problematic of Christianity for the racist projects of white nationalists is chiefly an ethical one insofar as the commitment to racial protectionism figures as the white nationalist object of "ultimate concern." Thus any subscription to a religious moral framework at odds with the ethic of racial protectionism potentially disrupts the obligation to protect the white

---

13. Berry makes an important observation about religion on this point: "The relationship between racial protectionism and Christianity reveals that religion is itself a significant site of contest and strategy for American white nationalists, even for those who profess to be atheists." Berry, *Blood and Faith*, 4.

14. Betty Dobratz, "The Role of Religion in the Collective Identity of the White Racialist Movement," *Journal for the Scientific Study of Religion* 40, no. 2 (2001): 299.

15. Berry, *Blood and Faith*, 2–3, 191–98.

race and jeopardizes the consummation of the imagined racial community. Wherever moral obligations collide with the ethical project of racial protectionism, the strategy of twenty-first-century white nationalists has been to suppress, or at the very least manage, alternative religious preferences. However, as elucidated by Berry, the rejection of Christianity in particular, which provides the basic moral framework of the mainstream conservative movement, compounds the problem of Christianity for white nationalists as they try to gain influence within American conservatism more broadly.

Attempts by white nationalists to enter the "mainstream" of American conservatism have been met mostly with resistance in recent decades, as most segments of the conservative movement have sought to distance themselves in the post–civil rights era (i.e., the second redemption) from explicitly racist groups and their activism. However, one group that has recently emerged with some success on this score is the alt-right, a group for whom the multivalent problem of Christianity described above has been true. In fact, one could very well characterize the alt-right as a movement founded precisely to be a "vehicle for White Nationalist entryism" into the political mainstream.[16] This is according to Greg Johnson, a self-identified sympathizer with the racist Right, who provocatively claimed in August 2016 that the "Alternative Right [i.e., alt-right] means White Nationalism—or it means nothing at all."[17] Alt-right leaders, however, are quick to argue that theirs is not merely a "race movement," but one that is equal parts conservatism, white nationalism, and populism. This is in large part a concession to appeal to conservatives who would otherwise resist association with any form of explicit racism. While there is some truth in their concession on this point, it is a deceptive half-truth, an attempt to mask the racist ideology that drives and unites them. The alt-right is fundamentally a movement for racial protectionism.

The alt-right has developed a strategy to convince conservatives that they represent a brand of white supremacy not encountered before in American history—intelligent, civil, clean-cut, not like the "hillbilly racists" of ages past—an image calibrated to convince those otherwise suspicious of them that they in fact deserve a seat at the table of mainstream American social and political life. Their strategy plays upon assumptions that racism is

16. Greg Johnson, "The Alt-Right Means White Nationalism . . . or Nothing at All," *Counter-Currents*, August 30, 2016, http://www.counter-currents.com/2016/08/the-alt-right -means-white-nationalism.

17. Johnson, "The Alt-Right Means White Nationalism . . . or Nothing at All."

the provenance of poor, uneducated white folks. As I have argued elsewhere, however, there is a strong connection between their movement and violent white supremacist activism.[18]

This connection is perhaps nowhere more evident than in the case of Dylann Roof, the self-professed white nationalist gunman who carried out one of the most violent religiously inflected acts of white terrorism in twenty-first-century America—the Charleston church shooting. On the evening of June 17, 2015, Roof walked into (Mother) Emanuel African Methodist Episcopal Church in Charleston, South Carolina, and, after sitting with members during a Bible study for the better part of an hour, opened fire, killing nine black churchgoers and injuring others. He was sentenced to death in January 2017. In his journal and during court proceedings, Roof acknowledged that alt-right propaganda websites (e.g., the Council of Conservative Citizens) were responsible for his "racial awakening."[19] It is also revealing that several alt-right leaders have admitted that Roof expressed "legitimate concerns" regarding America's "race problem."[20] Further analysis of Roof's writings and his court statements reveals a racial ideology strikingly congruent with the alt-right, one consistent even with the thought of the movement's self-styled "intellectuals" (e.g., Jared Taylor and Richard Spencer).[21] Yet, leaders of the alt-right worked furiously to distance themselves from Roof's violence and extremism, trying to convince American conservatives that their adherents are not Dylann Roof and their racial ideology is somehow culturally appropriate in a way that was not the case with groups like the KKK.[22] Their strategy proved

18. See Joel A. Brown, "Dylann Roof, the Radicalization of the Alt-Right, and Ritualized Racial Violence," *Sightings*, January 12, 2017, https://divinity.uchicago.edu/sightings/dylann-roof-radicalization-alt-right-and-ritualized-racial-violence.

19. "The Dylann Roof Trial: The Evidence," *New York Times*, December 9, 2016, www.nytimes.com/interactive/2016/12/09/us/dylann-roof-evidence.html. Frances Robles, Jason Horowitz, and Sheila Dewan, "Dylann Roof, Suspect in Charleston Shooting, Flew the Flags of White Power," *New York Times*, June 18, 2015, www.nytimes.com/2015/06/19/us/on-facebook-dylann-roof-charleston-suspect-wears-symbols-of-white-supremacy.html?_r=0.

20. [Richard B. Spencer], "Dylann Roof and Political Violence," *Radix Journal*, June 23, 2015, https://www.radixjournal.com/2015/06/2015-6-23-dylann-roof-and-political-violence.

21. See Brown, "Dylann Roof, the Radicalization of the Alt-Right, and Ritualized Racial Violence."

22. Since their initial organization in the nineteenth century, white supremacist groups have relied on similar stratagems, playing on notions of cultural respectability and assuming the guise of intellectualism to give the impression of a novel, more sophisticated incarnation of white supremacy. But "the alt-right only appears novel if we ignore the con-

quite effective in this regard. Over the last few years, the alt-right has successfully moved from the racist fringe in American culture and politics to wield an influence within the "mainstream" of conservative political life. It has gained popularity within traditional conservative circles, including in the religious discourse of certain pockets of evangelical Christianity, and it has found a place in the now very mainstream political battles over immigration and multiculturalism.

As demographics in the United States continue to trend toward the end of a white majority, it is increasingly likely that white Americans, and perhaps particularly white evangelicals, will be susceptible to the racial ideology of groups like the alt-right, although there is some evidence that conservative Christian leaders recognize the incompatibility of alt-right ideations concerning race and ethno-nationalism with the Christian value of love.[23] Yet racial protectionism does not have its provenance with the alt-right's new brand of racist activism in the United States. In fact, it is a timeworn practice of white America that one could argue has been its modus operandi throughout American history and up to the present day. And, perhaps to the surprise of some, white Christians are hardly immune to this kind of racist ideology, often even when they believe themselves to be nonracist.

---

tinuum of 'intellectual' white supremacy from which it emerged: scientific racism in the 19th and early 20th centuries, the national Ku Klux Klan of the 1920s, and the Citizens Councils of the 1950s and '60s" (Kelly J. Baker, "White-Collar Supremacy," *New York Times*, November 25, 2016, https://www.nytimes.com/2016/11/25/opinion/white-collar-supremacy.html).

23. Following the 2016 presidential election, in which the alt-right became a recurring feature of public discourse, the Southern Baptist Convention, one of the most conservative and reliably Republican Christian denominations in the United States, voted to denounce white supremacy in general and the alt-right in particular (Nathan Rott, "Southern Baptist Convention Votes to Condemn White Supremacy," *NPR*, June 14, 2017, http://www.npr.org/sections/thetwo-way/2017/06/14/532998287/southern-baptist-convention-votes-to-condemn-white-supremacy). For the Pew findings, see Michael Lipka, "U.S. Religious Groups and Their Political Leanings," Pew Research Center, February 23, 2016, http://www.pewresearch.org/fact-tank/2016/02/23/u-s-religious-groups-and-their-political-leanings). The fact that the SBC vote was contentious and not supported by an overwhelming majority betrays the extent to which nationalism has made inroads into evangelical Christian circles, yet the controversy confirms that Christianity is both a perceived and a real "problem" for white nationalist groups like the alt-right. See Damon T. Berry, "Religious Strategies of White Nationalism at Charlottesville," *Religion & Culture Forum*, October 13, 2017, http://voices.uchicago.edu/religionculture/2017/10/13/religious-strategies-of-white-nationalism-at-charlottesville.

The Sin We All Commit: White Protestants, Color Blindness, and Structural Racism

In examining white resistance to civil rights for racial minorities in the United States in the first decades of the new millennium, it is easy and perhaps even reasonable to focus on the movements and activism of what we might call "explicit" or "extreme" racism. Much of the scholarship surveying the phenomenon of twenty-first-century white supremacy has zeroed in on its most extreme manifestations in our political climate (e.g., the explicit nativist and racist rhetoric of the 2016 presidential campaign of Donald Trump) and in the groups and associations that promote racist agendas, such as the resurgent Ku Klux Klan, the alt-right, and neo-Nazis. Largely overlooked, however, have been the common structural forces that have at once oppressed black Americans and stoked antiblack resentment among white Americans, especially among poor, rural white Americans. And, perhaps to the surprise of many, the architects of these structures are not those explicitly racist groups named above but rather more mainstream actors with whom many Americans might identify. This section considers the subtler force of structural racism and Christian complicity in it in an effort to situate our current moment vis-à-vis the complicated and oft-tenuous relationship between religion and racism.[24]

There is a popular narrative in parts of America, including in many white Christian churches, that we have "triumphed over race," or that we have entered a "postracial" era in American history, especially since the election of a black president. Yet this "color-blind consensus" has in fact functioned to blind many white Americans to the realities of race in the United States.[25] Particularly important for our line of inquiry—that is, investigating the dynamics of white resistance to civil rights in America in regard to religion—is what Michelle Alexander calls the remaking of a "racial caste system" in America in the new millennium in her groundbreaking book *The New Jim Crow*.[26] Contrary to the widely accepted narrative of a

---

24. My argument here is primarily a historical one, drawing largely from two significant works on the history of racism in America: Michelle Alexander, *The New Jim Crow: Mass Incarceration in the Age Colorblindness*, rev. ed. (New York: New Press, 2011), and Carol Anderson, *White Rage: The Unspoken Truth of Our Racial Divide* (New York: Bloomsbury, 2016).

25. For a helpful resource for investigating the problematic notion of a "postracial America," see Sandhya Rani Jha, *Pre-Post-Racial America: Spiritual Stories from the Front Lines* (Saint Louis: Chalice, 2015).

26. Alexander, *The New Jim Crow*, 2.

postracial America, which undergirds strategies of color blindness, the sin of remaking a racial caste system in America belongs not only to the white nationalists and reactionary racists, but also to everyday Americans who are complicit in it to some degree, even ones who believe themselves not to be racist. Structural racism is a collective sin from which white Christian churches are hardly exempt.

Alexander's explanation of the rebirth of a racial caste in the United States proceeds from the premise that it "may be impossible to overstate the significance of race in defining the basic structure of American society." Her rehearsal of the long history of the continual remaking of the racial caste as one of the fundamental activities of the American project is helpful to anyone trying to get a better grasp of the place of race in American history.[27] She demonstrates that racism is highly adaptable and compellingly explains white privilege's "preservation through transformation" at every major turning point in American history.[28]

The New Jim Crow, and its recounting of a Twain-like historical rhyme in the continual remaking of America's racial caste, has significant import for understanding the relationship of religion to white racial resistance to civil rights. In particular, by describing the continually re-created racial caste system, Alexander alerts us to the reality that the ostensibly nonracist strategy shared by most Christian churches—attempting to solve American race relations by ignoring race—has actually helped to produce an extraordinary system of racialized social control.[29] In this sense, the victims of the racial strategy of color blindness are two groups. On the one hand, the rhetoric of color blindness, as Alexander demonstrates through the establishment of a biased system of mass incarceration, has effectively guaranteed that those who bear the brunt of its effect are those who are swept into this newest incarnation of America's racial undercaste, a population overwhelmingly comprised of black- and brown-skinned

---

27. Alexander, *The New Jim Crow*, 20–58.

28. See also Michael Omi and Howard Winant's notion of "racial projects," in *Racial Formation in the United States: From the 1960s to the 1990s* (New York: Routledge, 1996), 84–91.

29. Mark Hearn explains that "color-blind racism develops when persons ignore color in people and see them simply as individuals." Additionally, "As persons of color in racialized societies such as the United States are unequally treated on account of their color, the issue becomes a matter of faith and religious experience as religious leaders and educators, who disregard color, overlook important aspects of a person's ability to live wholly and abundantly." Hearn, "Color-Blind Racism, Color-Blind Theology, and Church Practices," *Religious Education* 104, no. 3 (2009): 272.

people.[30] On the other hand, white people who believe themselves to be nonracist are likewise victimized by color blindness insofar as their ostensibly well-intentioned attempts to mitigate the racial divide in America by "looking past race" actually function to perpetuate and strengthen the effects of structural racism. In other words, color blindness, which is a bedfellow of the highly problematic idea of a "postracial America," is sinister in its application, making worse the very thing it purports to resolve, and in the process implicating even the most well-intentioned white Christians who believe themselves not to be racist.

The cruel effects of color-blind approaches to race are seen in the effective resegregation of churches, public schools, and neighborhoods.[31] In the 1970s and '80s, just decades following landmark decisions and legislation aimed precisely at effecting structural desegregation (e.g., *Brown v. Board of Education*, 1954; Civil Rights Act, 1964; Voting Rights Act, 1965), courts and lawmakers took steps to dismantle enforced desegregation, premised on the belief that such measures were no longer necessary, such that by the early 1990s the Bush-Reagan courts had dismantled nearly every court-ordered desegregation plan, effectively ending the effort to enforce desegregation in public schools.[32] By the close of the 1990s, judges had gone so far as to prohibit public school boards from using considerations of race as justification for maintaining integrationist policies and standards.[33] This systematic process of resegregating American public schools was accelerated by what some scholars have identified as the "suburbanization of American cities," and more critically by other scholars of race as "white flight."[34] This happened when middle-class parents of white students (as well as a much smaller

30. Alexander, *The New Jim Crow*, 101–3.

31. John Charles Boger, "Willful Colorblindness: The New Racial Piety and the Resegregation of Public Schools," *North Carolina Law Review* 78 (September 2000): 1719–96.

32. Jacquelyn Dowd Hall, "The Long Civil Rights Movement and the Political Uses of the Past," *Journal of American History* 91, no. 4 (March 2005): 1233–63.

33. Sheryll Cashin, *The Failures of Integration: How Race and Class Are Undermining the American Dream* (New York: Public Affairs, 2004), 212. Also, see Gary Orfield, Susan E. Eaton, and the Harvard Project on School Desegregation, *Dismantling Desegregation: The Quiet Reversal of Brown v. Board of Education* (New York: New Press, 1996), and Gary Orfield, "Schools More Separate: Consequences of a Decade of Resegregation," July 2001, at www.civilrightsproject.ucla.edu/research/k-12-education/integration-and-diversity/schools-more-separate-consequences-of-a-decade-of-resegregation-1/schools-more-separate_orfield.pdf. See also Hall, "The Long Civil Rights Movement," 1257–58.

34. Kevin Kruse, *White Flight: Atlanta and the Making of Modern Conservatism*, Politics and Society in Twentieth-Century America (Princeton: Princeton University Press, 2005).

number of families of color) in cities felt pressure to move to neighborhoods with more reputable, better-funded schools. White flight left inner cities "hypersegregated," with schools overwhelmingly populated by students of color.[35] White flight is thus but one example of the subtle-but-sinister power of structural racism at work in modern America, a phenomenon that has not spared Christian churches in the United States, finding itself particularly at home among evangelical Christians.

Scholars who have studied the interrelated phenomena of white flight and urban resegregation have tended to overlook the pivotal role that religion and religious institutions have played in the dual construction of race and space in the United States. In his book *Shades of White Flight: Evangelical Congregations and Urban Departure*, Mark T. Mulder analyzed the white flight of several evangelical churches from neighborhoods on Chicago's South Side and found that they left their neighborhoods because of fear and concern for "self-preservation."[36] His study reveals that churches who share a "congregationalist" or "autonomous" polity, as do the vast majority of American evangelical churches, tend to rely on a "survivalist impulse" in the decisions they make.[37] And, significantly, this survivalist mode of decision making has encouraged a mass exodus of white evangelical churches from the city to the suburbs.[38] For the evangelical churches in his study, "departure represented the only viable means of survival" when faced with racial tension, and their congregational polity allowed them a "higher level of mobility" than Catholic and Protestant mainline churches in the same neighborhoods, which tend more toward a "parish model" and were thereby more committed to the geographic space in which they existed. Mulder helps us recognize that the congregationalism characteristic of the polity of most evangelical churches in the United States can inhibit the healing of the American Christian racial divide.

35. John Charles Boger, "Education's 'Perfect Storm'? Racial Resegregation, High Stakes Testing, and School Resource Inequities: The Case of North Carolina," *North Carolina Law Review* 81 (May 2003): 1375–1462. The No Child Left Behind Act (2002) actually exacerbated rather than resolved the inequalities in public school funding by encouraging competition between overwhelmingly white suburban schools and inner-city schools predominately made up of students of color.

36. Mark T. Mulder, *Shades of White Flight: Evangelical Congregations and Urban Departure* (New Brunswick, NJ: Rutgers University Press, 2015).

37. Mark T. Mulder, "Evangelical Church Polity and the Nuances of White Flight: A Case Study from the Roseland and Englewood Neighborhoods in Chicago," *Journal of Urban History* 38, no. 1 (2012): 16–38.

38. Mulder, "Evangelical Church Polity," 17, 33–34.

However, church structure is not the only variable that makes evangelical Christianity particularly susceptible to structural racism, including white flight. In their book *Divided by Faith: Evangelical Religion and the Problem of Race in America*, Michael Emerson and Christian Smith argue that the very nature of evangelical Christianity prohibits it from being an antiracist force. Evangelical Christianity often does just the opposite, contributing to the construction and perpetuation of highly racialized institutions and societies.[39] Emerson and Smith contend that, to understand evangelical strategies intended to remedy what evangelicals commonly refer to as "the race problem," we must first consider the "evangelical cultural toolkit." The toolkit consists of three elements undergirding evangelical engagement with society: accountable freewill individualism (the belief that individuals are not guided by structural or institutional forces but by their own choices),[40] relationalism (the belief that personal and local relationships are fundamental, over and against the social and systemic), and antistructuralism (a rejection of explanations for phenomena, such as racism and poverty, based on social structural influences). Taken together, these "tools" shape both how evangelical Christians perceive race relations and how they try to solve the distinct phenomena of racism and racial inequality. Thus, Emerson and Smith teach us that, "while many evangelicals may want to see an end to race problems, they are constrained by their religiocultural tools to call only for voluntaristic, faith-based solutions that would achieve the desired effects gradually and incrementally, such as converting people to Christianity and forming strong cross-racial relationships."[41]

Not to be lost, here, is the irony that white evangelical strategies to fight racism ultimately lead to greater, more entrenched forms of racial oppression. Due in large part to its singular focus on the individual as the locus of salvation (i.e., the fundamental belief that each person is responsible for his or her salvation through Christ and for maintaining that relationship), combined with a denial that structural racism exists, white evangelical theology exhibits a fundamental inability to address the structural forces that divide Americans along the "color line." Emerson and Smith show this

39. Michael O. Emerson and Christian Smith, *Divided by Faith: Evangelical Religion and the Problem of Race in America* (New York: Oxford University Press, 2000).

40. Emerson and Smith, *Divided by Faith*, 76.

41. Eric Tranby and Douglas Hartmann, "Critical Whiteness Theories and the Evangelical 'Race Problem': Extending Emerson and Smith's *Divided by Faith*," *Journal for the Scientific Study of Religion* 47, no. 3 (2008): 344.

to be the case even when evangelical Christians are ostensibly opposed to racism. White evangelical antiracist rhetoric focuses almost solely on individual racial prejudice while failing to account for the structural character of American racism. Notably, this idiosyncrasy of evangelical theology is often appealed to as justification for Christian aloofness in the political sphere surrounding issues of racial injustice. In this view, Christians should seek after and promote "spiritual means" for solving the "race problem" and avoid "coercive" political strategies (e.g., the ubiquitous evangelical dismissal and rejection of Black Lives Matter).

The evangelical racial strategy of color blindness—the default setting for evangelical race relations for most of the last century—combined with evangelicals' unwavering commitment to a "principled conservatism" of individualist, antistructural ideals and discourse, encourages evangelicals to look beyond skin color and to seek the "transformation of the heart," not the political system, for solving social ills such as racism and racial injustice.[42] This translates into what we might call "racial moderatism" on the part of evangelicals and often justifies disengagement from political discourse and action aimed at mitigating structural racism. As Mulder concludes in his study on evangelical white flight, "Though not necessarily intentional, the nature of white evangelical religion—with its inability to address fundamental and structural stratifications—has functioned to perpetuate racial barriers."[43] It is indeed a sad, perhaps even tragic, irony that the efforts of many white Christians to overcome racism have actually contributed to strengthening racist institutions and perpetuating racial oppression and inequality in this era of the second redemption.

---

42. For more on the history of evangelical Christian racial strategies, see Joseph L. Thomas, "Crossing the Color Line: A Brief Historical Survey of Race Relations in American Evangelical Christianity," in *This Side of Heaven*, ed. Joseph L. Thomas and Douglas A. Sweeney (New York: Oxford University Press, 2007), 111–26; Peter Heltzel, *Jesus and Justice: Evangelicals, Race, and American Politics* (New Haven: Yale University Press, 2009); and Curtis J. Evans, "White Evangelical Protestant Responses to the Civil Rights Movement," *Harvard Theological Review* 102, no. 2 (2009): 245–73. For more on the strategy and effect of evangelical color blindness strategies and theology, see Hearn, "Color-Blind Racism, Color-Blind Theology, and Church Practices," 272–88; Tranby and Hartmann, "Critical Whiteness Theories," 341–59.

43. Mulder, "Evangelical Church Polity," 18.

White Christian Habitus: Toward an Explanation
for White Christian Racial Resistance

This chapter has attempted to explore the general landscape of white Christian resistance to civil rights for racial minorities in twenty-first-century America. The current era in American history, which I have described as "the second redemption," is hardly immune to the kind of racism and racial oppression that has plagued previous generations in American history. As much as the myths of progress and American exceptionalism try to convince us that America's original sin of slavery has been forgiven and that we are marching toward a postracial America (if we are not there already), this brief survey reveals a dramatic counternarrative. By focusing on two different manifestations of racism in America—extreme or reactionary racism (e.g., white nationalism) and structural racism (e.g., white flight)—and their consequences for Christianity, this chapter has made clear that racism and racial oppression and inequality are very much alive in the new millennium. What is more, this reality presents one of the greatest stumbling blocks for the church's witness of Christian unity. Yet, as much as it has been made clear that racism presents a real and serious threat to the unity of the Christian church in America, important questions remain to be explored, perhaps especially, Why do white Christians who believe themselves not to be racist, unknowingly (and sometimes even knowingly) aid and abet systems and institutions that result in racial division and oppression?

Explaining and theorizing about white Christian racial (or racist) resistance is a difficult yet necessary task. Even while this chapter mostly refrains from theorizing about this resistance, the preceding study provides some important clues. The former analysis uncovers a common motivation shared by both white nationalists and ostensibly nonracist white Christians who nonetheless are complicit in structural racism: namely, their participation in different forms of racism proceeds from a similar impulse of racial preservation or protectionism. For white nationalists and other extreme racists, this is obvious and self-professed. But this same survivalist impulse motivates white Christians, even those who believe themselves to be nonracist, to act in ways that betray racial prejudice and capitalize on racial privilege. White Christians and white nationalists alike sense a threat to white political and cultural hegemony, whether knowingly or not, and they react in ways (albeit in drastically different ways) that intend to protect their racial group, often at the expense of racial minorities. Everyday white Christians thus, no less than other white Americans, participate in the project of preserving and protecting whiteness.

This finding comports with recent data-driven analysis of white Christian social and political activity over the past two decades vis-à-vis issues pertaining to race in the United States. In his book *The End of White Christian America* (released just a few months before the 2016 election of Donald Trump to the presidency), Robert P. Jones, CEO of the Public Religion Research Institute (PRRI), wrote that white (and especially white evangelical) Christians have "lost much cultural power while still retaining—at least in the southern enclaves—the remnants of significant political clout."[44] As demographics in the United States continue to trend toward what Jones calls "the twilight of white Christian America," white evangelical and mainline Protestants increasingly will sense not only the eclipsing of their racial majority but also the waning of their cultural and political influence. When this happens, if history is any guide, the descendants of white Christian America will continue to act on their survivalist impulses. They will likely either retreat into disengaged enclaves (the sectarian response) or band together to launch what sociologist Nathan Glazer has called "defensive offensives," in which "a formerly powerful majority recasts itself as a beleaguered minority in an attempt to preserve its particular social values."[45] Faced with an increasingly unfamiliar cultural landscape that threatens the supremacy of whiteness, these defensive offensives will likely play upon a nostalgic mythos, conjuring up images of better ages past. This strategy of a nostalgic resistance to a multicultural (and notably less white) future was expressed by many white Americans, including the majority of evangelicals, in the surveys conducted by the PRRI.[46]

Also, as anyone who paid attention to the rhetoric of Trump voters in the 2016 election could affirm, nostalgia of this sort has proven politically efficacious. Yet, as Robert Jones cautions, "nostalgia is not only unfaithful

---

44. Robert P. Jones, *The End of White Christian America* (New York: Simon and Schuster, 2016), 230–31.

45. Nathan Glazer, "Fundamentalism: A Defensive Offensive," in *Piety and Politics: Evangelicals and Fundamentalists Confront the World*, ed. Richard John Neuhaus and Michael Cromartie (Washington, DC: Ethics and Public Policy Center, 1987), 250–51. See Jones, *End of White Christian America*, 43–44. This is also largely consistent with white evangelical racial strategies of recent decades, insofar as these strategies "do not advocate for or support changes that might cause extensive discomfort or change their economic and cultural lives" (Emerson and Smith, *Divided by Faith*, 130).

46. Jones, *End of White Christian America*, 227–34.

to the past; it also threatens the integrity of the present."[47] Whatever forms the white Christian response takes, however, we can be almost certain they will ultimately serve to protect whiteness (i.e., white values, white norms, white privilege, white people, white power, etc.), whether white Christians are conscious of it or not. But why do we do this? How can we so confidently predict a response of racial protectionism?

White racial protectionism, which this study contends is the default (meaning the uncritical and often unconscious) reaction of white Americans when whiteness is threatened, should not be imagined only as the willful decision to defend one's imagined racial community—although it can be (e.g., white nationalism)—but it is more often the unconscious response of well-meaning white people who believe themselves to be nonracist. Racial protectionism, in this latter sense, is a socially and historically conditioned disposition—a function of what Pierre Bourdieu calls the "habitus."[48] Bourdieu's notion of habitus is one way, among others, to make sense of white racial protectionism, particularly as it occurs among people who otherwise believe themselves not to be racist. More specifically, it provides a helpful framework for understanding the religious dimension of white racial protectionism, which I argue constitutes a uniquely "white Christian habitus."[49]

Bourdieu is interested in explaining why certain "seemingly natural" actions (both collective and individual ones) can be performed without conscious deliberation. Bourdieu defines habitus as a set of cultural schemes, or practices, laid down in the earliest stages of an individual's life, and therefore the products of past conditions, that make a constructed world seem "natural" and a structured way of being in the world appear as "common sense." Habitus functions as a "map" of the individual's social worlds, generating dispositions within the confines of the historical and social conditions within which they are produced and reproduced.[50] Habitus makes "coherence and

47. Jones, *End of White Christian America*, 230.

48. See especially Pierre Bourdieu, *Practical Reason: On the Theory of Action* (Stanford: Stanford University Press, 1998), and Bourdieu, *Outline of a Theory of Practice*, Cambridge Studies of Social Anthropology 16 (Cambridge: Cambridge University Press, 1977).

49. I am here adapting Eduardo Bonilla-Silva's concept of "white habitus," which he describes as a "racialized, uninterrupted socialization process that *conditions* and *creates* whites' racial taste, perceptions, feelings, and emotions and their views on racial matters. . . . [Consequently,] it promotes a sense of group belonging (a white culture of solidarity) and negative views about nonwhites." In *Racism without Racists: Color-Blind Racism and the Persistence of Racial Inequality in America*, 5th ed. (Lanham, MD: Rowman and Littlefield, 2018), 121.

50. It is neither "mechanical submission nor a conscious consent to an order. . . . The social world is riddled with *calls to order* that function as such only for those who are pre-

necessity out of accident and contingency," effectively turning history into nature.[51] One senses what is appropriate or reasonable in a given situation precisely because one is predisposed to act in ways that are in accord with the habitus one received. Members of the same class and racial group, for instance, would share a relatively homogenous habitus because they have in common many formative experiences, family structures, and fundamental religious beliefs, among other things. Because they share a similar internalized social map, they are able to act "appropriately," that is, in such a way that aligns with and in fact reproduces the very "set of dispositions" they embody.

If we consider whiteness as a kind of habitus (the dominant American habitus, in fact), such that whiteness (e.g., white values, white ways of being religious, political, social, etc.) provides the norm for what it means to be appropriately and fully American (or Christian, for that matter), then we can understand how a threat to that habitus as the dominant social map for navigating authentic American-ness would seem "unnatural" and unsettling, evoking an instinctive, even if unconscious, reaction and resistance.[52] Bourdieu suggests that when such a threat is sensed, those for whom the threatened habitus has been internalized will seek to "keep distance" in order to mitigate the threat, whether strategically or unknowingly.[53] Such resistance is almost automatic and unavoidable, as though ingrained in one's social DNA. When this shared habitus is threatened and made vulnerable—for instance, when advances and civil rights for minorities entail increased cultural, political, and economic influence for nonwhite groups—individuals of the dominant group act in predetermined ways orchestrated by their shared habitus to safeguard its place of dominance, sometimes intentionally and knowingly but often not so. For instance, by resisting otherwise antiracist movements such as the civil rights movement or Black Lives Matter because they appear to disrupt the (seemingly) natural order of society, white Chris-

---

disposed to heeding them as they *awaken* deeply buried corporeal dispositions, outside the channels of consciousness and calculation. It is this doxic submission of the dominated to the structures of a social order of which their mental structures are the product that Marxism cannot understand insofar as it remains trapped in the intellectualist tradition of the philosophies of consciousness" (Bourdieu, *Practical Reason*, 54–55). Elsewhere he identifies this as the "hysteresis effect" (Bourdieu, *Outline of a Theory*, 182).

51. Pierre Bourdieu, "Outline of the Theory of Practice: Structures and the Habitus," in *Practicing History: New Directions in Historical Writing after the Linguistic Turn*, ed. Gabrielle M. Spiegel, Rewriting Histories (New York: Routledge, 2005), 179–80.

52. See Tranby and Hartmann, "Critical Whiteness Theories," 341–59.

53. Bourdieu, *Outline of a Theory*, 185.

tians act out of the habitus of whiteness and perpetuate systems of racism that result in racial oppression. White racial resistance of this sort is not a recent invention or an aberration in American history; it is the modus operandi of a society structured by a habitus of whiteness.

Breaking the Dams

This would be a sad place to end the chapter, offering little hope for overcoming the multifarious and insidious force of racism in America. However, the Christian witness holds that there is in fact hope for liberation, freedom even for white Christians controlled by what religion scholar Willis Jenkins calls the "quotidian monster of white supremacy."[54] It will require hard work, to be sure, and Christians and scholars alike must continue to probe what Edward Blum has termed "the spiritual wage of whiteness"—that is, the conflation of whiteness with godliness that has been created, challenged, and re-created time and again in American history.[55] This is to suggest that religion is often complicit in racial ideologies of domination that Bourdieu would remind us are often unseen in their sinister machinations, and religious actors and the scholars who study them must be willing to bring it out of the shadows and into the light for critical analysis. Blum offers a poignant challenge:

> [We] will find much in the study of race and whiteness. The spiritual wage of whiteness has been, at the very least, compensation and justification. It has facilitated, without much internal conflict, the transformation of colonial freedom searchers into slaveholders, of Progressive-era churchgoers into lynch mobs, and of modern suburbanites into civil rights opponents. W. E. B. Du Bois prophesied in 1920 that, while many believed that whiteness would lead them to heaven, it actually carried them on a "descent to Hell." It is to that inferno that scholars of American religion and culture must travel. Unlike the Divine Comedy, though, there is no promise of paradise at the journey's end.[56]

54. Willis Jenkins, "Moral Trauma," *Medium*, August 28, 2017, https://medium.com/@willisjenkins/moral-trauma-f4c17866ad8c.

55. Edward J. Blum et al., "Forum: American Religion and 'Whiteness,'" *Religion and American Culture: A Journal of Interpretation* 19, no. 1 (Winter 2009): 1–35.

56. Blum, "American Religion and 'Whiteness,'" 4, 9–10.

Whether evangelical, Reformed, mainline, Orthodox, Catholic, or otherwise, white Christians would do well to consider afresh the words that Martin Luther King Jr. wrote over half a century ago to white religious leaders during the most crucial days of the fight for African American civil rights:

> I must confess that over the past few years I have been gravely disappointed with the white moderate. I have almost reached the regrettable conclusion that the Negro's great stumbling block in his stride toward freedom is not the White Citizen's Counciler or the Ku Klux Klanner, but the white moderate, who is more devoted to "order" than to justice; who prefers a negative peace which is the absence of tension to a positive peace which is the presence of justice; who constantly says: "I agree with you in the goal you seek, but I cannot agree with your methods of direct action"; who paternalistically believes he can set the timetable for another man's freedom; who lives by a mythical concept of time and who constantly advises the Negro to wait for a "more convenient season." Shallow understanding from people of good will is more frustrating than absolute misunderstanding from people of ill will. Lukewarm acceptance is much more bewildering than outright rejection. . . . I had hoped that the white moderate would understand that law and order exist for the purpose of establishing justice and that when they fail in this purpose they become the *dangerously structured dams* that block the flow of social progress.[57]

Our hope is that the Christian witness of the twenty-first century will not be one of racial division and "the dangerously structured dams" of racism, but rather of unity, justice, liberation, and reconciliation. May it be that Jesus's plea on the cross on behalf of humanity, "forgive them, for they know not what they do," is heard so that in this century we may discover redemption of another kind.

---

57. Martin Luther King, "Letter from Birmingham City Jail" (1963), in *A Testament of Hope: The Essential Writings of Martin Luther King, Jr.*, ed. James Melvin Washington (San Francisco: Harper and Row, 1986), 289–302 (emphasis added).

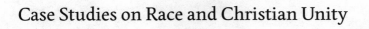

Case Studies on Race and Christian Unity

Women, Race, and Unity in the Stone-Campbell Movement

Loretta Hunnicutt

The intersection of race, gender, and unity in American Christianity has confronted the nation with some of its most difficult challenges. If racial segregation and male dominance have been defining characteristics in American history, the experiences of churches document this well. Few institutions have reflected so clearly the racial separation and male privilege in American society. Unfortunately, accounts of religious history have generally privileged the experience of whites and males, thus further obscuring the visibility of nonwhites and women in American Christianity. Catherine Brekus argues that most religious history has relegated women's experiences to the margins.[1] Thus, the religious experiences of both black and white religious women have fallen into an abyss in the writing of American history.

Racial segregation in churches has presented one of the great challenges to Christian unity for most religious traditions in the United States. Few lines have divided the church more. One of the most significant lenses through which to examine the religious experiences of black and white women and Christian unity is the Stone-Campbell Movement.[2] Born out of the post-Revolutionary religious environment, this movement's experi-

---

1. Catherine A. Brekus, *The Religious History of American Women: Reimagining the Past* (Chapel Hill: University of North Carolina Press, 2007), 1.

2. For more information on the Stone-Campbell Movement, see D. Newell Williams, Douglas A. Foster, and Paul Blowers, *The Stone-Campbell Movement: A Global History* (Saint Louis: Chalice, 2013). For more information on race relations in the Stone-Campbell Movement, see Wes Crawford, *Shattering the Illusion: How African American Churches of Christ Moved from Segregation to Independence* (Abilene, TX: Abilene Christian University Press, 2013); Barclay Key, "Race and Restoration: Churches of Christ and the African American Freedom Struggle" (MA thesis, University of Florida, 2007); Brenda M. Cardwell and William K. Fox, *Journey toward Wholeness: A History of Black Disciples of Christ in the Mission of the Christian Church* ([Nashville]: National Convocation of the Christian Church [Disciples of Christ], 1990); Carroll Pitts Jr., "A Critical Study of Civil Rights Practices, Attitudes and Responsibilities in Churches of Christ" (MA thesis, Pepperdine University, 1969).

ences with gender, race, and unity bear particular scrutiny for several reasons. First, the movement itself originated in a desire for Christian unity (at times including race) that rejected all written creeds and emphasized congregational autonomy (as patterned by first-century churches) to achieve that goal.[3] Second, though blacks and whites at times interacted very little, the movement did not officially splinter into separate black and white denominations.[4] Third, it numbered among its members one of the highest concentrations of white slaveholders, and thus charted a difficult course in racial reconciliation.[5] Similar to women in other Protestant traditions, black and white women of the movement figured prominently in its attempts to bridge the racial gap between its members. While racial unity has remained largely elusive, Stone-Campbell women, both black and white, have provided significant leadership in what racial unity the movement has achieved. Though not often occupying pulpits or holding official titles of leadership, female leaders incorporated many of the central functions of the movement such as educating preachers, speaking at church meetings, and publishing articles in movement journals.[6] Race relations and the impact of Stone-Campbell women followed a long arc in the movement from integration during the era of slavery to increasing separation during the Jim Crow era and finally to a slow but growing movement toward integration in the civil rights era.

Complicating any analysis of race, gender, and unity in the Stone-Campbell Movement are the widely disparate streams of the movement formed by a series of significant divisions. Though sharing common origins in the theology and teaching of Alexander Campbell and Barton Stone (among many others), the members of the movement bearing their name have over time separated over a myriad of issues. Stone and Campbell had

3. See Douglas A. Foster, "Unity, Christian," in *The Encyclopedia of the Stone-Campbell Movement*, ed. Douglas A. Foster et al. (Grand Rapids: Eerdmans, 2004), 754-58.

4. See Williams, Foster, and Blowers, *The Stone-Campbell Movement*, 44-45.

5. Winfred Ernest Garrison and A. T. DeGroot, *The Disciples of Christ: A History* (Saint Louis: Christian Board of Publication, 1948), 468.

6. For women in the Stone-Campbell Movement, see Loretta M. Long, "Christian Church/Disciples of Christ Tradition and Women," in *Encyclopedia of Women and Religion in North America*, ed. Rosemary Skinner Keller, Rosemary Radford Ruether, and Marie Cantlon (Bloomington: Indiana University Press, 2006), 1:296-307; Loretta M. Long, *The Life of Selina Campbell: A Fellow Soldier in the Cause of Restoration* (Tuscaloosa: University of Alabama Press, 2001); Williams, Foster, and Blowers, *The Stone-Campbell Movement*, 61-75; Debra B. Hull, Kathy J. Pulley, and Eleanor A. Daniel, "Women in Ministry," in Foster et al., *Encyclopedia of the Stone-Campbell Movement*, 776-81.

each embraced a theology that focused on the rejection of the creeds adopted by most Protestant traditions (which they deemed the cause of most conflict in Protestantism) in favor of uniting on Scripture alone. They and their supporters eventually withdrew from all denominational traditions and sought a form of church organization and worship style patterned after the first-century church, relying on Scripture alone for guidance in faith and practice.

Despite members' goal of Christian unity, disputes arose in the movement from its beginning. The leadership of Alexander Campbell initially supported the cohesion of the movement, but his death in 1866 and the impact of the Civil War brought significant strain to his followers. One group (largely centered in the North) sought a more structured organization to the church in order to support efforts at evangelization and fund-raising. They were successful in founding the American Christian Missionary Society to support mission efforts, but when this organization pushed through resolutions condemning slavery in the 1860s, the Southern churches felt threatened. Numerous issues driven by the sectional conflict during and after the Civil War created such tension in the postbellum era that, by the beginning of the twentieth century, the movement had split into largely Southern (Church of Christ) and Northern (Christian Churches) streams. Different theological proclivities (e.g., should the Bible's silence on practices such as using missionary societies or instruments in worship be interpreted as permissive or restrictive?) exacerbated the social divisions of the emerging Southern and Northern societies in industrial America. In the North, a second division occurred among the Christian Churches that in some ways reflected the divisions brought about by the fundamentalist-modernist controversy. The conservative group became known as the Christian Church (though some congregations are called Church of Christ), and the progressive group as the Christian Church (Disciples of Christ).

Among blacks, though doctrinal disagreements resembled those among whites, the dividing lines also represented in part attitudes toward the church's role in confronting racism, with the more activist-oriented believers favoring the Disciples and the more conservative believers aligning with the Churches of Christ. Despite the challenge of addressing the wide array of approaches to gender and race relations represented in the movement, there is great opportunity as well. The different approaches to gender and race relations among church members from the same theological origins represent a unique window into the nature of male-female and black-white relations in American Christianity.

Women and Race in the Stone-Campbell Movement

During the era of black enslavement, both black and white women in many Protestant traditions figured prominently in issues critical to race relations, such as the antislavery movement, the integration of black members into white churches, and church-sponsored efforts to educate black men and women. Slavery cast a long shadow over race relations before the Civil War. This is very evident in the relationships among black and white members of the churches. Many early churches had both black and white members.[7] The relationships between these two groups varied significantly from church to church. In some churches black members had their own leadership, but in others they had little role other than attending worship. Overall, the system of slavery and its expectations of race relations conditioned whites to expect blacks to occupy menial positions in every element of human interaction. The church was no different.

Women played central roles in race relations in many American religious traditions. For instance, religious women dominated the ranks of the antislavery movement from the 1830s through the 1850s.[8] Additionally, enslaved women represented a significant percentage of church members throughout the South, especially in Baptist and Methodist traditions. Similarly, in the early era of the Stone-Campbell Movement, black women served as members and some white women spoke out against slavery and promoted the inclusion of blacks in the church and other movement institutions, especially universities. Unfortunately, little is known of the numerous black women who joined early Stone-Campbell churches apart from their names. Few surviving sources provide any detail on these women and the role they played in churches. At best, most early record keepers note the woman's name and perhaps her status of servitude (enslaved or free), and possibly the name of her "owner." For instance, Rachel Hunter, a free black woman, joined the Walnut Spring congregation in Strasburg, North Carolina, in 1825 and was identified as a "member of the

---

7. For an analysis of interracial Protestant churches in the South during slavery, see John B. Boles, *Masters and Slaves in the House of the Lord: Race and Religion in the American South, 1740–1870* (Lexington: University Press of Kentucky, 2015). For details on interracial churches in the Stone-Campbell Movement, see R. H. Peoples, *The Historical Development of Negro Work and Its Relation to the Organized Brotherhood Life*, as quoted in R. L. Jordan, *Two Races in One Fellowship* (Detroit: United Christian Church, 1944), 26.

8. See Elizabeth J. Clapp and Julie Roy Jeffrey, *Women, Dissent, and Anti-Slavery in Britain and America, 1790–1865* (Oxford: Oxford University Press, 2011).

Church of Christ."[9] However, we know very little about her motivation for joining or the position she occupied in the church. Yet her presence in this church represents one of the earliest attempts at racial unity in the early Stone-Campbell Movement. Indeed, churches represented a rare space of fellowship between blacks and whites in a society that otherwise enforced a rigid hierarchy between the two races. For instance, blacks in Stone-Campbell churches were listed as "members," the same as white church attendees. Surviving records indicate that black women, reflecting women in American Christianity in general, were much more likely than black men to attend Stone-Campbell churches.[10] They persevered in joining these churches despite being relegated figuratively and literally to the margins of the church.

Not only did black women provide the earliest encounters between black and white members of the churches, they also contributed to the growth of the movement, especially in the South. According to N. Robert Gill, the First Christian Church of Savannah, Georgia, originated in the efforts of Sheldon Dunning and "an old Negro woman" in the 1830s. Gill's history does not indicate her precise role, but for several years she and Dunning were the only adherents in Savannah to the tenets that defined the early Stone-Campbell Movement.[11] Mary, an enslaved woman, worshiped with the Buffalo Creek Christian Church in Elizabethton, Tennessee, which was likely founded by her master. The treasurer's book from that era lists financial contributions she made to the congregation.[12] While it is difficult to discern her motivations in contributing to a church inaugurated by the man who kept her in bondage, her commitment to the congregation seems evident.

---

9. Minute Book of the Christian Church in Strasburg at the Walnut Spring School House, as quoted in Robert O. Fife, *Teeth on Edge* (Grand Rapids: Baker, 1971), 56.

10. Displaying proportions typical of many early churches, the minutes of the Roberson Fork Church of Christ in Lynnville, Tennessee, in the 1830s and 1840s list ten male black members and sixteen black females. See Minutes of the Roberson Fork Church of Christ (Giles County, Tennessee), 1838–1842, Tennessee State Library and Archives, Nashville. Another, smaller example is the First Christian Church of Richmond, Kentucky, which recorded seven black women and two black men as members prior to the Civil War. See Katherine Phelps Caperton, *History of the First Christian Church of Richmond, Kentucky* ([Richmond, KY]: [First Christian Church], 1944), 19.

11. N. Robert Gill, *150 Years in God's Service: This Great Brotherhood of Ours in Savannah* (Savannah, GA: First Christian Church, 1969), 59.

12. Mary Hardin McCown and Josephine Carpenter Owen, *100th Anniversary, History and Directory, 1871–1971, First Christian Church, Johnson City, Tennessee* (Johnson City, TN: Tri-Cities Lithographing, 1971), 97.

During the era of black enslavement, few whites in the Stone-Campbell Movement challenged slavery. They thus reflect the majority of Southern Christians, who rarely questioned slavery publicly. Significantly, Stone-Campbell adherents were twice as likely as members of most Protestant traditions to own slaves.[13] Moreover, the movement's founders themselves were slaveholders and at best refused to support the abolition of slavery; at worst they privileged the interests of fellow slaveholders. Alexander Campbell, the most prominent voice, refused to affirm that slavery was inherently evil, opposed immediate abolition, and made racist comments in his influential journal the *Millennial Harbinger*. His son, Alexander Campbell Jr., married a Southern woman and served as a colonel in the Confederate army.[14]

Despite the general support for slavery in the Stone-Campbell Movement before the Civil War, women were prominent among the few who raised their voices against the practice both in and out of the church; some of them openly challenged Campbell's position on the issue. Campbell's sister Jane Campbell McKeever, founder of the Pleasant Hill Seminary in Washington, Pennsylvania, was one of the most prominent Stone-Campbell members to reject the institution of slavery. Her views gained public attention when John Boggs, one of the few openly antislavery editors in the movement, published a letter from her in his *North-Western Christian Magazine* in 1856. In a clear challenge to her brother, she writes (emphases are hers), "I truly rejoice to find that ONE of *our brotherhood* has had the fortitude, and independence of mind, to rise superior to the reproach and opposition of so many of his *professed christian* [sic] *brethren*, in behalf of the poor, oppressed and degraded slave."[15] But McKeever did more than just write letters to journals. She and her husband, Matthew, operated a station on the Underground Railroad ferrying enslaved Africans to freedom in the North. They probably used the school they operated as cover for the movement of extra food and supplies to support the escaped slaves they housed.[16] Additionally, two of Campbell's other sisters, Dorothea Bryant

---

13. Garrison and DeGroot, *The Disciples of Christ*, 468.

14. See Williams, Foster, and Blowers, *The Stone-Campbell Movement*, 35–39; Don Haymes, Eugene Randall II, and Douglas A. Foster, "Race Relations," in Foster et al., *Encyclopedia of the Stone-Campbell Movement*, 619–22.

15. Jane McKeever, "Interesting Letter," *North-Western Christian Magazine* 1 (November 1854): 153.

16. Bernice Bartley Bushfield, *McKeever History, with Allied Families of West Middletown, Washington County, Pennsylvania* ([Toronto, OH?]: n.p., 1959), 138.

and Alicia Clapp (and their spouses), also operated stations on the Underground Railroad.[17] Another woman, Marcia M. Bassett Goodwin, later the editor of two significant Stone-Campbell journals, the *Christian Monitor* and *Missionary Tidings*, published a poem critical of slavery that appeared in the *Anti-Slavery Bugle* (New Lisbon, Ohio) in 1861.[18] Given the overall rare criticism of slavery from within the movement, the actions of these women are significant.

Women, Race, and Education

While members of the Stone-Campbell Movement disagreed about a host of theological and social issues, one interest that linked them was education. Throughout American religious history, Christian traditions have sponsored colleges and universities to educate their young people in Christian principles and promote the evangelization of the nation. Christian traditions brought much of the energy to higher education during the nineteenth century.[19] From the Stone-Campbell Movement's origins there had been a strong push to provide a Christian education to the next generation as a method of ensuring correct interpretation of scriptural mandates.[20]

The colleges and seminaries formed by Stone-Campbell members served as a key battleground where the theology and identity of the movement emerged. The outcome of this battle often determined who retained authority to lead the movement and who remained on its margins. This battleground was defined by several key factors. First, the movement founded dozens of colleges within the first two generations of its existence that, in a congregationally organized movement, functioned as a quasi-denominational structure where faculty instructed on doctrinal questions and new generations of leadership were shaped by their teaching. Second, the leaders of the movement's first generation, nearly all male, had at one point in their careers made their living in whole or in part by educating young men and women, so the movement's origins were inextricably linked with edu-

17. John H. Hull, "Underground Railroad Activity among Western Pennsylvania Disciples," *Discipliana* 57, no. 1 (Spring 1997): 7–8.

18. Marcia M. Bassett, "The Cry for Freedom," *Anti-Slavery Bugle*, May 4, 1861.

19. Christopher J. Lucas, *American Higher Education: A History*, 2nd ed. (New York: Palgrave Macmillan, 2016), 120.

20. See John L. Morrison, "Education, Philosophy of," in Foster et al., *Encyclopedia of the Stone-Campbell Movement*, 292–94.

cational endeavors.[21] Third, until the 1870s, none of the dozens of schools founded by members of the movement accepted black women as students. Thus, education stood as a hallmark of the movement, and those excluded from obtaining it faced significant marginalization.[22]

After the Civil War, Stone-Campbell educators joined those of other Christian traditions, including the Presbyterian, Baptist, and Methodist denominations, to sponsor efforts to educate black children.[23] Black and white members encountered each other in the movement's educational institutions in significant ways. Because black students were not admitted to the colleges of the movement, the main interactions between blacks and whites took place in the church buildings. However, after the war ended, and similar to the actions of black Methodists, Baptists, and Presbyterians, many black members of Stone-Campbell churches withdrew from white majority congregations and sought autonomy from white racism by forming their own churches.[24] This division had the potential to separate the races entirely, as blacks and whites would no longer encounter each other in the churches or in other movement gatherings, but efforts at educating formerly enslaved people led to points of interaction between blacks and whites in the postwar era. Black and white women emerged as a key force in championing education for black students.

Though in number of institutions and resources allocated the efforts to provide education for blacks in the Stone-Campbell Movement never approached those for white students, several black and white women initiated important efforts toward educating black students early in the movement. For instance, one biographer of Jane Campbell McKeever suggests that she

21. Williams, Foster, and Blowers, *The Stone-Campbell Movement*, 31.

22. For example, Alexander Campbell operated the Buffalo Seminary beginning in 1818 (see Selina Huntington Campbell, *Home Life and Reminiscences of Alexander Campbell* [Saint Louis: J. Burns, 1881], 120); Thomas Campbell, Alexander's father, operated a series of schools, including one in Burlington, Kentucky, where he was prevented from instructing black students (see Robert Richardson, *Memoirs of Alexander Campbell, Embracing a View of the Origin, Progress and Principles of the Religious Reformation which he Advocated* [Philadelphia: J. B. Lippincott, 1868], 1:494); Walter Scott, Thornton F. Johnson, and David Staats Burnet organized the first college of the movement, Bacon College in Georgetown, Kentucky, in 1844, which did not admit black students (see Richard L. Harrison, "Bacon College," in Foster et al., *Encyclopedia of the Stone-Campbell Movement*, 55).

23. Lucas, *American Higher Education*, 166.

24. Cardwell and Fox, *Journey toward Wholeness*, 7; Hap Lyda, "Black Disciples in the Nineteenth Century," in *The Untold Story: A Short History of Black Disciples* (Saint Louis: Christian Board of Publication, 1976), 12.

may also have provided religious education for the black servants in her employ even before the end of slavery.[25] Another woman, Myrtilla Miner, directly challenged the prohibitions against black female education in the antebellum South. Miner, though born in New York, accepted a teaching position at Newton Female Institute in Whitesville, Mississippi, in 1846. Dr. David Phares, an early convert of Alexander Campbell in the South, opened the school in 1842, and it continued to operate "under the influence" of the Christian Church until 1865.[26] After her arrival, Miner was struck by the plight of black women living in the community and proposed to Phares that she provide them with instruction in her free time. In response, Phares suggested that "Northern philanthropists had a vast work to do at home to elevate their own free colored people," effectively denying her request.[27] Eventually, Miner acceded to his observation and moved to Washington, DC, where she opened one of the first schools in the nation for black women.[28] But Miner's experiences in Mississippi offer a rare if predictable public look at how Stone-Campbell leaders viewed education for blacks prior to the end of slavery. Education was largely reserved for white members, despite the connection between education and the development of faith.

In the struggle over slavery, while the Stone-Campbell Movement did not officially split into racially divided denominations, blacks formed congregations of their own that reflected the increased segregation occurring in other arenas of American life. As a result, education became one of the few areas of contact between white (mostly female) instructors and black students in the movement. With the arrival of the Civil War, church member Letitia Faurot pioneered among Stone-Campbell leaders in expanding education opportunities for black students, especially among those who would form the nucleus of the Disciples wing of the Stone-Campbell Movement. She established schools beginning in 1864 for blacks living in the Tennes-

25. Ethelene Bruce White, "Jane Campbell McKeever: Her Life and Beliefs with Selected Comparison to Her Brother Alexander Campbell" (unpublished paper, Harding University Graduate School of Religion, 2008), 107. Portions of the unpublished paper also appeared in White, "Jane Campbell McKeever (1800-1871): A Brief Biography with Comparison to Her Brother Alexander Campbell on the Issue of Slavery and Abolition," *Stone-Campbell Journal* 13, no. 1 (Spring 2010): 3-16.

26. "First Academies in County," *Woodville (MS) Republican*, July 19, 1924, 9.

27. Lester Grosvenor Wells, "Myrtilla Miner," *New York History* 24, no. 3 (1943): 362.

28. For more information on Miner's teaching career, see Wells, "Myrtilla Miner," 358-75; Ellen M. O'Connor, *Myrtilla Miner: A Memoir* (Boston: Houghton-Mifflin, 1885); Sadie Daniel, "Myrtilla Miner: Pioneer in Teacher Education for Negro Women," *Journal of Negro History* 34, no. 1 (January 1949): 30-45.

see "contraband camps" she visited with her husband, a Disciples preacher who served as a chaplain for the Union army.[29] Her actions during the war proved only the beginning of her career in education. Faurot played a key role in establishing the most significant black college among the Disciples, the Southern Christian Institute (SCI). The school originated with Faurot's interest in evangelizing blacks in the South, and comported with the goals of the president of the General Christian Missionary Convention, Thomas Munnell. Both had taken note of the work of other denominations in this area since the end of slavery and agreed that the Disciples should launch their own efforts. SCI in Mississippi would educate thousands of black students, many of whom emerged as leaders in Disciples churches throughout the nation.

Graduate of SCI and member of the Twelfth Street Christian Church in Washington, DC, Oletha Brown Blayton provided critical leadership in racial integration in Washington, DC. Though born in Louisiana, she relocated to the nation's capital during World War I and found work in a factory that made uniforms for soldiers.[30] After decades of service as president of a women's group at Twelfth Street, Blayton had by the 1940s helped organize a combined meeting of the women of the Twelfth Street congregation and the National City Christian Church women, who were mostly white. Local laws in Maryland and Virginia forbade black and white women from socializing (and especially sleeping) in the same space except as master and servant. According to Blayton, the women of Twelfth Street agreed to serve the National City women, and the retreat went forward—a remarkable testimony to the dedication of the Washington, DC, women.[31]

While SCI largely originated in the white desire to evangelize blacks, other important institutions would emerge from the desires of the black community itself. Lawrence Burnley's study of race and education in the Christian Church documents "the interconnectedness of literacy and religion" for African Americans.[32] "In general," he notes, "Blacks in the U.S. came to accept the evangelical belief that reading the Bible for one's self was an essential part of the process of achieving a 'right' relationship with

---

29. Letitia Faurot, letter to the editor, *Indiana School Journal* 9, no. 6 (June 1864): 170–71.

30. "Oletha Brown Blayton," in *Christian Women Share Their Faith: A Book of Herstories*, ed. Carole Coffey and Disciples of Christ Department of Church Women (Indianapolis: Division of Homeland Ministries, 1985), 68.

31. "Oletha Brown Blayton," 68.

32. Lawrence A. Q. Burnley, *The Cost of Unity: African-American Agency and Education in the Christian Church, 1865–1914* (Macon, GA: Mercer University Press, 2008), 4.

God. The Bible and the Christian religion represented the promise of a better world for many enslaved and free Africans alike."[33] Several black women led in the effort to provide education for black children and successfully enlisted the support of white women in the cause. Mary Alphin, a black teacher and state organizer for the Disciples of Christ in Texas, launched a key fund-raising effort in support of a school for blacks in Texas in 1906.[34] She motivated churches by emphasizing the need for trained leadership that a school would provide.[35] After her election as president of the Texas Woman's Missionary Society in 1908, she appealed to the Christian Woman's Board of Missions for funds to build the school. After repeated requests by the black women's society, the white board offered to fund the school if the black churches raised the first thousand dollars.[36] Alphin accepted the offer, and over the next few years raised the money among black Disciples.[37] She also played a key role in convincing Ida Van Zandt Jarvis of Fort Worth, Texas, an officer on the white board, to donate the land for a new school. In 1912, Jarvis Christian Institute (now Jarvis Christian College) opened and for several years functioned under the oversight of the Christian Woman's Board of Missions as the only accredited high school for blacks in the Hawkins, Texas, area (until 1937).[38]

Race relations and Christian education among the Churches of Christ encountered even more significant complications than among the Disciples. First, since these congregations clustered largely in the South, they operated in a more racially hostile climate that favored segregation and racial separation. Second, they eschewed parachurch institutions such as missionary societies that they believed undermined New Testament Christianity. This made it more challenging to develop initiatives to create institutions for black learning. Third, Churches of Christ also favored more conservative interpretations of Scripture that placed more limits on women's role in church leadership. All these factors tended to put roadblocks in the way for

---

33. Burnley, *The Cost of Unity*, 3.

34. Lou Mallory, "The Early Days of Jarvis Christian College," *Hawkins–Holly Lake (TX) Gazette*, February 3, 2007, http://www.hlrgazette.com/wchistory020307.htm.

35. Mary Alphin, "Report to the Board," *Gospel Plea* 28, no. 2 (June 1910): 35.

36. E. B. Bynum, *These Carried the Torch: Pioneers of Christian Education in Texas* (Dallas: W. F. Clark, 1946), 23.

37. Giley Elizabeth Nixon Griffin, *Faith Keepers: African American Women Leaders in Texas, 1846–2000, in the Christian Church (Disciples of Christ)* (Dallas: Griffin, 2000), 5.

38. F. Erik Brooks and Glenn L. Starks, *Historically Black Colleges and Universities: An Encyclopedia* (Santa Barbara, CA: ABC-CLIO, 2011), 156.

more racial interactions desired by black and white women. Nevertheless, black education represented a key area of interaction between blacks and whites where women provided key leadership.

Among the Churches of Christ, the Nashville Christian Institute (NCI) emerged as one of the most important schools for blacks. Black educators demonstrated significant leadership among the Churches of Christ. But they also faced a central dilemma. Though they preferred to direct their own educational interests, a lack of financial resources constantly threatened this desire. Although the NCI was initially funded by black Churches of Christ in the Nashville area, a chronic lack of resources forced the school eventually to turn to local whites for funding.[39] In general, black education received less attention among the more socially conservative churches that separated from the Disciples of Christ. In a way, this allowed several black schools to operate more independently, as they likely benefited indirectly from white indifference. A lifelong quest for education shaped Annie Tuggle, one of the most significant leaders among black Churches of Christ. Though opportunities for female leadership in the denomination were limited, and for black women even more so, Tuggle would emerge as a key figure in the organization and fund-raising efforts of black schools. She enlisted influential white church members David Lipscomb and A. M. Burton in the cause of black education and helped secure funding for several black schools, including the Silver Point Institute founded by G. P. Bowser and the NCI. She also championed the cause in the pages of significant journals edited by white church leaders, including the *Gospel Advocate*, which was edited by one of the most influential Church of Christ leaders, David Lipscomb. Tuggle successfully enlisted Lipscomb's support for black education.[40]

Ironically, one of the best histories of black education among the Churches of Christ is Tuggle's autobiography. Entitled *Another World Wonder*, Tuggle's 1973 book documented several decades of the struggle among black Churches of Christ for education and revealed her central role in connecting potential white financial supporters to black schools. Black agency in founding schools was more evident among Churches of Christ than among the Disciples of Christ, perhaps due to the more conservative outlook of white Church of Christ leadership. White leaders among Churches

---

39. Crawford, *Shattering the Illusion*, 44–46.

40. For details on Tuggle's relationship with black Church of Christ schools, see Annie C. Tuggle, *Another World Wonder* (n.p.: n.p., 1973); Edward J. Robinson, *I Was under a Heavy Burden: The Life of Annie C. Tuggle* (Abilene, TX: Abilene Christian University Press, 2011).

of Christ were more supportive of segregation and did not prioritize black education. Thus, blacks pursued their own institutions with some autonomy. Prominent black preacher G. P. Bowser, for example, created and operated a series of schools intending to provide key education opportunities for black students.[41] Women played a key role in these schools. They often made up the majority of teachers and certainly were the majority of support staff (including housecleaning, meal preparation, and other forms of labor).

Another woman, Mary Campbell of Nashville, provided key leadership for the NCI and its mission of educating black preachers. In the process, she represents the important role women played in the limited racial cooperation among Churches of Christ. Campbell taught public speaking during the entire existence of the NCI, and several black preachers attributed to her much of the success of their careers. For instance, Durden Stough's history of the Catoma Street Church of Montgomery, Alabama, includes a narrative from a former Baptist preacher who studied with Campbell at the NCI. This unnamed preacher claimed, "[I] learned more in six weeks under Brother Brents' instruction in Bible and in the class of public speaking conducted by Sister Lambert Campbell than I learned in six years studying at various other schools."[42] Other preachers had similar opinions. Campbell and her husband often hosted students in their home while they completed their education. These students testified to Campbell's extensive hospitality and full support for black students—even to the point of defying the racial conventions of the day. For instance, one of these students, David Jones, claimed, "I remember meeting [Mary Campbell] downtown, anywhere, she'd just grab you and hug you, and that was just unheard of back in the 1950s and '60s."[43]

Despite the differences between the approach to education among the Disciples and the Churches of Christ, both black and white women formed the nucleus of the staff that sustained the colleges founded by each. At the SCI, Jarvis, and NCI, women often made up the majority of the teaching staff. They also performed the majority of the support functions such as boarding the students and cleaning the facilities. In the end, they were the people on the front lines of these pivotal racial interactions. These kinds

41. R. Vernon Boyd, "Bowser, George Philip (1874–1950)," in Fowler et al., *Encyclopedia of the Stone-Campbell Movement*, 97.

42. Durden Stough, *A History of the Catoma Street Church of Christ, 1879–1973* (Montgomery, AL: Catoma Street Church of Christ, 1973), 61.

43. Ted Parks, "One Pulpit for 50 Years: For a Half-Century, Jones Has Fostered Hands-On Ministry," *Christian Chronicle*, December 1, 2012, http://www.christianchronicle.org/article /one-pulpit-for-50-years-for-a-half-century-jones-has-fostered-hands-on-ministry.

of interactions may explain why Campbell was a rarity among Church of Christ women in challenging racial norms. Moreover, for black women this was one of the few opportunities to contribute to the growth of the movement.

While educational institutions, through the labor of both black and white women, provided grounds for racial interaction, they did not often lead to racial unity, particularly from the black perspective. The influence of broader cultural notions of white superiority placed severe barriers between black and white church members throughout the history of the movement. First, black colleges were only necessary because white colleges in the movement remained strictly segregated (with the exception of Pepperdine University) until the mid-1960s. Second, white church members often championed the spiritual equality of black church members but rarely viewed black church members as social equals. More importantly, they could not view the church through the eyes of blacks—a situation that continued for over a century. For instance, echoing the belief of most whites in the late nineteenth century, Letitia Faurot's educational endeavors were laced with paternalism and a belief in fundamental black inferiority. In 1864, she reported, "I have spent hours in huts, talking to Negros on the necessity of cleanliness, economy &c, as they need instruction in the first rudiments of life. I called the mothers of my school together weekly and talked to them on these and religious subjects." She clearly did not see her students as fundamentally capable of overseeing their own interests, which establishes a clear line of demarcation between their abilities and her own authority.[44] Faurot's attitude may also help explain why many black church members desired to establish their own independent congregations in the postwar era.

On the other hand, Faurot's desire to provide a real service to black students of all ages was also clear and reflective of the complexity of race relations. She believed that the students of the Murfreesboro school evinced a "talent to learn" that was "about on par with other children I have taught." In her report to the Western Freedmen's Aid Commission regarding the school, she further claimed that she "never met any other children so eager to have it come to their turn to read, or who could quite equal them in enduring cold and uncomfortable positions to have the privilege of reciting their lessons."[45]

44. Faurot, letter to the editor, 171.
45. Western Freedmen's Aid Commission, *Second Annual Report Western Freedmen's Aid Commission* (Cincinnati: Methodist Book Concern, 1865), 38.

Though her support of black autonomy in education was certainly limited, she showed definite admiration for their commitment to education.

Ida Van Zandt Jarvis's attitude toward blacks demonstrates how the nineteenth-century notions of black inferiority also characterized the twentieth century. Though Jarvis would contribute significant leadership and funding to the creation of Jarvis Christian Institute, her family had been slave owners and she grew up in close but very paternalistic relationships with the black workers installed in her household. Jarvis clearly inherited paternalistic ideas from her family slaveholding experiences. While her mother took the unusual step of attempting to teach the black residents of their household to read the Bible, Jarvis recalls that "they had little ambition and the teaching was an uphill business." Not surprisingly from a contemporary perspective, she also noted that these same reluctant learners found more ambition after they gained their freedom.[46] Nonetheless, Jarvis's paternalism demonstrates the challenges in achieving racial unity in the Stone-Campbell Movement.

Similarly, while Mary Campbell championed the cause of black education among the Churches of Christ, even volunteering her time at the NCI, she too often fell prey to the racial expectations of the era. This is particularly evident when she advised David Jones, "use your mind well, stay out of trouble, and you'll have plenty of time to fix things."[47] This was a standard attempt to keep blacks from seeking civil rights as a way to address white racism and instead encourage them to conform to white superiority as the path to success.

The writing of history itself has further supported the marginalization of black contributions to the church and thereby hindered opportunities for real integration. This is clearly reflected in the histories of black education. Stone-Campbell educational histories, according to Lawrence Burnley, tended to immortalize the efforts of white church members (mostly male) to establish schools for blacks and downplay the key role black church leaders (both male and female) played in establishing important schools.[48] Burnley clearly notes how this historiographic blind spot diminishes black agency in significant ways. If the role of black agency in Stone-Campbell education has been sidelined, then the role of black women has been all the more ne-

46. Ida V. Jarvis, "How to Lift the Black Man's Burden," *Missionary Tidings*, February 1905, 368.

47. Parks, "One Pulpit for 50 Years."

48. Burnley, *The Cost of Unity*, 13. Burnley offers a clear summary of the shortcomings of the major histories.

glected. For instance, most major studies of black education in the movement say little about key figures such as Mary Alphin and Mary Campbell.

Histories of black education follow a different path in the Churches of Christ. Here women's role is more clearly evident. Ironically, the greater influence of white racial superiority within the Churches of Christ led to more independence and autonomy for black educators. White indifference to black education opened up more space for autonomous efforts of blacks to secure their own education. Tuggle's autobiography documents this phenomenon. At the same time, it also represents a significant history of education among black Churches of Christ that clearly places blacks themselves at the center of the narrative.

Civil Rights and Integration

In the 1960s, the Churches of Christ reacted to the civil rights movement much as did many conservative church traditions in the North and the South that, according to Barry Hankins, believed the church should focus on evangelism and converting the lost rather than turning back segregation.[49] The integration of Church of Christ schools in the 1960s eventually led to the closing of most black institutions and inaugurated a new era of interaction between blacks and whites concerning racial divisions in the church. Many of the histories exploring racial integration in the Stone-Campbell Movement have focused on public interactions between black and white preachers and other male leaders.[50] However, though less well documented, women also pursued a path of racial reconciliation.

As an author and speaker in black Churches of Christ, Thelma Holt's career represents a clear commitment to racial unity and the role of women in achieving that goal. In 1971 she delivered the lecture "Race Relations," later included in a book of her writings, that emphasized the role of both races in reconciliation. First, she placed black and white women on equal footing as "in need of forgiveness." "We are prejudice [sic] and don't know it," she argued. "Prejudice has been with us a long time."[51] Though she does

49. Barry Hankins, *American Evangelicals: A Contemporary History of a Mainstream Religious Movement* (Lanham, MD: Rowman and Littlefield, 2008), 126.

50. See, for example, Crawford, *Shattering the Illusion*, and Cardwell and Fox, *Journey toward Wholeness*.

51. Thelma M. Holt, "Race Relations: Lecture—1971," in Holt, *My Task* (Florence, AL: Success Publications, 1978), 80–83.

not identify which prejudices she is addressing, she clearly seeks to find common ground rather than exploit division. Second, she does not deny the very real effects of racism and acknowledges the tremendous struggles prejudice created, including its physical and moral dimensions. Nonetheless, she still calls upon black women to seek faith-based solutions to solving social problems (including racial discrimination) in American culture. In this she reflects the clear Church of Christ preference for working from within the church rather than creating alliances with social movements. Her work led to some success in integration, as her writings appeared in journals sponsored by white women, including the *Gleaner*, a missionary publication begun by the women of the Park Row Church of Christ in Arlington, Texas, and *Christian Woman*, the oldest and most widely circulated publication for women in the Churches of Christ.[52]

Those who aimed to bring down racial barriers in white Churches of Christ faced an uphill battle. Despite the integration of Church of Christ schools, separate black and white churches operated almost entirely independently, with their own conferences and social gathering networks. The largely conservative theological and social commitments of the Churches of Christ meant that the majority of church members did not seek substantive change to this arrangement. They tended to favor church initiatives and mistrust social justice movements whose motives might not be entirely compatible with their faith commitments.

Though the success of efforts at racial integration was limited, a small but vocal group of women did use their voice to try to pierce the curtain separating blacks and whites in Churches of Christ.[53] In 1966, one of them, Joyce Hardin, a white educator and missionary to Korea, published an article in the *Gleaner* supporting racial integration in the church and in American culture. Her article focused on white fears of integration, which she equated with "Hitler's prejudices concerning Jews."[54] Drawing on her experience as a missionary and as the adoptive mother of a child born in Korea, Hardin encouraged women not to fear those of another culture but instead to "teach our mutual need for love and security, our common standard of good, and

---

52. *The Best from the Pen of Thelma M. Holt* (Florence, AL: Success Publications, 1972), 18–20.

53. Several works explore race relations among the Churches of Christ in good detail, including Crawford, *Shattering the Illusion*; Robert C. Douglas, *The Exercise of Informal Power within the Church of Christ: Black Civil Rights, Muted Justice, and Denominational Politics* (Lewiston, NY: Edwin Mellen, 2008); and Williams, Foster, and Blowers, *The Stone-Campbell Movement*, 46–60, 204–9.

54. Joyce Hardin, "One Family," *Gleaner* 1, no. 1 (1966): 7.

the intelligences that are common to all people." Hardin clearly understood much of the challenge of racial integration in Churches of Christ. For instance, after noting that presentations at the churches on "world brotherhood" tended to emphasize how people of other cultures looked or behaved differently, she encouraged white women to cease the focus on labeling people by appearance and behavior in favor of promoting the similarities of people worldwide.[55]

Additionally, Joyce Hardin and Thelma Holt shared the perspective that the key to improved race relations was the next generation. Hardin argued that "the secret to world peace lies with our children. We can teach them to hate or let them love."[56] In this, she recognized the learned nature of racial separation and encouraged church members to rise above it. Holt's focus on young people emphasized listening to the frustration they felt with the social problems, including racism, that they encountered. Here she echoes the Church of Christ skepticism about social movements, but at the same time she affirms that Christian women play a key role in developing the racial attitudes of the young.[57]

By the 1960s, *Christian Woman*, published since 1933, emerged as a forum for women's voices on racial integration. As one of the most widely read publications among Church of Christ women, *Christian Woman* provided a key venue for discussing race relations within the churches. Bettye Nichols and Ona Belknap, consecutive editors of the magazine from the 1950s to the 1970s, spearheaded much of this emphasis. During the editorial tenure of both, the magazine published articles by, for, and about black women—a rarity for most Church of Christ publications. Significantly, the articles by and about black women did not focus exclusively on race relations but included issues of interest to all readers, which went several steps toward an integrated women's publication. Among these articles were a biographical portrait of Thelma Holt by her daughter and a discussion of the importance of women seeking their own personal and professional development authored by Pat Evans.[58]

Beyond simply publishing articles, in 1969 Belknap also partnered with Holt to conduct a dialogue on race between black and white women in

55. Hardin, "One Family," 10.

56. Hardin, "One Family," 10.

57. *The Best from the Pen of Thelma M. Holt*, 134.

58. Geraldine Holt Doby, "Profile of a Woman: Thelma Holt," *Christian Woman*, July-August 1969, 16-17; Pat Evans, "The Challenge of Being a Whole Woman," *Christian Woman*, January 1969, 12-13.

Detroit; this constituted one of the most striking attempts at racial recon-ciliation in the history of Churches of Christ. The dialogue attracted over two hundred women representing churches from several states. At the first meeting, attendees described scenes of confessing faults, joined hands, and emotional embraces. Becky Tilotta, one of these attendees, noted the com-plexity of the enterprise these women had embraced. She described how white women's ignorance of the plight of their black sisters was lessened, but some black attendees feared the dialogue offered only "Band-Aids on a cancer."[59] In the end, Holt was named chairwoman of the organization that emerged from the dialogue, Operation Hope. Operation Hope continued for several years and spread to several other states.[60]

The most significant white religious support for the black civil rights movement came from liberal Protestant traditions such as the United Church of Christ and the American Baptist Church.[61] Thus Disciples churches, which had much in common with liberal Protestantism by the 1960s, faced fewer obstacles to racial reconciliation than did the Churches of Christ, as Disciples more openly embraced the integration of blacks and whites promoted by the civil rights movement. Though there were signifi-cant failures, this continued to be an important, if limited, pattern of racial reconciliation long pursued by Disciples churches. Here too women played key roles. Black women, for instance, had a long history of service to the Disciples stream of the Stone-Campbell Movement. Sarah Lue Bostick had served as an organizer among black churches for the Christian Woman's Board of Missions (CWBM) in the early twentieth century and significantly supported the establishment of the Jarvis Christian Institute. The CWBM adopted the practice of appointing a black woman to promote the work among black churches, and Rosa Brown Bracy served in this capacity after 1914. Both women were important bridges between the work of black and white women in the early twentieth century. Bracy would go on to serve as executive secretary of the National Missionary Convention, the main body of the black Disciples. Eventually, Carnella Jamison Barnes served as the first black president of the International Christian Woman's Fellowship, the main women's organization of the Disciples churches (and successor to the Chris-tian Woman's Board of Missions), from 1974 to 1978.

59. Carolyn Montgomery, "Bridges of Understanding," *Christian Woman*, March 1971, 17, 18.

60. Montgomery, "Bridges of Understanding," 18.

61. Hankins, *American Evangelicals*, 126.

While histories of both the Disciples churches and Churches of Christ have long focused on men's role in racial unity (if they addressed the topic at all), women's efforts have produced significant results especially among the laity. Though not in traditional positions of power, black and white women exerted influence over their households, their congregations, and their communities. Through their roles as teachers, authors, and group leaders, both black and white women pursued integration even in the face of resistance from their fellow church members. American Christianity still wrestles with how to achieve racial unity. Racial segregation continues to present challenges to most congregations among the Stone-Campbell Movement, just as in most other Protestant traditions. Given their past activities, women will most assuredly continue to be at the center of the efforts that support greater racial unity in their churches and in their communities.

The Civil Rights Movement and Interracial Unity within the Christian Church (Disciples of Christ)

Lawrence A. Q. Burnley

What role did the civil rights movement play in the mid-twentieth century as an agent of religious unity? Conversely, what role did this movement play in exacerbating preexisting racial divisions? This chapter will focus primarily on the construction of race; thus, efforts to achieve *interracial unity* will be the subject under discussion. That being said, it is important to note the existence of multiple identities such as gender, sexual orientation, class, various forms of cognitive and physical ableness, and religion/spirituality, just to name some; the myriad ways they intersect; and the various ways they have been influenced by socioeconomic and political forces associated with the civil rights movement. A single chapter cannot adequately examine the complex topic of interracial unity, so our discussion here will be limited to the social construction of race.

This chapter will examine ways "interracial unity" has been conceived and the manner in which these conceptions found expression before, during, and after the civil rights movement. After defining terms revolving around Christian unity and race relations, the chapter analyzes the influence of the civil rights movement on interracial unity in American society in general before exploring the Stone-Campbell Movement in particular, focusing on the Christian Church (Disciples of Christ). In the end, the civil rights movement has had mixed results in its influence on interracial unity within the Christian church. For both civil rights and interracial unity in the church, the gains have been enormous, but we still have a long way to go.

Interracial Unity

Any response to the aforementioned questions must begin with clarifying what we mean by "unity." On the one hand, unity from the perspective of some European American (white) leaders within Protestant Christian movements can be understood as a salutary theological idea that has impacted race relations both negatively and positively, as Gardiner Shattuck Jr. describes in *Episcopalians and Race: Civil War to Civil Rights*. Shattuck writes,

> White leaders in the Episcopal Church have generally understood unity—the unity of humankind, created by God, redeemed (as the Nicene Creed says) by "one Lord Jesus Christ," and gathered by the Holy Spirit in the church—as a salutary theological concept. Yet in spite of the undeniable religious truth of that ideal, it has also been misapplied and used to repress divergent voices and concerns within the church. Thus, the quest for ecclesiastical and social unity has had negative as well as positive consequences for African Americans and, akin to the myth of the harmonious, biracial plantation of the Old South, has tended to promote the invisibility (to use Ralph Ellison's famous metaphor) of black people within decision-making areas of the Episcopal Church.[1]

On the other hand, religious unity—specifically interracial unity within Protestant ecclesial expressions of the Christian faith—can be understood as the development and implementation of collaborative interracial strategies, policies, and practices committed to understanding, identifying, and dismantling all forms of racism (structural, systemic, and individual) within the church and the broader society. An example of an articulated intent to demonstrate interracial unity understood in this way is a General Synod resolution of the United Church of Christ (UCC), which calls for the UCC to be an "antiracist church." The "2003 General Synod Multiracial/Multicultural Addendum to 1993 Pronouncement and Proposal for Action" reads in part,

> WHEREAS, racism is rooted in a belief of the superiority of whiteness and bestows benefits, unearned rights, rewards, opportunities, advantages, access, and privilege on Europeans and European descendants; and
>
> WHEREAS, the reactions of people of color to racism are internalized through destructive patterns of feelings and behaviors impacting their physical, emotional, and mental health and their spiritual and familial relationships; and

---

1. Gardiner H. Shattuck Jr., *Episcopalians and Race: Civil War to Civil Rights*, Religion in the South (Lexington: University of Kentucky Press, 2000), 4.

> WHEREAS, through institutionalized racism, laws, customs, traditions, and practices systemically foster inequalities; . . .
>
> THEREFORE LET IT BE RESOLVED, that the United Church of Christ is called to be an antiracist church and that we encourage all Conferences and Associations and local churches of the United Church of Christ to adopt anti-racism mandates, including policy that encourages anti-racism *programs* for all United Church of Christ staff and volunteers; and
>
> LET IT BE FURTHER RESOLVED, that Conferences and Associations and local churches facilitate programs within their churches that would examine both historic and contemporary forms of racism and its effects and that the programs be made available to the churches.[2]

This pronouncement reflects the UCC's understanding of the systemic and structural dimensions of racism, the complex ways racism impacts certain expressions of the human family, and their belief that an authentic commitment to following Christ involves actions that are antithetical to efforts that seek to advance racism. The pronouncement seeks, or at least creates the possibility, to critically examine complex issues tied to race. It identifies some of the conditions leading to the creation of race as a social category and the ways this social construction has privileged some and disadvantaged others—and continues to do so—in both historical and contemporary contexts. In this way, the quest for unity is positioned not only to achieve equality from a theological standpoint, but also to address conditions that allow for persistent systemic inequities that disproportionately impact persons based on real or perceived racial identity.

Unity, particularly within the context of interracial engagement, as it was framed by Shattuck, is misleading and paternalistic at its core and constitutes another form of racism. In his review of Shattuck's monograph, Clark M. Brittain underscores this point with this observation:

> Prior to the *Brown* decision, the racism of white Episcopalians took the form of paternalism: their lesser but certainly beloved black members needed the guidance of their white brethren. Shattuck says Episcopal leaders accepted segregation and did not believe that

---

2. "Anti-Racist Church," United Church of Christ, accessed December 31, 2017, http://www.ucc.org/justice_racism_anti-racist-church.

change would occur soon. Moreover, despite the genuine desire of many African American Episcopalians to remain within the Anglican Tradition, the sometimes more blatant racism of many laypeople, such as Jessie Ball duPont, always relegated blacks to a powerless place in the Church. Thus the Episcopal Church's rhetoric of unity clearly did not extend to the practice of equality among its black members.[3]

Conversely, and for the purpose of this chapter, Christian interracial unity is an outcome of interracial social relationships grounded in an understanding of the gospel of Christ, intentionally functioning in direct and purposeful opposition to all forms of racism. Put simply by James Cone, "racism is incompatible with the Gospel of Christ."[4]

Interracial unity understood in this way results in members of the body of Christ seeking to transcend racialized divisions in the church and broader society, compelled as followers of Christ to understand and dismantle racism in all its forms. Interracial unity begins with naming, examining, and understanding what race actually is. This includes an intentional and ongoing examination of socioeconomic and historical forces that created this false social construct and its persistent and pervasive impact on the human condition. According to Joseph Barndt, "Race is an arbitrary (specious, false) socio/biological construct created by Europeans during the time of world wide colonial expansion and adapted in the political and social structures of the United States, to assign human worth and social status, using themselves as the model of humanity, for the purpose of legitimizing White power and White skin privilege."[5]

First and foremost, interracial unity begins with a willingness of all members within the body of Christ to talk about race. As simple as this may seem, efforts to achieve interracial unity are often thwarted due to reluctance, largely by whites, to engage in such conversations. This concern led Beverly Daniel Tatum to ask the question, "Can we talk about race?" She writes,

---

3. Clark M. Brittain, review of *Episcopalians and Race: Civil War to Civil Rights*, by Gardiner H. Shattuck Jr., *Journal of Southern Religion* 4 (2001), http://jsr.fsu.edu/2001/reviews/brittain.htm.

4. James Cone, *Black Theology of Liberation*, C. Eric Lincoln Series in Black Religion (Philadelphia: Lippincott, 1970), 49.

5. Joseph Barndt, *Understanding and Dismantling Racism: The Twenty-First Century Challenge to White America* (Minneapolis: Fortress, 2007), 72.

> Can we talk about race? Do we know how? Does the childhood segregation of our schools and neighborhoods [and our churches] and the silence about race in our culture inhibit our capacity to have meaningful dialogue with others, particularly in the context of cross-racial relationships? . . . Can we get beyond our fear, our sweaty palms, our anxiety about saying the wrong things, or use the wrong words, and have an honest conversation about racial issues? . . . Can we talk about race? By "we": I mean those of us who are in leadership positions in education—as faculty, as administrators, as men and women of influence [and as clergy, lay leaders, and followers of Christ].[6]

Talking about race—or the choice to avoid such engagement—continues to play a role in the church's ability to achieve interracial unity.

Civil Rights Movement

For many African Americans, and later others, any notion of interracial unity was fundamentally flawed apart from addressing issues of power and reparations. After efforts by African Americans and their allies to achieve equality and racial justice were met with outright and sometimes violent rejection by whites both within and beyond the church, a call for black empowerment and the creation and control of separate spaces emerged in various forms. Prohibited from equitable access to spaces of worship, education, employment, health care, business ventures, and civic engagement, African Americans were forced either to accept an imposed dehumanizing status of second-class citizenry or create spaces for themselves that responded to their needs. The conditions gave birth to what Albert Raboteau referred to as the "invisible institution," which would eventually become a visible institution known as the black church. Created by various methods of de jure and de facto segregation, the black church became itself a form of self-segregation.[7] I discuss in *The Cost of Unity* the historical conditions that informed the creation of the black church and the choice by African Americans to form and sustain these spaces.

6. Beverly Daniel Tatum, *Can We Talk about Race? And Other Conversations in an Era of School Resegregation*, Race, Education, and Democracy (Boston: Beacon, 2007), xiii.

7. Albert Raboteau, *Slave Religion: The "Invisible Institution" in the Antebellum South* (Oxford: Oxford University Press, 1978; updated 2004).

It would be a gross understatement to say that freedom in church worship was important for blacks. Before and after manumission, worship provided a great many blacks with one of the few opportunities to express fully—with mind, body, and spirit—the pain wrought from the brutality of chattel enslavement. It also enabled them to express the pain of other forms of racial, class, and gender oppression as well as vocal moans born of unimaginable emotional, psychological, and physical pain. Conversely, worship also provided the opportunity for many to express the joy born of experiencing the evidence of God's grace and love in the midst of seemingly insurmountable circumstances, a joy that surpasses rational understanding. To be able to engage in such expression without fear of white reprisal or judgment is a point often missed by historians and other religious scholars. Church was where blacks could express their hope for a better day while living in ostensibly hopeless situations. It was hope rooted in the belief that God could make a way when there seemed to be no way at all. This form of worship required a rational decision to believe and trust in a God that could not be seen, yet it also embodied a faith that transcended the dimension of reason.[8]

Today, groups within the Stone-Campbell Movement that experienced persistent marginalization and paternalistic treatment by whites have maintained separate spaces and organizational structures. These, as in years past, allow for greater value of their voices in theological discourse and affirmation of their culture's attention to concerns of these groups. Within the Disciples of Christ, groups with primary racial/ethnic identity include the National Convocation (African American), the North American Pacific/Asian Disciples, and Hispanic Ministries.

Martin Luther King Jr.'s observation and critique that "it is appalling that the most segregated hour of Christian America is eleven o'clock on Sunday morning" rings as true today as when he spoke these words in 1960. When given the opportunity to worship apart from white control, and undoubtedly when they formally separated from white congregations, blacks worshiped in ways that gave expression to their cultural orientation and were both responsive to and informed by their socioeconomic and political situation. Freedom to worship allowed black people to express their lived experiences

---

8. Lawrence A. Q. Burnley, *The Cost of Unity: African-American Agency and Education in the Christian Church, 1865–1914* (Macon, GA: Mercer University Press, 2008), 118–19.

in a way that was responsive to their socio-emotional and spiritual needs. Black Christians were an extremely ecumenical group. It was not unusual for black members of churches affiliated with the Stone-Campbell Movement to worship together and have pulpit exchanges with Baptists, Methodists, and others. Surely both emotion and reason would find full expression in these services.

Contrary to any desire to achieve interracial unity with whites, African American leaders before and during the civil rights movement—Richard Allen, Denmark Vesey, Jarena Lee, Sojourner Truth, David Walker, Edward Wilmot Blyden, Marcus Garvey, Albert Cleage, and Elijah Muhammad, to name only a few—led movements aimed at separation, self-empowerment, and self-sufficiency. Theological constructions of black empowerment, a reframing of the gospel message, and reinterpretations of the African past that challenged dominant Eurocentric presentations predate James Cone's *Black Theology and Black Power* in 1969; Kwame Ture's[9] call for black power; and El Hajj Malik El-Shabazz's clarion call for freedom, justice, and equality "by any means necessary."[10] These and others were convinced that attempts at achieving liberation and equality with whites through racial integration were futile.

Rightly or wrongly, the genesis, advancement, leadership, and eventual decline of the civil rights movement are often tied to the life, ministry, and death of Martin Luther King Jr. Some scholars have located the earliest stages of this movement in the efforts, largely by women, to desegregate the armed forces during the decade leading to the start of World War II. Some point to the "Double V" (victory at home and victory abroad) during the war. Others trace the most significant and organized push to achieve civil rights by and for black people to the efforts of veterans who, after gallant service in defense of the nation and the democratic principles upon which it was built, returned home to persistent racist policies and practices in the United States. Still others mark the start of the movement with *Brown v. Board of Education of Topeka* (1954), which was met with celebration by some and resistance by others.

Without question, the most celebrated, and in some circles the most vilified, figure associated with this movement is Martin Luther King Jr.

9. Former name: Stokely Carmichael.
10. El Hajj Malik El-Shabazz (Malcolm X), "Malcolm X's Speech at the Founding Rally of the Organization of Afro-American Unity," New York, June 28, 1964, BlackPast.org, accessed January 5, 2018, http://www.blackpast.org/1964-malcolm-x-s-speech-founding-rally -organization-afro-american-unity.

Canonized, and not by accident,[11] in our collective historical memory are the words spoken from the steps of the Lincoln Memorial on August 28, 1963, in which he cast a prophetic vision of racial justice and unity within and beyond the church. He said, in part: "I have a dream that my four little children will one day live in a nation where they will not be judged by the color of their skin but by the content of their character. I have a dream today [that] . . . little black boys and black girls will be able to join hands with little white boys and white girls and walk together as sisters and brothers."[12] Once this freedom is achieved, according to King, the church, indeed the human family, will be positioned to accelerate movement toward the realization of what he would later describe as the "beloved community." "And when this happens, and when we allow freedom to ring . . . we will be able to speed up that day when all of God's children, black men and white men, Jews and Gentiles, Protestants and Catholics, will be able to join hands and sing in the word of that old Negro spiritual, 'Free at last! Free at last! Thank God almighty, we are free at last!'"[13] Speaking about her late husband's vision of the beloved community, Coretta Scott King stated, "Dr. King's Beloved Community is a global vision in which all people can share in the wealth of the earth. In the Beloved Community, poverty, hunger and homelessness will not be tolerated because international standards of human decency will not allow it. Racism and all forms of discrimination, bigotry and prejudice will be replaced by an all-inclusive spirit of sisterhood and brotherhood."[14]

To be clear, while the beloved community envisioned racial justice and unity, it did not presuppose the absence of conflict. The King Center in Atlanta, Georgia, expands on this point: "Dr. King's Beloved Community was not devoid of interpersonal, group or international conflict. Instead he rec-

---

11. Historians have influenced our collective memory of King in a way that does not cultivate a nuanced understanding of his political, ideological, and theological evolution. This is due largely to the massive exposure to the last two minutes of his famous 1963 speech, "I Have a Dream," with little consideration of his views toward the end of his life. Of particular note is his critique of the war in Vietnam as outlined in his "Beyond Vietnam" speech, discussed below. It was a powerfully complex critique, but in my experience very few people know much about King's views as articulated in this speech.

12. Martin Luther King Jr., "I Have a Dream . . ." (speech at the March on Washington, August 28, 1963, Washington, DC), 5. Text available at the National Archives, https://www.archives.gov/files/press/exhibits/dream-speech.pdf.

13. King, "I Have a Dream . . . ," 6.

14. Jeff Ritterman, "The Beloved Community: Martin Luther King Jr.'s Prescription for a Healthy Society," *Huffington Post*, updated December 6, 2017, https://www.huffingtonpost.com/jeffrey-ritterman/the-beloved-community-dr-_b_4583249.html.

ognized that conflict was an inevitable part of human experience. But he believed that conflicts could be resolved peacefully and adversaries could be reconciled through a mutual, determined commitment to nonviolence. No conflict, he believed, need erupt in violence. And all conflicts in The Beloved Community should end with reconciliation of adversaries cooperating together in a spirit of friendship and goodwill."[15]

Throughout his life, King identified not only spiritual barriers to achieving racial justice and unity, but also fundamental structural barriers preventing the realization of the beloved community. Toward the end of his life—again in the prophetic tradition of the church—King named the destructive, powerful, and complex forces that thwart efforts to achieve racial justice, unity, and the establishment of the beloved community: poverty (a by-product of extreme materialism), racism, and militarism. In a speech delivered at Riverside Church in New York City April 4, 1967, entitled "Beyond Vietnam: A Time to Break the Silence," King said:

> When machines and computers, profit motives and property rights, are considered more important than people, the giant triplets of racism, extreme materialism, and militarism are incapable of being conquered. . . . Our only hope today lies in our ability to recapture the revolutionary spirit and go out into a sometimes hostile world declaring eternal hostility to poverty, racism, and militarism. With this powerful commitment we shall boldly challenge the status quo and unjust mores, and thereby speed the day when "every valley shall be exalted, and every mountain and hill shall be made low; the crooked shall be made straight, and the rough places plain."[16]

Today, we find ourselves dealing with painful reminders that King's beloved community continues to be a vision not only hoped for and not yet seen, but also at times seemingly unattainable. Gains in civil rights, access to health care for the most vulnerable, and immigration reform are just

15. The Martin Luther King, Jr. Center for Nonviolent Social Change, "The King Philosophy," accessed January 5, 2018, http://www.thekingcenter.org/king-philosophy.

16. Martin Luther King Jr., "Beyond Vietnam: A Time to Break the Silence" (address delivered to the Clergy and Laymen Concerned about Vietnam, Riverside Church, New York, April 4, 1967), in *A Call to Conscience: The Landmark Speeches of Martin Luther King, Jr.*, ed. Clayborne Carson and Kris Shepard (New York: IPM/Warner Books 2001), 157–58. Text also available in *King Encyclopedia*, Stanford University, http://kingencyclopedia.stanford.edu/encyclopedia/documentsentry/doc_beyond_vietnam.

some of the advances made during the administration of President Barack Obama. At one point, some argued the nation had entered into a "postracial" period. On the contrary, despite gains achieved with the election of the first African American president, current events provide graphic evidence that what James Cone referred to as "America's original sin"—racism—is alive and well. Indicators of racist ideology, policy, and practice persist in our religious institutions and the broader society: pervasive shootings of unarmed black men with impunity by law enforcement officers; disproportionate sentencing of black men; and racial disparity in household income, employment, health, infant mortality, sentencing, academic achievement, public education expenditures, and school suspension and expulsion.[17]

In his award-winning book *Stamped from the Beginning: The Definitive History of Racist Ideas in America*, Ibram X. Kendi, professor of history and director of the Antiracist Research and Policy Center at American University, examines the history of racial progress and the progression of racism in the United States. In an interview discussing his book, Kendi writes, "When Black people have broken through barriers, new barriers have been put in place to hold them back. . . . Barack Obama represents racial progress and Donald Trump represents the progression of racism. And typically, the progression of racism has followed racial progress."[18] Other examples of this pattern include the period of Reconstruction following the Civil War followed by the creation and administration of Jim Crow laws and the founding of the Ku Klux Klan. The gallantry of black troops and the migration of southern blacks to northern cities to secure jobs during the First World War were followed by widespread lynching and race riots during the "bloody summer" of 1919. In the years leading up to and during the Second World War, progress was made by black women to remove the barriers of segregation in the military. During this period, racist stereotypes that questioned the bravery and leadership abilities of black men were refuted by the gallant service of the Tuskegee Airmen and other men and women who served in the armed forces. This progress was followed by limited access to, and sometimes denial of, the GI Bill and the practice of "redlining," which denied African Americans access to fair housing.

African Americans and other people of color who have been and continue to be the objects of racist thought, practice, and policies understand-

17. For a more detailed examination of socioeconomic and political benchmarks for African Americans, see the most recent *State of Black America Report* (New York: National Urban League, 2017).

18. David Pluviose, "Ibram Kendi Directs Nation's Focus to History of Racism," *Diverse Issues in Higher Education*, January 9, 2017, http://diverseeducation.com/article/90948.

ably ask, where are our white Christian brothers and sisters in response to the pervasive, systemic, and structurally embedded racism? Where is the evidence of being "one in Christ" in response to white supremacy and the behaviors that sought and continue to seek ways to advance "America's original sin"? M. Shawn Copeland, professor of systematic theology at Boston College, provides a response to this question. She states,

> For white people living in the United States, the entanglement of Christianity with chattel slavery and antiblack racism forms a set of deep and confusing paradoxes. As a nation, we understand ourselves in terms of freedom, but we have been unable to grapple with our depriving blacks of freedom in the name of white prosperity and with our tolerance of legalized racial segregation and discrimination. As a nation, we have been shaped by racism, habituated to its presence, indifferent to its lethal capacity to inflict lingering human damage. Too often, Christians not only failed to defy slavery and condemn tolerance of racism; they supported and benefitted from these evils and ignored the very Gospel they pledged to preach [and embody].[19]

It must be noted, however, that history does provide evidence of sincere and authentic efforts to achieve interracial unity, albeit motivated by conflicting concepts of unity. Some of these efforts include:

· Antislavery/abolition movement
· Underground Railroad
· African colonization movement[20]
· Education reform/literacy access and development
· Antilynching movement
· School desegregation

19. M. Shawn Copeland, "Black Theology and a Legacy of Oppression," *America*, June 24, 2014, https://www.americamagazine.org/faith/2014/06/24/black-theology-and-legacy-oppression.

20. A number of motivations, often conflicting, among blacks and whites informed support for African colonization. Some whites viewed African colonization as a gradual form of abolition. Many white abolitionists, who were convinced of what they believed to be an innate inferiority of African people, were not desirous of creating an egalitarian, racially integrated society. Many enslaved and free Africans were convinced that their best hope to achieve a sustained freedom, self-sufficiency, and empowerment was to return to Africa or parts of the Caribbean and Central America.

- Social Gospel movement
- Labor movements
- Niagara movement and the creation of the NAACP
- Freedom schools
- Organized marches (Washington, Selma, Chicago, etc.)
- World Council of Churches
- Clergy Opposed to the War in Vietnam
- Participation in the National Council of Churches[21]

These and many other efforts provide examples of attempts at achieving interracial unity. But again, the theological constructions, as well as the ontological and anthropological assumptions that informed them and the goals persons attempted to achieve with them, were mixed. Many of them were fundamentally paternalistic and not driven by a vision of deconstructed racialized hierarchies or the achievement of the beloved community as articulated by King.

Christian Church (Disciples of Christ) on Interracial Unity

The Christian Church (Disciples of Christ), one of three major streams of the Stone-Campbell Movement, provides an interesting case study for examining the effects of the civil rights movement on interracial unity in American Christianity.[22] In response to a divided Protestant Christianity, the Stone-Campbell Movement came into existence in the early nineteenth century with a plea for Christian unity on the basis of the Bible alone. As this unity movement eventually endured internal divisions, the Christian Church (Disciples of Christ) emerged as the mainline stream of the movement, firmly committed to the goal of Christian unity as illustrated in its efforts in the ecumenical movement. Therefore, this denomination provides a helpful example of the opportunities and challenges of interracial unity in American Christianity. Efforts to achieve interracial unity within the Stone-Campbell Movement before, during, and following the civil rights

21. While serving as president of the National Council of Churches, Disciples of Christ lay leader J. Irwin Miller stated, "Racial discrimination violates Christian love and is man's denial of God's rule." See D. Newell Williams, Douglas A. Foster, and Paul M. Blowers, *The Stone-Campbell Movement: A Global History* (Saint Louis: Chalice, 2013), 204.

22. See the introduction of this book for more information on the Stone-Campbell Movement.

movement have reflected patterns of progress/regression and support/resistance as experienced in other parts of the nation. They can be viewed as forms of interracial unity as conceived by Shattuck.

An example of the type of paternalism Brittain noted about the Episcopal Church (i.e., the rhetoric of unity did not translate to the practice of racial equality) is demonstrated in the Stone-Campbell Movement, whose silence on slavery is well documented. This silence was fueled largely by the leadership's acquiescence to the demands of Southern members of this movement for maintaining unity within the church.[23] Also well documented is the comparatively slow response by churches within the Stone-Campbell Movement (within the context of Northern Protestant movements in the United States) to establish schools with and on behalf of enslaved and, later, formerly enslaved African people in North America.

There is evidence of whites within the movement who demonstrated unity with those seeking to abolish slavery. One example is an Indiana preacher named Pardee Butler, who moved to Kansas in 1855 to help stem the spread of slavery in the western territories. Proslavery activists tarred and feathered him and threatened to hang him if he persisted in his work.[24]

It could be argued that the work of the Christian Woman's Board of Missions (CWBM) to establish schools for African Americans in the South is an example of interracial relations. On the surface, this appears to be an example of interracial unity in an effort to advance African American freedom and empowerment. A closer examination, however, reveals other motives at play. I address this in *The Cost of Unity*:

> It is arguable whether or not white Disciples of Christ leaders "could not" or simply chose not to keep the curriculum and training at their schools in concert with technological advances. There is no evidence to support that CWBM or their predecessors were committed to pro-

23. The Stone-Campbell Movement's response to slavery and the provision of education for blacks is examined in Burnley, *The Cost of Unity*, and David E. Harrell Jr., *Quest for a Christian America, 1800–1865: A Social History of the Disciples of Christ*, vol. 1 (Nashville: Disciples of Christ Historical Society, 1966; reprint, Tuscaloosa: University of Alabama Press, 2003). Citations refer to the University of Alabama Press edition.

24. Burnley, *The Cost of Unity*, 126. In fairness to Barton Stone, he freed those he enslaved and proposed disfellowship of owners of enslaved African people in his early career as a minister. Nonetheless, as his movement grew in the early 1800s, he capitulated to demands of Southern members of the Christian Churches who were owners of enslaved Africans and rejected disfellowship on the basis of owning enslaved people.

viding the best education that would facilitate black self-determination and empowerment. The brand of education supported by agencies controlled by white Disciples was always dictated first by what best reinforced the dominant social norms of the South. Disciples of Christ mission agencies demonstrated little, if any, interest in maintaining schools for blacks whose curriculum was responsive to trends in the industrial labor markets.[25]

The paternalistic nature of CWBM's form of mission for and among African Americans is consistent with Shattuck's and Brittain's observations regarding the Episcopal Church.

As early as 1915, there is clear evidence that African American Disciples understood the Scriptures as containing a mandate to condemn racist policies and practices or any notion of the superiority of one race over another. Samuel R. Cassius (1853–1931) was an outspoken black minister who left the Disciples of Christ branch of the Stone-Campbell Movement as a direct result of his experience with racism within the church. Cassius cited Acts 17:26 as evidence of a biblical mandate for not only church unity but also interracial unity: "[God] hath made of one blood all nations of men for to dwell on all the face of the earth, and hath determined the times before appointed, and the bounds of their habitation" (KJV). Around 1915, Cassius proclaimed, "That one verse ought to serve every purpose of a Christian's mind and cause him not to think more highly of himself than he ought to think, because it teaches there is no superiority in color and no difference in race."[26] Cassius went on to unite with the Churches of Christ, which had separated from the Disciples of Christ in 1906. Though the Churches of Christ were viewed as more theologically conservative, Cassius believed they offered a more equitable fellowship for blacks: "The great uplift of the ten million of American Negroes is now up to the Church of Christ." He held this position largely because of his understanding of the Church of Christ's approach to biblical interpretation: "We teach that the word of God means just what it says and is not subject to any man's private interpretation."[27]

25. Burnley, *The Cost of Unity*, 204.

26. Quoted in Don Haymes, Eugene Randall II, and Douglas A. Foster, "Race Relations," in *The Encyclopedia of the Stone-Campbell Movement*, ed. Douglas A. Foster et al. (Grand Rapids: Eerdmans, 2004), 620. Also see Samuel Robert Cassius, in Edward J. Robinson, ed., *To Lift Up My Race: The Essential Writings of Samuel Robert Cassius* (Knoxville: University of Tennessee Press, 2008).

27. Haymes, Randall, and Foster, "Race Relations," 620.

African Americans who remained in the Christian Church (Disciples of Christ) beyond 1914 were committed to both church union and racial justice. Tensions created by polarized realities convinced many Disciples leaders of the need to empower themselves by developing separate institutional structures under their control while remaining in fellowship with the Disciples of Christ. This of course was not a new concept among black Disciples. Consistent with aforementioned efforts by African Americans to empower themselves, black Disciples established fully autonomous state conventions, schools, and other organizational structures beyond local congregations to address their spiritual, socioeconomic, and political concerns as they defined them.

Black discontent with the refusal of white Disciples to support higher education for their constituencies found substantive and sustained organizational expression with the formation of the National Christian Missionary Convention (NCMC) in 1917. Under the leadership of Preston Taylor, African American Disciples gathered in Nashville, Tennessee, September 5–9, 1917, to organize NCMC. This was perhaps the most decisive, proactive, and widely embraced organizational reaction by black Disciples in nearly one hundred years of enduring racist policies and practices within the Christian Church. The organization of NCMC addressed the needs of African Americans within the church and society. Chief among these needs were the provision of Disciples-related schools with higher education curricula and the development of educated Christian leadership.

In 1969, a second merger took place between the NCMC, the United Christian Missionary Society, and the International Convention of the Christian Church (Disciples of Christ). With this merger, the NCMC ceased to exist as a staffed organization with an annual assembly; it became primarily an investment-holding corporation. The merger also gave birth to the National Convocation of the Christian Church (Disciples of Christ) (NCCC[DC]), a body that is embedded in the national structure of the denomination. The NCCC(DC) was intended to exemplify racial equity and inclusiveness as well as a model of Christian unity more in line with what was mandated in Scripture. The administrative secretary of the NCCC(DC) became a member of the Christian Church's general minister and president's staff and had the responsibility to monitor the delivery of services of the general church to predominantly African American, Hispanic, and Asian Disciples of Christ. The primary goal of the second merger agreement and the creation of the NCCC(DC) was to achieve more substantive equity, access, and unity across racial lines throughout the church. Raymond E. Brown Sr. was elected the first president of the NCCC(DC).

African American Disciples actively communicated their distress with ongoing racial discrimination, which was pervasive during this period. Organizationally, expressions of protest and calls for racial justice were not unusual and can be seen in the recommendations of the Social Actions Committee of the NCMC. Meeting August 23–28, 1966, at Park Manor Christian Church in Chicago, the convention passed two resolutions in response to racial injustice within the church and beyond. One resolution, "Support for Chicago Housing Protests," supported "protests currently being led in the Chicago area by Dr. Martin Luther King Jr., against such un-American housing practices." The other resolution, "Racially Discriminatory Employment of Ministers," addressed discriminatory practices by local churches, seminaries, and state and national manifestations of the church in ministerial call and field placements for seminarians. Both resolutions were approved.[28]

Clergy and laypersons routinely participated in the civil rights movement in local, regional, and national contexts. William H. Hannah, who would later serve as associate general minister and president and administrative secretary for the National Convocation, and other black Disciples clergy and lay leaders were vocal supporters of a number of demands in the National Black Economic Development Conference's "Black Manifesto." Formally titled "Manifesto to the White Christian Churches and the Jewish Synagogues in the United States of America and All Other Racist Institutions," it was a call for economic reparations in the amount of $500 million and was presented by James Forman to a meeting of the National Council of Churches in New York City in April 1969. At the 1969 General Assembly in Seattle, the Disciples of Christ rejected the demands of the "Black Manifesto" but agreed to commit $30 million to combat poverty and racial discrimination.

In its 1971 meeting at Louisville, Kentucky, after years of internal and external struggles for racial justice in the church and broader society, the General Assembly of the Christian Church passed Resolutions 7147 and 7148, establishing a Department of Black Ministry and a Reconciliation Program. Other initiatives tied to achieving interracial unity during this time were established, including the following: the Short-Term Employment Experiences in Ministry Program to prepare African Americans and

28. Minutes of the Business Session of the National Board of the National Christian Missionary Convention, Fiftieth Annual Assembly, Chicago, August 1966, 12–13.

Latinos for ministry; the David Kagiwada scholarship for Asian American seminarians; the Central Pastoral Office for Hispanic Ministries; and the North American Pacific/Asian Disciples office.

The 1997 General Assembly Resolution 9728 summarizes the church's formal response to the socioeconomic and political issues addressed by the civil rights movement. The civil rights struggle of African Americans in the 1950s and 1960s led to the merger of staff and services of the NCMC with the United Christian Missionary Society (UCMS) in 1960, and the merger of the NCMC and the International Convention of the Christian Churches (Disciples of Christ) in 1969 (Resolution 6844). The 1965 riots by African Americans in major urban centers and the 1968 publishing of the Black Manifesto led the General Board to do the following: send a message to Disciples congregations suggesting responses to the accusations of the Black Manifesto; set a 20 percent quota for employment of minorities by units of the Christian Church and a 20 percent quota for membership on the decision-making boards of the Christian Church (1969 General Assembly Resolution 19, "A Message from the General Board of the Christian Church [Disciples of Christ]"); and review and reaffirm its 1969 action in 1975 through action GB-78-0475.[29]

Clearly, the civil rights movement prompted the Disciples of Christ to take steps toward interracial unity, but progress has been slow going for this denomination, just as it has for others in American Christianity and American society.

The Way Forward

In American Christianity's effort to achieve existential interracial unity within the church, what is the best way forward? Can the language and goal of reconciliation be productive? In her book *Dear White Christians: For Those Still Longing for Racial Reconciliation*, Jennifer Harvey posits,

> [The] "racial reconciliation paradigm" as I call it here has failed us. The fact that we have been working for interracial, multiracial, di-

---

29. *1998 Yearbook of the Christian Church (Disciples of Christ)* (Saint Louis: Chalice, 1998), 304–11. Resolution 9728 also is available at Christian Church (Disciples of Christ) in the United States and Canada, accessed January 5, 2018, http://disciples.org/wp-content/uploads/ga/past assemblies/1997/resolutions/9728.pdf.

verse and just reconciled faith communities for some time and have yet to see almost any sustained movement toward realizing such communities is a powerful indictment of the adequacy of reconciliation. Moreover, our failure to have realized these communities should also command our attention and lead us to the insight that, perhaps, something different is required. More powerful still is the reality that in clinging to a reconciliation paradigm for understanding race, we have basically ignored what actually transpired in this nation, but also within the church, in the final years of the civil rights movement. While we rightly find historical and theological precedent for today's visions of reconciliation in the civil rights movement, by the end of the 1960s many, many Christians of color (I should say Black Christians specifically) were insistent and clear that our integrationist visions of reconciled beloved communities were utterly inadequate. But when Black Power offered its analysis, firing the imagination and conviction of many Black Christians, white Christians' response was not to respond to what we heard. Instead we fled.[30]

Actually, the "fleeing" of white Christians was a response. They fired back and retreated to spaces of safety where they could control the discourse and interpretations of history and analyses of contemporary phenomena. For many white Christians, the rhetoric of power, reparations (the paradigm supported by Harvey), and a reframing of the gospel message through the lens of marginalized narratives was immediate and concise. These voices, beginning with black and Latino theologies of liberation[31] that critiqued Eurocentric, male, and heteronormal perspectives, were met with charges of heresy and intellectual invalidity from white lay leaders, scholars, and clergy.

The civil rights movement had varied impacts on interracial unity within and beyond the Stone-Campbell Movement. Greater depth in interracial relationships, increased commitments to combating racism, and deepened racial divisions in social and political spaces were all outcomes of this movement. As such, King's response to a question of how far the

---

30. Jennifer Harvey, *Dear White Christians: For Those Still Longing for Racial Reconciliation* (Grand Rapids: Eerdmans, 2014), 2–3.

31. Authors of these theologies were largely male; their work would later be critiqued and strengthened by women from these communities.

country has come in race relations rings as true today as it did in 1964: "On the one hand I must affirm that we have come a long, long way in the struggle to make civil rights a reality for all of God's children. But on the other hand, I must say that we still have a long, long way to go before the problem is solved."[32]

32. Martin-Luther King Jr. speech delivered at University of Dayton Fieldhouse, Dayton, Ohio, November 28, 1964, 3. Transcript available at University of Dayton, accessed January 5, 2018, https://udayton.edu/news/images/documents/mlk_dayton_transcript.pdf.

Racial Cooperation in the Jim Crow and Civil Rights Eras

EDWARD J. ROBINSON

Standing in the "symbolic shadow" of the Lincoln Memorial in 1963, Martin Luther King Jr. (1929–1968) delivered his famous "I Have a Dream" speech. "One hundred years later," lamented King, "the Negro still is not free; one hundred years later, the life of the Negro is still sadly crippled by the manacles of segregation and the chains of discrimination."[1] King pointed out that the Emancipation Proclamation, which transformed the Civil War from a war to save the Union into a war to free enslaved Africans, helped to liberate black people, but it did virtually nothing to eradicate racism and racial discrimination.[2] The failure of the first Reconstruction necessitated a second Reconstruction, namely, the civil rights movement.[3]

The Compromise of 1876 had awarded the disputed presidential election to Rutherford B. Hayes, even as it killed congressional Reconstruction and mandated the withdrawal of federal troops from the South. The withdrawal of Union soldiers meant that formerly enslaved Africans had to fend for themselves in a racially hostile environment. Scholar W. E. B. Du Bois (1868–1963) captured the social and political plight of most black southerners by asserting: "The slave went free; stood for a brief moment in the sun;

1. Cited in David Howard-Pitney, *Martin Luther King Jr., Malcolm X, and the Civil Rights Struggle of the 1950s and 1960s: A Brief History with Documents* (Boston: Bedford/St. Martin's, 2004), 104. See also James Melvin Washington, ed., *A Testament of Hope: The Essential Writings and Speeches of Martin Luther King, Jr.* (San Francisco: Harper, 1986), 271.

2. The author accepts George M. Frederickson's definition of racism, namely, the "hostile or negative feelings of one ethnic group or 'people' toward another and the actions resulting from such attitudes." He added: "Racism exists when one ethnic group or historical collectivity dominates, excludes, or seeks to eliminate another on the basis of differences that it believes are hereditary and unalterable." See Frederickson, *Racism: A Short History*, Princeton Classics (Princeton: Princeton University Press, 2002), 1, 170.

3. This is the essential argument of Eric Foner, *Reconstruction: America's Unfinished Revolution, 1863–1877*, New American Nation Series (New York: Harper and Row, 1988; rev. 2011).

and then turned again toward slavery."[4] The return toward chattel enslavement was swift, harsh, and brutal—essentially "slavery by another name."[5]

In 1886, Atlanta journalist Henry Grady (1850–1889) announced to a
New York audience that there was a "New South,"[6] touting the region's push
for a new economy. The so-called New South, however, proved both old and
oppressive for people of African descent. Three years before Grady's pronouncement the United States Supreme Court had ruled unconstitutional
the Civil Acts of 1875, which prohibited racial segregation in public facilities
(except schools). The 1883 ruling presaged *Plessy v. Ferguson* (1896), which
legalized segregation across the South. As historians John Hope Franklin and
Evelyn Brooks Higginbotham have pointedly observed: "In the segregated
South, the meaning of 'we the people' as the polity and citizenry did not
include African Americans."[7]

Physical violence often accompanied legalized segregation, for between
1882 and 1903, more than two thousand black southerners were victimized
by lethal white mobs.[8] In the waning years of the nineteenth century, black
Americans also lost their premier leader when Frederick Douglass died in
1895. His demise led to the rise of Booker T. Washington (1856–1915), who
openly endorsed racial segregation. Ida B. Wells (1862–1931), William Monroe Trotter (1872–1934), Du Bois, and others, however, vehemently assailed
Washington's leadership philosophy on race.[9]

4. W. E. B. Du Bois, *Black Reconstruction: An Essay toward a History of the Part Which
Black Folk Played in the Attempt to Reconstruct Democracy in America, 1860–1880* (New York:
Harcourt, Brace, and Co., 1935; New York: Russell and Russell, 1966), 30.

5. Douglas A. Blackmon, *Slavery by Another Name: The Re-Enslavement of Black Americans from the Civil War to World War II* (New York: Anchor Books, 2009), 4, points out that
after the abolition of chattel enslavement, there developed a "system in which armies of free
men, guilty of no crimes and entitled by law to freedom, were compelled to labor without
compensation, were repeatedly bought and sold, and were forced to do the bidding of white
masters through the regular application of extraordinary physical coercion."

6. John Hope Franklin and Evelyn Brooks Higginbotham, *From Slavery to Freedom: A
History of African Americans*, 9th ed. (New York: McGraw-Hill, 2011), 263.

7. Franklin and Higginbotham, *From Slavery to Freedom*, 271.

8. Philip Dray, *At the Hands of Persons Unknown: The Lynching of Black America* (New
York: Modern Library, 2002), vii–xi. See also Franklin and Higginbotham, *From Slavery to
Freedom*, 282–83.

9. August Meier, *Negro Thought in America, 1880–1915: Racial Ideologies in the Age of
Booker T. Washington* (Ann Arbor: University of Michigan Press, 1963). For the racial stance
of Booker T. Washington, see his *Up from Slavery* (Garden City, NY: Doubleday, 1901; New
York: Oxford University Press, 1995), 129. For Du Bois's attack of Washington's leadership
philosophy, see his *The Souls of Black Folk* (Chicago: A. C. McClurg, 1903; Boston: Bedford/

Antiblack literature and media outlets enflamed race hatred across the United States. Thomas Dixon Jr. (1864–1946), a Baptist minister-turned-novelist, in 1905 published a novel, *The Clansman*, which portrayed black men as degenerate beasts who roamed southern communities raping white women. A decade later, Dixon collaborated with motion picture director D. W. Griffith (1875–1948) to produce the movie *Birth of a Nation*, which theatrically replayed *The Clansman*'s themes. United States president Woodrow Wilson watched the film in the White House and reportedly endorsed it as "history in lightning,"[10] but S. R. Cassius, a black minister in Churches of Christ, exposed the real aim of Dixon's novel and Griffith's movie: "to poison the minds" of white supporters against all black people.[11]

To counter such racist propaganda, James Weldon Johnson (1871–1938), a black novelist, musician, and politician, profoundly expressed in his 1912 novel, *The Autobiography of an Ex-Colored Man*, the emotional struggles black people commonly encountered. The light-skinned narrator, who chose to pass for white, overheard a black man say: "It's no disgrace to be black, but it's often very inconvenient." Such inconvenience prompted the narrator to identify as white because of his "shame at being identified with a people that could with impunity be treated worse than animals. For certainly the law would restrain and punish the malicious burning alive of animals."[12] Johnson's literary efforts and his alignment with the National Association for the Advancement of Colored People (NAACP) did little to stem the rising tide of antiblack rhetoric. Rather, such racist literature as that of Dixon and the venomous production of Griffith prevailed and helped divide the nation to such a degree that a second Ku Klux Klan revived under the leadership of a Methodist minister, William J. Simmons (1880–1945), in 1915 in Stone Mountain, Georgia.[13]

St. Martin's, 1997), 62–72. For Ida B. Wells's brief tenure as leader of African Americans after the death of Frederick Douglass, see Linda O. McMurry, *To Keep the Waters Troubled: The Life of Ida B. Wells* (New York: Oxford University Press, 1998), 233.

10. Joel Williamson, *A Rage for Order: Black/White Relations in the American South Since Emancipation* (New York: Oxford University Press, 1986), 115. See also Raymond Allen Cook, *Fire from the Flint: The Amazing Careers of Thomas Dixon* (Winston-Salem, NC: John F. Blair, 1968).

11. Edward J. Robinson, *To Save My Race from Abuse: The Life of Samuel Robert Cassius*, Religion and American Culture (Tuscaloosa: University of Alabama Press, 2007), 141; *To Lift Up My Race: The Essential Writings of Samuel Robert Cassius*, ed. Edward J. Robinson (Knoxville: University of Tennessee Press, 2008), 110.

12. James Weldon Johnson, *The Autobiography of an Ex-Colored Man* (Boston: Sherman, French, and Co., 1912; Mineola, NY: Dover, 1995), 72, 90.

13. David M. Chalmers, *Hooded Americanism: The History of the Ku Klux Klan* (Durham, NC: Duke University Press, 1981).

In this racially charged and racially divided milieu, sanctioned as well by white religious leaders, two men—one white and one black—reached across the racial divide attempting to build the kingdom of God in Jim Crow America. This chapter seeks to tell the courageous and complex story of James L. Lovell (1896–1984) and Richard N. Hogan (1902–1997); it argues that the dynamic duo collaborated in an epoch of rigid racial separation and helped expand the reach of their chosen religious fellowship nationally and globally.

A Black and White Southerner Meet in the West

Determined to make up for lost time and ignored opportunities, Lovell, a white leader in Churches of Christ, sought to elevate African Americans spiritually by gathering financial support for Richard N. Hogan, a dynamic black evangelist of the same fellowship. Churches of Christ trace their origins back to four principal leaders: Barton W. Stone (1772–1844), Thomas Campbell (1763–1854), Walter Scott (1796–1861), and Alexander Campbell (1788–1866)—men who sought to "restore" primitive or apostolic Christianity in the modern world.[14] Like many other religious groups, white Churches of Christ generally excluded black people from their congregations. Lovell and Hogan, however, cooperated during an era of economic stress and racial strife to plant black congregations across the United States.

Born and reared in Robertson County, Tennessee (near the town of Portland), Lovell by age nine had lost both parents, and at age thirteen became a member of Churches of Christ. After serving in World War I, Lovell worked as a salesman for the Dupont Corporation in Denver, Colorado. In 1924, Lovell relocated to Salt Lake City, Utah, where he met and married Vivian Dorothy Peterman. After a dozen peripatetic years, Lovell and his family

14. Important studies of the history of Churches of Christ include: David Edwin Harrell's two volumes: *A Social History of the Disciples of Christ, Quest for a Christian America: The Disciples of Christ and American Society to 1866* (Nashville: Disciples of Christ Historical Society, 1966) and *The Social Sources of Division of the Disciples of Christ, 1865–1900*, Social History of the Disciples of Christ 2 (Atlanta: Publishing Systems, 1973); Leroy Garrett, *The Stone-Campbell Movement: An Anecdotal History of Three Churches* (Joplin, MO: College Press, 1987); Richard T. Hughes, *Reviving the Ancient Faith: The Story of Churches of Christ in America*, 2nd ed. (Abilene, TX: Abilene Christian University Press, 1998); Henry E. Webb, *In Search of Christian Unity: A History of the Restoration Movement* (Abilene, TX: Abilene Christian University Press, 2003).

returned in 1936 to Denver, where they resumed worshiping at the South Sherman Church of Christ. Lovell then began publishing his biweekly religious paper, the *Colorado Christian*.

Like Lovell, Hogan was a southerner. A native of Monroe County (Blackton), Arkansas, Hogan, after his father's death, lived with his grandparents until they placed him under the tutelage of George P. Bowser (1874–1950), an influential African American educator and preacher in Churches of Christ. With Bowser's careful grooming, Hogan received biblical and ministerial training in the Silver Point Christian Institute in Silver Point, Tennessee. From 1916 to 1919, young Hogan earned some renown as the "boy evangelist" by converting over seventy people. After marrying Maggie Bullock in Tennessee, Hogan enjoyed preaching stints in Tennessee, Arkansas, Kentucky, Michigan, and Illinois. By the end of 1936, Hogan, while working with a congregation in Muskogee, Oklahoma, had established eleven churches and baptized approximately one thousand people.[15]

The paths of Lovell and Hogan crossed in Denver in the summer of 1937, when the latter preached at the Ogden Church of Christ and baptized twenty-five people. Lovell called the meeting "one of the most successful meetings in the history of the work in Colorado both from the standpoint of additions and attendance." Lovell testified that "I had heard most of the leading white preachers of the church and many of our colored preachers, but hearing Hogan lifted me to new spiritual heights. My soul was stirred. I thought of the years that I proposed to be a worker for Jesus and the little I had ever done toward saving the souls of the colored people—my people." After the Denver revival, Hogan asked Lovell to direct his evangelistic campaigns, and Lovell immediately began booking and arranging Hogan's meetings and "assisting him in saving the souls of the Negro race."[16]

In a letter to a prospective white supporter, Lovell elaborated his plan to help Hogan in disseminating the gospel across the United States. "Jack, you know what Hogan can do," averred Lovell, "and it is to men who have heard him that I am asking to join me in directing his work. . . . I am ready to put in my time—burn the midnight oil, besides my money in helping him. I want 20 men in the United States to pitch in with me . . . to carry his work along and send him into destitute places and furnish him with a tent, loud

15. Richard N. Hogan, *Sermons by Hogan* (Austin, TX: Firm Foundation Publishing, 1940), vii–ix.

16. Lovell, "Sponsoring Colored Work," in James "Jimmie" L. Lovell Papers, 1930–1995, Center for Restoration Studies, Abilene Christian University, Abilene, Texas; hereafter cited as CRS.

speaking system, trailer and all that he needs to sweep this land for Jesus."[17] Lovell's desire to see lost souls saved inspired him to reach across the color line to aid financially and spiritually a gifted black evangelist in Jim Crow America.

Two things attracted Lovell to Hogan. First, Hogan's competent preaching impressed Lovell. "I have expressed before and I do so again, and that I consider R. N. Hogan one of the strongest gospel preachers in the church regardless of 'color.'" Lovell also considered Hogan a better expositor of Scripture than most white evangelists. "In all due respect to our white preachers, if any ordinary person wants to understand the Bible, it takes Brother Hogan to explain it so it can be understood. I have to admit, and I have heard hundreds of others say the same thing, that they learn more Bible from Hogan in one sermon than they do in a dozen sermons preached by the majority of the white preachers."[18] In an era when many white Americans deemed black people intellectually inferior and morally decadent, Lovell bestowed lofty praise on the black preacher Hogan.

Additionally, and more importantly, an encounter with a formerly enslaved African spurred Lovell's interest in the spiritual plight of black Americans. When visiting his hometown in Tennessee, Lovell visited Anna Oakley, a former slave then near death. When discussing spiritual matters, Mrs. Oakley stated: "I know the Baptist Church is not the church of the Bible. I know that the Church of Christ as you white people have there in town is the church Christ established, but you know that I could not come there and worship as I would like to have done." Lovell knew that a racist spirit of segregation excluded black people from congregations across the South, so Mrs. Oakley's words pierced his heart and pricked his conscience. "Where did she go? What do you think God will have to say in the last day," Lovell pondered, "and especially to whom will He talk about the case?" After his final meeting with "Aunt" Oakley, Lovell vowed to "give a part of my future life in the salvation of the souls of the people with whom I was reared and whom I love for their sincerity and sereness [sic] of heart." Lovell's providential encounter with Hogan in Colorado gave him "the opportunity" to fulfill his vow.[19]

For Lovell, then, the evangelization of American blacks was self-redemption. By assisting Hogan, he would indirectly uplift the very people he neglected during his youth.

17. Lovell to Jack Perry, September 19, 1937, in CRS.
18. Lovell, "Sponsoring Colored Work."
19. Lovell, "Sponsoring Colored Work."

I thought then of my life as a Christian—how little I ever did to assist colored people in the South, where I was born, in finding Jesus. . . . Even to this very day the gospel has never been preached to the colored people in my home forty miles north of Nashville, yet we have white churches of Christ every five miles throughout the country. When I heard Brother Hogan I wondered if God would use me in being a missionary to the people of my childhood days—people I have always loved so well—the most loyal, the kindest hearted people of the world? How could I be a missionary?[20]

Overwhelmed with a sense of guilt and divine obligation, Lovell launched a letter-writing campaign to inform fellow white Christians of his plan to propagate the gospel of Christ among African Americans through Hogan. In his paper, the *West Coast Christian*, Lovell began publishing a column, "Hogan's Helper," to assist the black evangelist's work. Lovell announced his scheme to "send Hogan to those thickly-populated colored sections like Louisiana and Mississippi, East St. Louis, Chicago, Detroit, Philadelphia, New York City—places where we do not have white churches able to fully support such a work alone." "Every contributor to Hogan's work will receive 'Hogan's Helper,'" explained Lovell, "which will keep you fully informed on what he is doing and how every dime of your money is spent."[21]

Hogan found his greatest effectiveness in the western states, however, and Lovell's appeals to white believers throughout the nation generated generous support, enabling the black preacher to purchase a tent and trailer for planting churches in Texas, Oklahoma, Kansas, and Utah. But in the end, Hogan accomplished his most impressive work in southern California. In 1937 Hogan, with Lovell's backing, traveled to the Golden State, baptized forty-four people, and planted the 110th and Wilmington Street Church of Christ in Los Angeles. The following year, Hogan relocated his family to Los Angeles and established the Forty-Eighth Street and Compton Avenue Church of Christ. As the congregation outgrew its facilities, Hogan in 1945 approached his friend George Pepperdine (1886–1962), founder and CEO of Western Auto Supply stores, for a five thousand dollar loan for a down payment. Hogan and his flock repaid the ten-year loan within ten months. In 1953, Hogan's congregation relocated, becoming the Figueroa Church of Christ in Los Angeles. Hogan, while evangelizing and establishing churches

20. Lovell, "Hogan's Helper," *West Coast Christian* 3 (May 1938): 4.
21. Lovell, "Explains His Efforts for the Colored Race," *Gospel Advocate* (1938): 81, 88.

throughout the country, served as minister to the Figueroa congregation for almost sixty years.[22]

Hogan not only preached and converted scores of African Americans to Churches of Christ, but he also influenced white listeners to follow the teachings of Jesus. Lovell, when promoting Hogan's evangelistic work, reported in 1940: "In a recent meeting in Bakersfield, Calif., he baptized 35 WHITE people—78 souls added to the Lord." By 1941, Lovell estimated that Hogan's exceptional preaching had engendered approximately six hundred converts.[23]

The "Place" of Race in the Hogan-Lovell Relationship

Notwithstanding Lovell's genuine affection for Hogan and his ardent support for the black evangelist, the relationship was not immune from racial and racist undercurrents. Lovell, a native southerner, clearly imbibed some of the paternalistic assumptions about Hogan particularly and black people generally. In a 1937 letter to J. W. Akin, a white believer in East Texas, Lovell applauded Hogan as "one of the greatest preachers in the brotherhood," but quickly added: "However, he is a negro, and very few of them know how to manage. I see where with proper supervision Hogan can be made a glorious instrument in the hand of God."[24] Here, Lovell paternalistically viewed Hogan and other African Americans as childlike, incompetent, and untrustworthy.

Scholar Joel Williamson has recognized three racial mentalities in the post–Civil War South: racial "liberals," "conservatives," and "radicals."[25]

22. Billie Silvey, "R. N. Hogan: From Nashville 'Boy Preacher' to Spiritual Reference Source for Christians," *Christian Chronicle*, August 1993, 7.

23. Lovell, "Progress of the Colored Brethren," *West Coast Christian* 3 (September 1940): 3. It is unclear whether Hogan himself baptized the thirty-five white people who responded to his preaching in Bakersfield. If Hogan literally baptized the white candidates himself, this act stamps him as very different from Marshall Keeble, who often reported that he always allowed white men to baptize white women who responded to his preaching in southern states. See Edward J. Robinson, *The Fight Is On in Texas: A History of African American Churches of Christ in the Lone Star State, 1865–2000* (Abilene, TX: Abilene Christian University Press, 2008), 51–65, and especially Robinson, *Show Us How You Do It: Marshall Keeble and the Rise of Black Churches of Christ in the United States, 1914–1968*, Religion and American Culture (Tuscaloosa: University of Alabama Press, 2008), 88.

24. Lovell to Akin, September 19, 1937, in CRS.

25. Williamson, *A Rage for Order*, 70–80, has observed that racial conservatives in the New South held to the idea of the biological inferiority of black people, thus assigning them

Atticus G. Haygood (1839–1896), a racial liberal and a leader in the Methodist church, believed that African Americans could experience social and spiritual elevation, as long as they were under the guidance and tutelage of white southerners. David Lipscomb (1831–1917) and William K. Pendleton (1817–1899), Anglo preachers in the Stone-Campbell Movement, lamented the abolition of chattel enslavement since black southerners were "turned loose in our midst without protectors and advisers."[26] In the view of Lipscomb and Pendleton, the enslavement of black people blessed them, but emancipation cursed them because they were no longer under the care and oversight of so-called superior white people.

Racial conservatives emphasized the importance of black people staying in their "place" of subordination. John M. McCaleb (1861–1953), a white missionary and hymnist, chided a young black man when he called a white woman by her first name, "Bessie." "That boy," fussed McCaleb, "was out of his place." Such racial radicals as Thomas Dixon Jr. viewed the abrasive and assertive "New Negro" as beasts who must be lynched. S. R. Cassius contested racial conservatives in the Stone-Campbell Movement by insisting that black evangelists required monetary support from white Christians, but not white supervision. To racial conservatives who harbored a deep fear of black men mixing with white women, Cassius replied: "The American Negro as a whole does not want to mix with any other people under heaven. We believe that we are just as good morally, and socially as any other people on earth." In response to the racial radicalism revealed in Dixon's novel and D. W. Griffith's movie, the black evangelist called their work a "compilation of falsehoods" that has "caused more lynchings and burnings than all other things that have been done or said."[27] Lovell, of course, was no racial radical,

---

a perpetual place of subservience. He also highlighted Virginia author Philip A. Bruce and North Carolina novelist Thomas Dixon Jr. as racial radicals, who viewed the "new Negro" as one who reverted to beastly behavior. See also C. Vann Woodward, *The Strange Career of Jim Crow*, James W. Richard Lectures in History, 3rd rev. ed. (New York: Oxford University Press, 1974), 31–65. For a black man in Churches of Christ who contested all three racial mentalities, see Robinson, *To Save My Race*, 59–78.

26. The quote is from David Lipscomb, "The Freedmen—Their Condition," *Gospel Advocate* 10 (1868): 199. See also William K. Pendleton, "The Great Want of the Colored People," *Millennial Harbinger* 40 (1869): 171.

27. Cited in Robinson, *To Save My Race*, 60, 67, 140. Dick Lehr, *The Birth of a Nation: How a Legendary Filmmaker and a Crusading Editor Reignited America's Civil War* (New York: PublicAffairs, 2014), 191, has recently shown that William Monroe Trotter, a Harvard graduate and editor of a black newspaper, the *Guardian*, stood as a principal opponent of Griffith's film, protesting that the movie's rationale was to "disparage the Colored race."

but he seemingly imbibed some of the sentiment of racial liberals and racial conservatives.

Consequently, Lovell not only admired Hogan for his preaching ability, but he also esteemed him highly because he embodied what white supporters considered to be traits of the "old Negro"—qualities of humility and fidelity. In a letter to Hogan, Lovell expressed: "Richard I am flooded with work all the time but I think of you daily and pray God to keep you TRUE and Faithful and Humble. You have what it takes to be a BIG preacher but if you turn out like so many of our BIG preachers do I had rather see you stay little, but I have confidence in you and as long as I have that I will stick with you and when I lose it I will fight you."[28] It seems that by staying "little," Lovell meant for Hogan to stay in what white Americans deemed "his place." For in 1937, Lovell wrote to Mrs. A. J. Allen, a white Christian in Coolidge, Texas, observing: "Brother Hogan has anything beat that I have ever heard, and he is just like Brother Keeble, humble as can be (otherwise I could not work with him)."[29] Lovell's meaning of "humble" bore more than theological significance; it also carried racial and social overtones. Lovell wanted to garner financial support for a black evangelist who would not disturb the racial status quo of Jim Crow America.

In 1941, Foy E. Wallace Jr. (1896–1976), a leading white preacher in Churches of Christ, castigated a young white editor of the *Christian Soldier* who admitted that he "roomed with the negro preacher, R. N. Hogan, and slept in the same bed with him two nights! And he seemed proud of it!" In Wallace's mind, the laws of Jim Crow and the precepts of Jesus Christ were virtually indistinguishable. "Aside from being an infringement of the Jim Crow law," decried Wallace, "it is a violation of Christianity itself, and of all common decency." After rebuking Hogan and some white Christians for "trying to make white folks out of the negroes or negroes out of the white folks," Wallace praised Marshall Keeble (1878–1968) and Luke Miller (1904–1962), African American preachers in Churches of Christ, who "know their place and stay in it, even when some white brethren try to take them out of it."[30]

Wallace's reprimand points to two instructive observations. First, Wallace, like many white southerners, feared the interaction of black men

28. Lovell to Hogan, October 16, 1937, in CRS.

29. Lovell to Allen, November 28, 1937, in CRS. For an insightful discussion of the contrasting traits of the "old Negro" and the "new Negro," see Leon Litwack, *Trouble in Mind: Black Southerners in the Age of Jim Crow* (New York: Vintage Books, 1998).

30. Wallace, "Negro Meetings for White People," *Bible Banner* 3 (March 1941): 7. See also Hughes, *Reviving the Ancient Faith*, 281–83.

and white women. Colin Kidd, in his study of race and religion, has noted:
"Behind white America's fear of the black male there lurked an abhorrence
of miscegenation."[31] Furthermore, Wallace clearly linked "humility" and
"meekness" with African Americans' compliance with Jim Crow codes. In
a personal letter to Lovell, Hogan divulged the real reason behind Wallace's
anger.

> Yes brother Lovell I saw the article in the Bible Banner written by
> brother Wallace. It did not take me by surprise for I felt sure that I
> would be hearing something of the kind; because he sent an appoint-
> ment to the churches in the [Rio Grande] Valley during my meeting
> in Weslaco and because the white people wouldn't stop attending my
> meeting to come and hear him he was provoked to the extent that
> he decided to give them a raking over through the columns of his
> paper. He is the first person, (so far as my knowledge is concerned)
> who has accused me of conducting myself in a way that shows that I
> am interested in "mixing with the white people" or "social equality."
> Such has NEVER [e]ntered my mind and is no part of the truth. I trust
> God will forgive brother Wallace and the like of him; but I know that
> before God will forgive him, he MUST repent.[32]

Wallace apparently envied Hogan, who attracted more white listeners to
his Texas meeting than Wallace did; more importantly, the Wallace-Hogan
incident reveals some of the antiblack sentiment that the black preacher
encountered in the white-dominated Churches of Christ.

In the opening years of the civil rights movement, Lovell continued to
heap praise upon Hogan. The former again rehearsed his own personal encounters with black Tennesseans as well as Hogan's rise from an understudy
of G. P. Bowser to a zealous and effective evangelist. "After I moved to Los
Angeles," wrote Lovell, "Brother Hogan and his family came. I stood by him
in getting a home and a new work started." Lovell continued his commen-
dation of Hogan: "There has never been a day in all this time that I was not
happy that way back yonder God saw fit to bring our lives together." Lovell
singled out Hogan as one of his three closest friends. "In all the church and
the hundreds of leaders I have known in the past 50 years, three men stand

31. Colin Kidd, *The Forging of Races: Race and Scripture in the Protestant Atlantic World,
1600–2000* (New York: Cambridge University Press, 2006), 41.
32. Hogan to Lovell, April 18, 1941, in CRS.

out, men whom I dearly love, respect, and upon whose faith I would pin my hopes of eternity—Marshall Keeble, Amos Cassius, Richard N. Hogan."[33]

From Evangelist to Integrationist: The Legacy of R. N. Hogan

If God brought Lovell and Hogan together in the throes of the Great Depression, the racial upheaval of the civil rights era led them down different paths. After toiling as a church planter and church builder in the 1930s and 1940s, Hogan turned his attention and energies toward shepherding and stabilizing African American Churches of Christ. In 1951, a year after his mentor G. P. Bowser died, Hogan assumed the coeditorship, with J. S. Winston (1906–2002), of the *Christian Echo*, a newspaper established for black Christians in 1902. This position gave him a greater voice and greater visibility among African Americans in Churches of Christ; indeed, after Marshall Keeble's demise in 1968, Hogan became one of the premier leaders in black Churches of Christ.[34]

Hogan's influence on African American Churches of Christ was first as a leading fund-raiser for Southwestern Christian College (SwCC). After the establishment of the Southern Bible Institute in Fort Worth in 1948, Winston and Hogan used the columns of the *Christian Echo* to promote the school financially. The following year, SwCC relocated to Terrell, Texas, and Hogan used his political ties in southern California to raise large sums of money for the fledgling black college. He became good friends with Kenneth Hahn (1920–1997), a white Christian and member of the Los Angeles Board of Supervisors for four decades, who used his influence to invite movie stars and celebrities to raise money for SwCC. It is difficult to estimate how much Hogan generated for the Christian college in Texas.

Additionally, just as G. P. Bowser had poured his life into training his young protégés, Hogan mentored many promising disciples. Calvin Bowers (1932–2014) succeeded Hogan as preaching minister at the Figueroa Church of Christ in Los Angeles in 1994; the former lauded the latter for his vision, leadership, and emphasis on "unity in the Lord's Church." Hogan so strongly

---

33. Lovell, "R. N. Hogan," *California Christian*, November 1952, 2; Lovell, "Love Binds Us Together in Jesus Christ," *California Christian* 11 (October 1955): 2–3.

34. Calvin Bowers, *Realizing the California Dream: The Story of Black Churches of Christ in Los Angeles* (Los Angeles: Calvin Bowers, 2001), 109, has noted: "Through the efforts of Jimmy [sic] Lovell within the state of California, and the calls that were coming in from the entire nation for evangelistic meetings, Hogan was rapidly becoming one of the two best-known evangelists in black Churches of Christ. Marshall Keeble was also quite popular at this time."

opposed congregational division, according to Bowers, that he often averred: "I'd rather have been the one who drove the nails into the hands and feet of my Lord than the one who divides His Church."[35] Jack Evans Sr., president of SwCC and renowned black preacher in Churches of Christ, was perhaps Hogan's most prominent understudy. Evans imbibed his mentor's debating and preaching techniques as well as his theological exclusivism.[36] Evans acknowledged: "I esteem him now as my mentor, supporter, and primary reason for remaining as president of Southwestern Christian College in these uncertain times of economic distress and hypocritical negativism from some 'prophets of doom.' R. N. Hogan, the king of preachers, is not only a royal, serving saint; he is my friend from here to eternity."[37] Evans doubtlessly spoke for many other African American preachers and members in Churches of Christ.

Furthermore, while Martin Luther King Jr. and other civil rights activists were busy toppling racial barriers in the broader American society, Hogan worked at eradicating racial discrimination within Churches of Christ. Hogan exposed the hypocrisy of a nation that denied civil rights to African American men who sacrificed for America's freedom. In the Second World War, Hogan observed, foreign enemies "tried to destroy the United States and her allies, but if the Germans and Japanese come to America today, they can go into any waiting-room, hotel, café, motel or any other public place and be treated with highest respect." He also noted that such foreigners can even attend white Church of Christ schools, but, he lamented, "not the Negro." Hogan highlighted Floyd Rose, a promising black preacher in Churches of Christ and a recent graduate of SwCC, who gained admission to McMurry University, a predominantly white school in Abilene, Texas, but could not attend the white Church of Christ school just a few blocks away, Abilene Christian College (ACC). Hogan sorrowfully lamented: "It looks as if these Methodists have more of Christ in them than the ones who claim to be Christians at A.C.C. What a shame, what a disgrace to the wonderful name 'Christian.'"[38]

In Hogan's view, race hatred was more than a social and political issue; he viewed racial segregation and racial discrimination as "sin." Because he

35. C. H. Bowers, "Thank You Brother Hogan," *Christian Echo* 81 (1990): 4.

36. C. Myer Phillips, "A Historical Study of the Attitude of the Churches of Christ toward Other Denominations" (PhD diss., Baylor University, 1983), 47–83. Like Keeble, Hogan and Evans were "radical exclusivists" who maintained that those who received baptism without understanding that it was "for the remission of sins" were not part of God's family. See Robinson, *Show Us How*, 62.

37. Jack Evans Sr., "A Royal Servant," *Christian Echo* 84 (January-February 1993): 3.

38. Hogan, "Racial Strife Continues," *Christian Echo* 56 (August 1961): 2, 4.

addressed the race problem in Churches of Christ so frequently and so force-fully, some white Christians labeled Hogan a "hater of white people." He de-nied the charge, adding: "I hate no one. I love my white brethren and that is one of the reasons that I am trying hard to get them to repent of this terrible sin." Hogan also admonished fellow black Christians: "To my Negro breth-ren, I admonish you to not let the sin of moral evils that our white brethren are committing against you, cause you to hate them, for you will lose your soul if you do. We must love them and it is better to suffer wrong than to do wrong yourselves. Remember that not all white brethren are guilty of this sin."[39] Hogan's editorials on race relations in Churches of Christ connote that Martin Luther King Jr.[40] partly influenced his thinking on America's racial turmoil, but his understanding of Scripture had a more decided impact on his views on racism, as his frequent references to Ephesians 2:14–16 and James 2:1–9 illustrate.[41]

Not only did Hogan appeal to the Bible to refute racist practices in Churches of Christ, he also summoned noteworthy white pioneers in the Stone-Campbell Movement who opposed racial injustice. Hogan lauded Da-vid Lipscomb, white editor of the *Gospel Advocate*, who in the post-Recon-struction era had the "intestinal fortitude and the love of God so inbedded [*sic*] in his heart that he spoke out in no uncertain terms in exposing the soul damning sin of racial prejudice and segregation in the Lord's church." Even though Lipscomb strongly rebuked white Christians who rejected black seekers from their congregations, the school that bore his name continued to practice racial discrimination until the mid-1960s. "The only reason for the ungodly practice of segregation that is so prevalent among our Christian brethren," surmised Hogan, "is the color of the Negro's skin."[42]

Hogan came to understand, however, that the black man's pigmenta-tion was not the only impetus behind white Christians' fear of integrating their schools. As noted earlier, many white Americans feared the poten-tial of black men sexually mixing with white women. Military counselor

---

39. Hogan, "Lest They Should Be Put Out of the Synagogue," *Christian Echo* 59 (June 1964): 4, 9.

40. In his book *The Strength to Love* (1963), King often urged his listeners to protest non-violently and to love their enemies genuinely, arguing: "Hate is rooted in fear, and the only cure for fear-hate is love." Cited in Washington, *A Testament of Hope*, 513.

41. Carroll Pitts Jr., "A Critical Study of Civil Rights Practices, Attitudes and Responsibil-ities in Churches of Christ" (MA thesis, Pepperdine University, 1969), 87, 90, 92.

42. Hogan, "Brother David Lipscomb Stood with God on Race Prejudice in the Church of Christ," *Christian Echo* 55 (June 1960): 2–3. See also Robinson, *The Fight Is On*, 132.

Margaret Halsey called biracial sex the "white American's Achilles heel," adding: "What the white people are afraid of is not that the Negro men will propose to the white girls, *but that the white girls will say yes.*"[43] Hogan, of course, understood this "sex fear,"[44] and he sought to alleviate white Christians' trepidation by emphasizing that most black men in Churches of Christ yearned to get a good Christian education and only desired "to be the white man's brother and *not* his brother-in-law."[45] In his 1976 debate with white Baptist preacher Vernon L. Barr, Hogan's protégé, Jack Evans Sr., declared: "The very heart of the racial problem in America, whether we admit it or not, is intermarriage."[46] By exposing the heart of America's racism, Hogan helped open the doors of opportunity to countless black youth in Churches of Christ, as white Christian colleges began opening their doors to African American students in the mid-1960s.

After helping to eradicate racial blockades from white Church of Christ schools, Hogan turned his attention to global missions. In the mid-1960s, the impassioned editor urged *Christian Echo* readers to support two black Churches of Christ preachers, F. F. Carson (1909–1987) and Billy Curl, in their missionary efforts to Africa.[47] A decade later, Lovell announced plans to send Hogan and a coterie of black workers to Lagos, Nigeria, for a 1976 campaign, "unlike any ever known by Billy Graham."[48] It remains unclear whether Hogan influenced Lovell's desire for global missions or whether Lovell led Hogan down the path to world evangelism. It is likely that the influence was mutual. What remains obvious, however, is that Hogan's impact on African Americans in Churches of Christ can be seen in his push for global missions.

If Hogan and Lovell shared a similar interest in worldwide evangelism, the duo most likely disagreed on congregational polity. Most whites in Churches of Christ viewed the elders as the true leaders of the local congregation, as Batsell Barrett Baxter (1916–1982) once affirmed: "the eldership is

43. Margaret Halsey, *Color Blind: A White Woman Looks at the Negro* (New York: Simon and Schuster, 1946), 101, 117.

44. Pete Daniel, *Lost Revolutions: The South in the 1950s* (Chapel Hill: University of North Carolina Press, 2000), 189–90, 274. King, in *The Strength to Love* (1963), observed: "Racial segregation is buttressed by such irrational fears as loss of preferred economic privilege, altered social status, intermarriage, and adjustment to new situations" (cited in Washington, *A Testament of Hope*, 513).

45. Cited in Robinson, *The Fight Is On*, 134.

46. Cited in Robinson, *The Fight Is On*, 134.

47. "Billy Curl to Enter Ethiopia in July," *Christian Echo* 59 (June 1964): 3; Hogan, "Let's Send Her with Him," *Christian Echo* 60 (January 1965): 1.

48. Jimmie Lovell, "Hogan to Africa," *Christian Echo* 74 (August 1975): 10.

the highest place which a man may achieve in the Lord's church. Everyone else, including preachers, is to serve under their guidance, for they 'exercise the rule' and 'have the care of souls.'"[49] Hogan did not share this perspective, however, arguing that the preacher and elders shared authority in the church. He then offered the following illustration: "here is a man out in the world living a filthy and ungodly life and I, an evangelist, go out there and preach the gospel of Christ to him. He hears and obeys the gospel and I continue to teach him until he is thought to be qualified for the office of an elder. As an evangelist, I appoint him an elder and as soon as he is appointed, I have to crawl under him. Pshaw! The Bible teaches no such thing." "It is a Biblical fact," he concluded, "that the evangelists and elders worked *together* and there was no arguments over who was over who."[50] As a white leader in Churches of Christ, Lovell perhaps would have disagreed with Hogan; yet there was no known open dispute over the preacher-elder relationship.

"The Tie That Binds": Two Soul Winners in Racially Divided America

Even if the duo viewed leaders' roles in the Church of Christ differently, their preoccupation with winning lost souls made such a matter insignificant. Furthermore, there is no known evidence suggesting that Lovell opposed Hogan's critique of racism in white Christian colleges; it is likely that the white missionary supported his black friend in pushing for the integration of Church of Christ schools. More significantly, Lovell looked beyond race to expand the borders of God's kingdom in segregated America. For this native white southerner, souls trumped race. "It has never been by design," confessed Lovell. "I love the souls of white, yellow, red, brown as I do those of the black race, but for some reason the Spirit has led me (and I believe it) toward those who were born black."[51] Lovell's passion for lost souls inspired him in 1972 to launch the World Bible School, a missionary outreach of Churches of Christ by correspondence courses; by the time of his death in 1984, his global missionary program had enrolled two million students in 107 countries.[52]

49. *Every Life a Plan of God: The Autobiography of Batsell Barrett Baxter* (Abilene, TX: Zachry Associates, 1983), 110.

50. Hogan, "The Relationship between the Evangelist and the Elder," *Christian Echo* 84 (March 1990): 2.

51. Lovell, "Hogan to Africa," 10.

52. Terry Cowan, "World Bible School," in *The Encyclopedia of the Stone-Campbell Movement*, ed. Douglas A. Foster et al. (Grand Rapids: Eerdmans, 2004), 783-84.

Yet, before reaching out to foreign countries, Lovell devoted his life to practicing charity at home. In an era when the humanity of African Americans was disputed and their equality denied, Lovell believed that black people had souls and that their souls were worth saving. Consequently, Lovell and Hogan joined hands to the gospel broom to "sweep this land for Jesus," to sweep away the sins of sectarianism and religious error. Hogan, however, appropriated Scripture to sweep away more than religious heresy; he devoted his time and energy to scrubbing away the demoralizing sins of racism in white Churches of Christ, which affected his own people so deeply.

In essence, the Lovell-Hogan relationship provides hope for race relations in twenty-first-century America. The authenticity of their bond was indisputable. G. P. Bowser, Hogan's principal mentor, offered a poem capturing the gist of this unique association in Jim Crow America:

Much credit is due one, Jimmie Lovell,
A white brother from the coast;
He picked up Hogan as his son,
And never stops to boast.[53]

Lovell indeed "picked up" Hogan, but the black evangelist in turn also gave life to the evangelistic cause of his white supporter and friend.

In our modern era, when political and social divisions are rife, when white nationalists have been emboldened, when unarmed black men have been brutally murdered by white police officers, and when the mass incarceration of black people spreads across our land, the story of these white and black Christian men can perhaps teach us something about racial peace and racial reconciliation. Lovell, burdened with a desire to see lost souls saved, summoned the monetary support of white Christians in the era of the Great Depression because he viewed African Americans as "my people." Hogan and the many black people he led into the fold of Churches of Christ benefited from white philanthropy and white altruism. Lovell's advanced perspective of black people, although imperfect, suggests that we must learn to look for the dignity and humanity in every human being. As Martin Luther King Jr. put it, "We must learn to live together as brothers or perish together as fools." Lovell and Hogan advocated and agitated whites and blacks in Churches of Christ to live as brothers in the Lord.

53. G. P. Bowser, "A Tribute to the Worth of R. N. Hogan," *Christian Echo* 39 (August 1944): 3.

Initiatives to Overcome Racism in the Christian Church (Disciples of Christ)

D. NEWELL WILLIAMS AND KAMILAH HALL SHARP

On July 9, 2017, the Reverend Teresa Hord Owens was elected general minister and president of the Christian Church (Disciples of Christ) in the United States and Canada, becoming the first African American woman chosen to head a mainline Protestant denomination. The Christian Church (Disciples of Christ), often referred to as the Disciples of Christ or simply as the Disciples, is the smallest in membership of the seven majority white denominations commonly identified as mainline, mainstream, or old-line churches; denominations that once composed the mainstream of Protestant churches in America. These denominations are known for their social and ecumenical commitments, and for many decades included the most influential leaders in the nation. The other six mainline denominations are, from largest to smallest, the United Methodist Church, the Evangelical Lutheran Church in America (ELCA), the Presbyterian Church (USA), the Episcopal Church, the American Baptist Churches USA, and the United Church of Christ.

The Christian Church (Disciples of Christ) is also one of the four North American streams of the Stone-Campbell Movement. The other three are the majority white Churches of Christ, the majority white Christian Churches and Churches of Christ (sometimes referred to as the Independent Christian Churches), and the majority black Churches of Christ, Disciples of Christ (sometimes referred to as the Assembly Churches). The movement from which these several streams emerged was born in the United States of the union in the 1830s of followers of Barton W. Stone, known as Christians, and followers of Thomas and Alexander Campbell, known variously as Reformers and Disciples of Christ. Though there were differences in theology and practice between the Stone and Campbell groups, leaders of both groups believed that Christians are called to unity in accord with Jesus's prayer in John 17:20-21.

As Rev. Owens began her service as general minister and president, she was not the only person of color at the general level of Disciples leadership. Of the denomination's ten general administrative units, referred to as general ministries, three were headed by African Americans: Disciples Home Missions, Overseas Ministries, and Higher Education and Leadership Ministries. Another general ministry, the Council on Christian Unity, was headed by an Asian American. In addition, three general racial and ethnic ministries were headed respectively by an African American, an Asian American, and a Hispanic American. The diversity evident in the second decade of the twenty-first century at the general level of this majority white denomination does not mean that racism and ethnic discrimination have been overcome in the Christian Church (Disciples of Christ). However, it may reflect the relative effectiveness of twelve initiatives that we (Williams and Hall Sharp) identified as potentially contributing to the overcoming of racism and ethnic discrimination within the denomination.

The first of these initiatives was launched by African American Disciples a century before the election of Rev. Owens. We offer a rudimentary description of the history of these attempts within the Disciples to address racism within their ranks over the last century. Attention to the footnotes will show that these initiatives, though distinctive, are in no way unique among mainline Protestant denominations. Broadly parallel efforts are noted in three mainline churches that, like the Disciples, have elected an African American as head of their denomination: the United Church of Christ, the Episcopal Church, and the Presbyterian Church (USA).[1]

Having described the history of each of these twelve initiatives, we share the results of telephone interviews conducted by Rev. Kamilah Hall Sharp in the spring and summer of 2017 with nineteen contemporary leaders of the Disciples of Christ. The purpose of these interviews was to determine the value of these different attempts to address racism in the Disciples of Christ. The nineteen leaders were asked to share their perceptions of the relative effectiveness in overcoming racial and ethnic discrimination of each of the twelve initiatives. They were also asked to describe current barriers to overcoming racial and ethnic discrimination in the denomination and to

---

1. The Reverend Dr. Geoffrey Black served as general minister and president of the United Church of Christ from 2009 to 2014; earlier, the Reverend Dr. Joseph H. Evans, whose election as secretary of the United Church of Christ (UCC) in 1967 made him the first African American elected to a national office of the UCC, served for one year as president of the UCC following the sudden death of the previous president; the Most Reverend Michael Bruce Curry was installed as the presiding bishop and primate of the Episcopal Church in 2015; and the Reverend Dr. J. Herbert Nelson was elected stated clerk of the General Assembly of the Presbyterian Church (USA) in 2016.

offer their recommendations for moving toward the denomination's stated priority of becoming an anti-racist/pro-reconciling church. The ultimate goal of this research is to help discern from a review and evaluation of past actions how racism may be most effectively addressed in current and future church communities.

All our interviewees stated that racism still exists in the Disciples of Christ. Many noted the influence of the culture at large on the culture of the church. Contemporary evidences of racism in the Disciples of Christ were identified. At the same time, a common theme among our interviewees was that the initiatives of the past century had been steps toward becoming an anti-racist/pro-reconciling church.

Background

African Americans were part of the Stone-Campbell Movement from the beginning. By the end of the nineteenth century, Hispanic Americans and Asian Americans were also part of the movement. Racism was evident from the start, though there had been isolated challenges to racist assumptions, such as Barton Stone's publication in 1835 of his response to fears that immediate emancipation of enslaved Africans, which he had come to support, would result in social chaos: "it is clear that the first step toward civilizing and christianizing the negro is to acknowledge that he is a man, whose confidence we have to gain by confessing that we have wronged him, and endeavoring to repair the injustice by abandoning forever the inhuman principle that man can hold property in man."[2] Expressions of racism, however, remained pervasive in the movement, such as Alexander Campbell's comment in relation to his opposition to slavery because of its negative impact on the white population: "Much as I may sympathize with a black man, I love a white man more."[3] Another example of racism in the early years of the movement was a Mississippi evangelist's 1851 appeal for financial assistance to a Northern church to support his ministry because the whites he was evangelizing were "of the same superior race as yourselves."[4] Statistics

2. New England Anti-Slavery Society, "Address to the People of the United States on Slavery," *Christian Messenger* 10 (May 1835): 97–98.

3. Alexander Campbell, "Our Position to American Slavery, No. VIII," *Millennial Harbinger*, June 1845, 263.

4. B. F. Manire, "Mississippi State Meeting," *Millennial Harbinger* 39, no. 10 (October 1868): 583.

from the American and Foreign Anti-Slavery Society of 1851 showed that members of the Stone-Campbell Movement owned 101,000 slaves, making them, per capita, the largest slave-owning religious body in the nation.[5]

In 1849, Disciples held their first general convention. This convention created the Disciples' first general organization, the American Christian Missionary Society. This organization was committed to sponsoring mission both at home and overseas. In the following decades, additional societies were organized by Disciples to advance the church's witness to Jesus Christ through benevolence to the sick and homeless, lending funds to build church buildings, and providing support to retired ministers and missionaries.[6]

For some African Americans, the racism in the movement was more than they could bear, especially as they experienced it in the general ministry organizations that are distinctive to the Disciples of Christ stream of the Stone-Campbell Movement. One such was Samuel Robert Cassius (1853–1931). Cassius denounced the white leaders of general ministry organizations who "preach about the goodness of God, and pray about loving one another, and being one in Christ, but . . . scorn me on account of my race and color, and tell me that their people will not tolerate me as an equal. I am compelled to say to all such, 'Thou hypocrite!' Do you believe the Bible when it says that God is no respecter of persons, or that God made of one blood all men?"[7]

In response to the Disciples convention's appointment in 1889 of a white man as superintendent of colored missions, Cassius exclaimed that the report of the meeting implied that blacks were so inferior intellectually and spiritually that it was impossible to find a black man "with enough common sense to do evangelistic work among his own people."[8] Despairing of ever being treated as an equal by white members of the movement, Cassius formed

---

5. *Annual Report of the American and Foreign Anti-Slavery Society* (New York: William Harned, Office Agent, 1851), 56. For further discussion of the range of views regarding slavery and race in the early Stone-Campbell Movement, see D. Newell Williams, Douglas A. Foster, and Paul M. Blowers, *The Stone-Campbell Movement: A Global History* (Saint Louis: Chalice, 2013), 35–39.

6. For further information regarding the development of general conventions and missionary societies (now referred to as general assemblies and general ministries) in the Disciples stream of the Stone-Campbell Movement, see Timothy C. Smith, "Conventions," in Foster et al., *The Encyclopedia of the Stone-Campbell Movement*, 237–40.

7. Samuel Robert Cassius, *The Letter and Spirit of Giving and the Race Problem* (1898), in *To Lift Up My Race: The Essential Writings of Samuel Robert Cassius*, ed. Edward J. Robinson (Knoxville: University of Tennessee Press, 2008), 74.

8. Samuel Robert Cassius, "A Colored Brother's Protest," *Christian-Evangelist*, November 14, 1889, 726.

in 1909 a regional black ministry in Oklahoma free from white control. Eventually, however, he came to oppose all regional and general organizations because of the racism of the white leaders of the movement and their refusal to support separate black organizations.[9]

Other African American members of the movement were not willing to give up on the possibility of a genuine partnership with the white leadership of the general ministries. Chief among these was Preston Taylor (1849-1931). Taylor was largely responsible for the first of the twelve initiatives that we discuss below.

Initiatives

What follows is discussion of the twelve initiatives we invited Disciples of Christ leaders to evaluate as to their relative effectiveness in overcoming racism and ethnic discrimination within the Christian Church (Disciples of Christ).

1. A General Organization Free from White Control

Preston Taylor's initiative was a general ministry organization free from white control that would partner with other general ministry organizations to advance the Disciples' educational and evangelistic mission among African Americans. Established in 1917, the organization was named the National Christian Missionary Convention (NCMC). In his inaugural address as president of the new organization, Taylor, having asserted that the relative lack of growth in the number of African American Disciples was largely the result of "the attitude of our white brotherhood on the race question," urged his audience, which included both black and white Disciples, to recognize the ecclesiological significance of affirming the full humanity of persons of color: "The Disciples of Christ, strange as it may seem, need the colored people, if for no other reason, as the acid test of Christian orthodoxy and willingness to follow the Christ all the way in his program of human redemption. For if the white brother can include in his religious theory and

---

9. Edward J. Robinson, *To Save My People from Abuse: The Life of Samuel Robert Cassius*, Religion and American Culture (Tuscaloosa: University of Alabama Press, 2007), 61-64, 75-76.

practice colored people as real brothers, he will have avoided the heresy of all heresies."[10] Though Taylor does not define "heresy of all heresies," given his acquaintance with the writings of Alexander Campbell, it is likely that he was using the term "heresy" in the way Campbell used it: to refer not to a theological teaching, but to division in the church that results from failing to receive "every person that the Apostles would receive."[11]

The NCMC was not the first attempt by black Disciples to establish an African American national missionary convention to support education and evangelism among African Americans in partnership with the white-dominated Disciples general organizations. The American Christian Evangelizing and Education Association (ACEEA), organized by a group of black ministers in Nashville in 1867, established several congregations in east Tennessee. Though the ACEEA appealed to a white-led general Disciples organization for support, it received little help from any source and collapsed by the early 1870s.[12] Preston Taylor had worked in 1873 with another African American Disciple to organize the National Convention of Churches of Christ. This organization had sought, without avail, to influence the white general convention in its work with African Americans.[13] But the NCMC was the first African American Disciples general organization to succeed in sustaining programs of its own and in developing partnerships with the white-dominated general ministries.[14]

10. Preston Taylor, "The Status and Outlook of the Colored Brotherhood," in *Report of the First General Convention of the Christian (Colored) Churches in the USA, held at Nashville, Tennessee, August 5–9, 1917* (Nashville: n.p., 1917), 23–24.

11. Alexander Campbell, *The Christian System*, 5th ed. (Cincinnati: Standard Publishing, 1901), 84.

12. Lawrence A. Q. Burnley, *The Cost of Unity: African-American Agency and Education in the Christian Church, 1865–1914* (Macon, GA: Mercer University Press, 2008), 214.

13. Burnley, *The Cost of Unity*, 215–16.

14. African American leaders in other mainline denominations also formed general organizations free from white control. The Christian Connection, one of the four traditions that came together with the formation of the United Church of Christ in 1957, included an Afro-American Christian Conference organized by blacks in 1892. See Samuel N. Slie, "The United Church of Christ and the Experience of the Black Church," in *Theology and Identity: Traditions, Movements, and Polity in the United Church of Christ*, ed. Daniel L. Johnson and Charles Hambrick-Stowe, rev. ed. (Cleveland: United Church Press, 2007), 41. Among Episcopalians, Alexander Crummell led in the formation in 1883 of the Conference of Church Workers among Colored People to lobby for recognition and respect in denominational affairs. See David Hein and Gardiner H. Shattuck Jr., *The Episcopalians*, Denominations in America 11 (Westport, CT: Praeger, 2004), 102. Within both the northern and southern branches of Presbyterianism, which reunited in 1983 to form the Presbyterian Church (USA), African

2. An Integrated Disciples Convention

The success of Taylor's vision helped to foster and facilitate a second initiative that addressed racism in the Disciples of Christ. One month after Taylor founded the NCMC in August 1917, Disciples adopted a revised constitution for their general convention that would be identified for the next fifty years as the International Convention of Disciples of Christ in the United States and Canada. Though black Disciples refused to give up their newly formed organization to become part of the International Convention, they voted to make the NCMC an auxiliary. Moreover, the NCMC did not duplicate services that could be secured through other general ministries. By the 1920s, a Joint Executive Committee with an equal number of members from the NCMC and the United Christian Missionary Society (UCMS) (created by the unification of a number of the earlier general ministries) oversaw services to predominantly African American congregations, with both organizations sharing the costs.[15] In 1944, this relationship was restructured to give full oversight for services to predominantly African American congregations to the NCMC, while adding representatives from the UCMS and other Disciples general ministries to the NCMC board, with each of those general ministries providing financial support to the NCMC.[16] These partnerships made it seem all the more obvious to denominational leaders that members of NCMC congregations should participate in the International Convention, to which all the other general ministries reported. Thus, in 1953, the International Convention adopted a resolution committing itself to a policy of nonsegregation in all convention sessions, in its constituent agencies, and in hotel and meal

American leaders formed special-purpose organizations designed to counter the confines of ecclesiastical segregation. The Afro-American Presbyterian Council, founded in 1894, and the American Negro Academy, formed a year earlier, both served as important conduits through which African American concerns and leadership eventually flowed into the white Presbyterian mainstream. See Randall Balmer and John R. Fitzmier, *The Presbyterians*, Religious Traditions in American Culture (Westport, CT: Greenwood Press, 1993), 105. See also Gayraud S. Wilmore, "Identity and Integration: Black Presbyterians and Their Allies in the Twentieth Century," in *The Diversity of Discipleship: The Presbyterians and Twentieth-Century Christian Witness*, ed. Milton J. Coalter, John M. Mulder, and Louis B. Weeks, Presbyterian Presence (Louisville: Westminster John Knox, 1991), 211-22.

15. Brenda M. Cardwell and William K. Fox, *Journey toward Wholeness: A History of Black Disciples of Christ in the Mission of the Christian Church* ([Nashville]: National Convocation of the Christian Church [Disciples of Christ], 1990), 21, 33, 38, 53-55.

16. Cardwell and Fox, *Journey toward Wholeness*, 61-64.

facilities. This resolution was monitored by a Social Action Commission formed by the NCMC. The Social Action Commission also encouraged NCMC members to become full participants in the life and work of the International Convention.[17] Through this initiative, African American Disciples were invited to be full participants in the International Convention, predecessor to the current General Assembly of the Christian Church (Disciples of Christ).

3. Admission to Disciples Seminaries

A third initiative dealt with the enrollment of African American students in the four Disciples-related theological schools. Though each school determined its own admissions policies, by the mid-1950s all four seminaries had opened enrollment to African American students.[18] Initially the number of black students was a small percentage of the total enrollment. However, over time many African American Disciples leaders earned graduate theological degrees from Disciples-related graduate theological institutions.[19]

17. Cardwell and Fox, *Journey toward Wholeness*, 81, 83–85. In 1955 the General Convention of the Episcopal Church responded to the issue of segregated facilities by moving their upcoming meeting from Houston to Honolulu. See Robert W. Prichard, *The History of the Episcopal Church*, 3rd rev. ed. (New York: Morehouse, 2014), 301.

18. These four schools in the order of their founding (though names and charters have changed over the years) are Lexington Theological Seminary (1865); Brite Divinity School at Texas Christian University (1895); Phillips Theological Seminary (1907); and Christian Theological Seminary (1925). Disciples also have foundations to provide financial aid, denominational instruction, and fellowship opportunities for Disciples graduate theological students at the University of Chicago Divinity School (Disciples Divinity House, established 1894); Vanderbilt University Divinity School (Disciples Divinity House, established 1927); and Claremont School of Theology, Pacific School of Religion, San Francisco Theological Seminary and Seattle University School of Theology and Ministry (Disciples Seminary Foundation, established 1960).

19. Within the UCC tradition, the 1931 merger of the Christian Connection and the Congregational denomination opened all the Congregational and Christian Connection seminaries to blacks. However, only a few blacks were deemed qualified for admission to these schools during that era. See Slie, "The United Church of Christ," 41. The first African American was admitted to the Episcopalians' flagship Virginia Theological Seminary in 1951. Bowing to negative publicity, the School of Theology at the University of the South opened admissions to African Americans two years later. See Hein and Shattuck, *The Episcopalians*, 124–25.

4. National Council of Churches Call for Civil Rights

In 1963 the National Council of Churches, under the leadership of Disciples lay leader J. Irwin Miller, called on churches to confess their sin of failing to affirm that every person is a child of God and to mobilize resources for securing civil rights for all Americans. Gaines M. Cook, executive secretary of the International Convention, with authorization from the convention's administrative committee, recommended that all Disciples agencies, boards, and institutions take immediate action. To facilitate Disciples efforts, the convention established the Coordinating Committee for Moral and Civil Rights.[20]

In response, the UCMS developed principles for staff involvement in civil rights demonstrations and direct action. A. Dale Fiers, UCMS president, modeled these principles by participating in civil rights marches in a number of southern cities. In addition, 561 Disciples ministers pledged to work for passage of the 1964 Civil Rights Act.[21] In 1963, and again in 1964, the Kentucky regional assembly adopted resolutions in support of civil rights.[22] Christian Theological Seminary (CTS) sent eight students to Washington, DC, to participate in the 1964 Theological Students' Vigil, and CTS dean Ronald E. Osborn participated in Indianapolis civil rights initiatives and the 1965 Selma-to-Montgomery voting rights marches.[23]

Of course, not all Disciples supported such efforts. Some members of the Coordinating Committee for Moral and Civil Rights were critical of its actions, leading several regions and congregations to withhold funds from the denomination. In 1966, Disciples leaders in Dallas tried to prevent Martin Luther King Jr. from speaking at the International Convention, which was to be held in their city. Ultimately leaders reached a compromise that allowed King to serve as one of four members of a panel.[24]

20. D. Duane Cummins, *Dale Fiers: Twentieth Century Disciple* (Fort Worth: TCU Press, 2003), 117.

21. Cummins, *Dale Fiers*, 119, 121–22, 124.

22. Richard L. Harrison Jr., *From Camp Meeting to Church: A History of the Christian Church (Disciples of Christ) in Kentucky* (Saint Louis: Christian Board of Publication, 1992), 284–85.

23. Keith Watkins, *Christian Theological Seminary, Indianapolis: A History of Education for Ministry* (Zionsville: Guild Press of Indiana, 2001), 151–52. For similar responses by another mainline denomination, see Slie, "The United Church of Christ," 45, and Barbara Brown Zikmund, ed., *The Living Theological Heritage of the United Church of Christ* (Cleveland: Pilgrim Press, 2005), 7:67–70.

24. Cummins, *Dale Fiers*, 119, 121–22. For further discussion of Disciples responses to the

5. Call for Opportunities in Housing and Church Employment

In reaction to white opposition to the International Convention's call to action on civil rights, African American Disciples expressed distress over the lack of support for racial justice among Disciples. The NCMC, at its August 23–28, 1966, meeting at the Park Manor Christian Church in Chicago, approved two resolutions. The first, titled "Support for Chicago Housing Protests," endorsed actions led by King in response to practices that restricted housing opportunities for African Americans in Chicago. The other, "Racially Discriminatory Employment of Ministers," condemned racial discrimination in ministerial call and field placement of seminarians by local Disciples churches, seminaries, and regional and general manifestations of the church.[25]

6. Call for Social and Economic Responses to Racism

At the same time that African American Disciples were expressing their distress over the lack of support for racial justice among Disciples, the nation was experiencing a series of long hot summers that included rioting in Watts in 1965 and rioting following the assassination of Dr. King on April 4, 1968. In response to urban unrest and calls by black Disciples for social and economic approaches to address racism, the denomination developed a program called Reconciliation. Beginning in 1968 with an initial two-year funding goal of two million dollars above regular budgets, Reconciliation supported programs and projects designed and proposed by congregations and other units of the church to help the urban poor in areas of employment, economic opportunity, housing, and educational programs. These programs were understood as addressing the root causes of poverty and the legacy of racism.[26]

1963 National Council of Churches appeal for action, see Williams, Foster, and Blowers, *The Stone-Campbell Movement*, 204–5.

25. Minutes of the Business Session National Board of the 50th Annual Assembly National Christian Missionary Convention, Chicago, August 1966, 12–13. Two months later, African American clergy of the UCC met at Plymouth UCC in Washington, DC, to discuss disappointment with the lack of progress within the UCC toward racial inclusiveness and freedom of opportunity, and they issued a statement addressing in greater detail the same two issues that the NCMC convention had addressed in August—equal opportunities for housing and an end to racial discrimination in ministerial call and placement across the church. See Zikmund, *The Living Theological Heritage*, 7:109–14.

26. Lester McAllister and William Tucker, *Journey in Faith: A History of the Christian Church (Disciples of Christ)* (Saint Louis: Christian Board of Publication, 1975), 483. This Disciples call for

Early in the twenty-first century, Reconciliation evolved into Reconciliation Ministry, and was charged with advancing the anti-racist/pro-reconciliation initiative adopted by the Disciples General Board. The primary means employed in advancing this initiative has been anti-racism training. This training has been offered to different general, regional, and congregational gatherings across the church. April Johnson, minister of reconciliation, has described the character of this training: "There is a large chasm of difference in the experience of systemic racism in our church and society. It is into this gap that we must enter with courage and commitment to be agents of individual, institutional and cultural change."[27]

7. Merger

In 1969 the NCMC completed a decade-long process of merger with the International Convention and the UCMS. Robert Hays Peoples, president of the

---

social and economic responses to racism emerged out of the work of the Interreligious Foundation for Community Organization (IFCO), which had been founded in 1967 by several mainline denominations, including the UCC, the Episcopal Church, and the northern Presbyterians, then known as the United Presbyterian Church in the United States of America (UPCUSA). IFCO's charge was to fund organizations cultivating self-determination and empowerment in poor communities. This charge included predominantly black urban areas and was a response to the impoverished conditions in which blacks continued to live despite the legal victories of civil rights. The call for social and economic responses to racism also led to the "Black Manifesto" delivered by James Forman at the historic Riverside Church in New York City on May 4, 1969. The manifesto demanded that white Christian churches and Jewish synagogues begin paying "reparations" of $500 million in response to the historic exploitation of blacks by white America. Funds were to be allocated to such projects as a southern land bank, publishing and printing industries, a research skills center, a black labor and defense fund, and a black university in the South. See Jennifer Harvey, *Dear White Christians: For Those Still Longing for Racial Reconciliation* (Grand Rapids: Eerdmans, 2014), 108–27. Ultimately rejected by all the mainline churches as too radical an expression of the call for social and economic responses to racism, the manifesto did result in a Presbyterian form of the Disciples' Reconciliation Program called the Program for Self-Development of People. See Wilmore, "Identity and Integration," 227. An Episcopal program growing out of the same call for social and economic responses to racism had begun operations in 1968 as the General Convention Special Program (GCSP). Differing in significant respects from the Disciples program (it made grants to agencies that did not have connections to the church, for example), the GCSP failed to gain popular support among the membership and was terminated in 1973. See Prichard, *History of the Episcopal Church*, 339–41, and Hein and Shattuck, *The Episcopalians*, 136–38.

27. April Johnson et al., "Justice Primer and Study Guide," *Disciples Advocate* 10, no. 1 (Spring 2012): 5. Justice Primer can be downloaded from Disciples Home Missions, https://www.discipleshomemissions.org/about-us/disciples-advocate/justice-primer.

NCMC, had called for such a merger in 1955, proposing that the NCMC remain as a "fellowship-assembly" for inspiration and education, and as a legal corporation that could hold property; its executive secretary was to be employed by the International Convention as its associate executive secretary. In 1959, an NCMC Commission on Merger identified the first step toward merger as transfer of program staff from NCMC supervision to UCMS staff positions with the same professional status as other staff performing similar jobs. The commission also called for the UCMS to maintain a minimum of four African American executive staff, to appoint African Americans to the policy-making boards of all agencies, to make African Americans visible in the public life of the church, and to form an Interracial Commission to promote employment of African Americans at all levels. A task force developed final steps, which the NCMC approved at its final meeting. The new organization would be named the National Convocation of the Christian Church (Disciples of Christ). The administrative secretary of the convocation would simultaneously serve as associate general minister and president of the denomination and would be selected by the General Office (formerly the Office of the Executive Secretary of the International Convention) in consultation with the convocation's executive committee and UCMS administration.[28] Later, this process was reversed, with the board of the National Convocation electing the administrative secretary in consultation with the general minister and president.

The preamble to the proposal approved in 1959 by the NCMC Commission on Merger remained the theological basis of the merger. "Christian Churches (Disciples of Christ) have always held the firm conviction that the church is one as Christ prayed, 'That they all may be one.' While this has been commonly applied to denominational divisions, our basic philosophy also affirms that there can be no wholeness if any segment is excluded because of culture, race, or national origin. The church is the creation of our Lord and Savior Jesus Christ, composed of all those who profess His Name."[29]

28. Cardwell and Fox, *Journey toward Wholeness*, 91–94, 123–25.

29. Quoted in Cardwell and Fox, *Journey toward Wholeness*, 98. The commitment to Christian unity appears to have been a powerful driver of efforts to overcome racism and ethnic discrimination not only in the Christian Church (Disciples of Christ) but also in the UCC—another of the mainline denominations that named Christian unity as being at the core of its identify. See Randi Jones Walker, *The Evolution of the UCC Style: History, Ecclesiology, and Culture of the United Church of Christ* (Cleveland: United Church Press, 2005), 25–52. Commitment to Christian unity had earlier led to a merger of black and white organizations

8. Affirmative Action

In the following decades, appointments to Disciples general and regional structures reflected an intentional dismantling of historic racial barriers to leadership. In 1971 Walter Bingham became the first African American elected as moderator of the General Assembly. John R. Compton served as the first director of the Reconciliation Program, and in 1977 became the first African American to serve as a regional minister. The 1982 General Assembly adopted guidelines for the implementation of affirmative action in church agencies. The next year, Compton was elected president of the Division of Homeland Ministries, becoming the first African American to serve as president of a general unit. Other milestones included the appointment in 1987 of Raymond E. Brown as senior vice president of the Board of Church Extension. Janice M. Newborn began her tenure as director of program implementation for the Department of Church Women in 1986. Edward L. Wheeler was elected president of Christian Theological Seminary in 1997. The twenty-first century saw the trend continue with Lois Artis elected president of the Church Finance Council in 2000, William Edwards appointed associate general minister and president in 2002, and Marilyn Fiddmont vice president of the Southwest Zone of the Christian Church Foundation in 2010. In recent years, several persons of color have been elected as regional ministers.[30]

---

in the UCC. The African American Convention of the South, formed in 1950 within the Congregational Christian Church, agreed to a breakup of their organization in response to the UCC constitution adopted in 1961. This constitution required that conferences and associations of the UCC include all the churches within their geographic area, not allowing for the continuation of racial/ethnic conferences. See Slie, "The United Church of Christ," 45; see also Percel O. Alston, "The Afro-Christian Connection," in *Hidden Histories in the United Church of Christ*, ed. Barbara Brown Zikmund (New York: United Church Press, 1984), 1:21–36. A similar commitment to Christian unity seems to have driven black participation among Presbyterians since the 1890s. See Wilmore, "Identity and Integration," 210–11.

    30. The call for affirmative action has been a common theme of the mainline churches. An affirmative action program resulted in thirteen African Americans being elected to the episcopate in United States dioceses of the Episcopal Church between 1971 and 1991. See Hein and Shattuck, *The Episcopalians*, 150. For examples in the United Church of Christ, see Zikmund, *The Living Theological Heritage*, 7:654, 709, 712, 729. In 1963 a group of leaders in the northern Presbyterian church formed the Presbyterian Interracial Council, which was instrumental in nominating and electing in 1964 the first black moderator of the northern General Assembly, Edler G. Hawkins. See Balmer and Fitzmier, *The Presbyterians*, 150.

9. New Congregations

In 1973 the National Convocation issued a strong call for the establishment of new black congregations. This appeal was repeated and approved by the 1975 General Assembly, which called for Church Extension to begin a new program for planting churches, noting that Disciples had "yet to mount an effective evangelistic thrust toward the masses of Blacks in urbanized areas."[31] As a result of this resolution, a succession of church-planting programs was initiated by Church Extension beginning in the 1980s. Although the goals established for the number of new African American churches were not met, new African American churches and other racial/ethnic congregations were established or recognized as Disciples of Christ. Possibly the best known of these new church starts was Ray of Hope Christian Church near Atlanta, which began in 1986 with a Bible study led by the Reverend Cynthia Hale. By 2010 the congregation numbered nearly five thousand members with an average worship attendance of eleven hundred.[32]

10. Growth of Hispanic Ministries

Hispanics have been numbered among Disciples since the last years of the nineteenth century. For most of this history, however, numeric growth of Hispanic Disciples in the United States has been slow. In 1991, in response to the initiative of Hispanic leaders, some of whom had come from Puerto Rico, where Disciples missionaries had planted a vital and growing denomination, the General Assembly recognized the Central Pastoral Office for Hispanic Ministries as a general ministry of the Christian Church (Disciples of Christ) in the United States and Canada. This general ministry has three objectives: to provide programs and pastoral care to Hispanic leaders and congregations, to advise the different regional and general ministries of the church on Hispanic ministry, and to be an advocate for Hispanic Disciples.[33]

31. Resolution 7569, approved by the 1975 San Antonio General Assembly, quoted in Harold R. Watkins, *Continuity, Conservation, Cutting Edge: A Research Book Surveying the History of the Board of Church Extension (aka Church Extension) of the Christian Church (Disciples of Christ)* (Indianapolis: Church Extension, 2005), 101.

32. Williams, Foster, and Blowers, *The Stone-Campbell Movement*, 234–35. See also Watkins, *Continuity, Conservation, Cutting Edge*, 101–4, 107–9.

33. Similar developments can be found in other mainline denominations. See Zikmund, *The Living Theological Heritage*, 7:639–42, and Prichard, *History of the Episcopal Church*, 346–

11. *Growth of North American Pacific/Asian Ministries*

Late in the nineteenth century, Disciples opened a mission to the Chinese in Portland, Oregon. In 1907, another Chinese mission opened in San Francisco. Both missions were closed in 1923 due to anti-Asian hostility reflected in the Chinese Exclusion Act. In 1901, a small group of Japanese came into contact with Disciples in southern California. By 1942, there were nine Japanese Christian churches. All nine were closed with the internment of Japanese Americans during World War II. Of the Asian Disciples churches founded in the first half of the twentieth century, only Filipino Disciples Church, founded in Los Angeles in 1933, has an uninterrupted ministry. A new wave of immigrants from Asia began with the Immigration and Nationality Act of 1965. In 1978, a consultation on Asian ministries was held in Indianapolis, out of which emerged North American Pacific/Asian Disciples (NAPAD). In 2009, in response to a request from the leadership of this organization, NAPAD was authorized by the General Assembly as a ministry parallel to the Central Pastoral Office for Hispanic Ministries. In contrast to that office, NAPAD's membership includes ethnic communities that do not share a common language.[34]

12. *Becoming an Anti-racist/Pro-reconciling Church*

In 2001 the General Assembly adopted "becoming an anti-racist/pro-reconciling church" as one of the major priorities of its 2020 Vision—a "whole

---

47. Following the reunion in 1983 of northern and southern Presbyterian churches as the Presbyterian Church USA, caucuses for racial/ethnic minorities were institutionalized in a single Racial Ethnic Ministry Unit. See Milton J. Coalter, John M. Mulder, and Louis B. Weeks, eds., *The Re-Forming Tradition: Presbyterians and Mainstream Protestantism*, Presbyterian Presence (Louisville: Westminster John Knox, 1992), 174–77. For a history of Hispanic Presbyterians, see Francisco O. Garcia-Teto and R. Douglas Brackenridge, "Hispanic Presbyterians: Life in Two Cultures," in Coalter, Mulder, and Weeks, *The Diversity of Discipleship*, 257–79.

34. Similar developments can be found in other mainline denominations. See Zikmund, *The Living Theological Heritage*, 7:637–39, and Prichard, *History of the Episcopal Church*, 343. For a history of Japanese American Presbyterians, see Michael J. Kimura Angevine and Ryo Yoshida, "Contexts for a History of Asian American Presbyterian Churches: A Case Study of the Early History of Japanese American Presbyterians," in Coalter, Mulder, and Weeks, *The Diversity of Discipleship*, 280–311. For a history of Korean American Presbyterians in the Presbyterian Church USA, see Sang Hyun Lee, "Korean American Presbyterians: A Need for Ethnic Particularity and the Challenge of Christian Pilgrimage," in Coalter, Mulder, and Weeks, *The Diversity of Discipleship*, 312–30.

church initiative" for the years 2001–2020. The groundwork for this priority had begun with approval by the General Assembly in 1997 of a Process of Discernment on Racism. This process helped raise awareness of the need for dealing with systemic racism. Most white Disciples had not understood racism as racial prejudice joined with power that allowed a dominant group to withhold resources, opportunities, and influence from others, nor had they recognized the power and privilege that white people have in American culture. The primary means employed in advancing this initiative has been the anti-racism training described as an outgrowth of the Reconciliation Program initiated in 1968 to address the social and economic character of racism.

Summary of Initiatives

This review of twelve initiatives for overcoming racism in the Christian Church (Disciples of Christ) should be humbling to the white majority of the denomination. With few exceptions, these initiatives would not have emerged or gained traction without the leadership of minoritized Disciples. White Disciples, while joining and affirming efforts initiated or led by minoritized persons, have not been in most cases the primary initiators or leaders of efforts toward full inclusion of minoritized communities in the Christian Church (Disciples of Christ). Worse yet, these initiatives have often met with apathy and even opposition from members of the white majority. From Preston Taylor's organization of the NCMC to the leadership of Hispanic and Asian American ministries, to the current Reconciliation emphasis on anti-racism training, progress toward full inclusion of diverse populations in the Christian Church (Disciples of Christ) has largely come through the efforts of minoritized Disciples—Disciples who valued the stated principles and goals of the Disciples of Christ and were determined to help advance the distinctive mission of the Disciples even when their needs and gifts were not appropriately addressed or recognized by other members of the denomination.

Interviews

How effective have these twelve initiatives been in overcoming racism in the Christian Church (Disciples of Christ)? That is the question that we raised in one-to-two-hour individual telephone interviews with a diverse group of nineteen leaders of the denomination. This sample of Disciples leaders included African Americans, European Americans, Hispanic Americans, and Asian Americans. Eight interviewees were women and eleven were men. Ages ranged from thirty-nine to ninety, with a median age of sixty. Interviewees lived throughout the United States. Each interviewee had at least ten years of experience as a lay or ordained leader in the Christian Church (Disciples of Christ).

What did we learn from these nineteen interviews?[35]

We asked all the interviewees whether racism still exists in the Christian Church (Disciples of Christ), to which we received a resounding "Yes." While each interviewee acknowledged that the denomination has made steady strides through various efforts, racism is still very much present within the various manifestations of the church. Some interviewees acknowledged the interlocking nature of racism, sexism, and classism within the church and society as a whole. Multiple interviewees highlighted the negative impact of the culture in the United States upon the culture of the church.

It is clear that many within the leadership of the church have taken the anti-racism training offered, as many of the interviewees use similar language and have similar definitions of race and racism. Most understand race as a social construct and racism as race prejudice plus power that influences institutional structures. The differences manifest themselves when they discuss their individual experiences.

Asked about contemporary evidences of racism, one interviewee said, "Racism is so insidious, it's such a strange disease that you can't always see it but you know it's happening." Some identified examples of people being denied positions due to race and the predominantly white faculties and boards of trustees at Disciples seminaries. Others cited the lack of financial support for the Reconciliation Ministry, Central Pastoral Office for Hispanic Ministries, and NAPAD as evidences of racism. For many, the financial struggles of each of these ministries call into question the commitment of the Christian Church (Disciples of Christ) to the work of overcoming racism and ethnic discrimination.

Numerous interviewees said the initiatives were somewhat effective because they viewed most of them as efforts in moving the church forward while acknowledging issues of racism. However, many believed there was

---

35. The information provided here is a summary of the findings. For more information about the interview process used in this study, see the appendix to this chapter. See the table for tabulation of the results.

not enough action behind the initiatives. One leader proclaimed, "I tell you it's wonderful that we have marched, but I was more concerned about what do we do after they stop marching? What do they say in their churches on Sunday morning?" Several remarked that desegregation of the seminaries in the 1950s allowed students from different racial/ethnic groups to interact with each other as human beings and to learn about each other's lives, but noted the challenges of dominant culture teaching styles, the curriculum, and the composition of faculties. For example, most of the faculties are predominately white and male, and the required readings for the courses consist primarily of works of white male authors. Thus, the interviewees expressed concerns that the experiences and contributions of minoritized people continue to be excluded. Some interviewees questioned if the efforts were widespread throughout the denomination or only in parts of the Disciples population. Quite a few responded that the efforts are more prevalent in the general leadership than among the laity and in certain regions of the church. As an example, an interviewee indicated the reluctance of some regions to require anti-racism training. Another noted that many congregations are disconnected from these initiatives.

Interviewees also asked if there was any action behind the words of the ninth initiative on attempting to establish new churches. This was the only initiative where many of the interviewees responded "not effective" in overcoming racism. One respondent acknowledged that numerous factors complicate establishing new churches, but questioned if establishing new churches was effective in overcoming racism. Another question that received mixed responses was the initiative on intentional dismantling of historic racial barriers to leadership. Nearly all recognized the increase of African American, Asian American, and Hispanic American leaders, but several noted that the increase has been very slow throughout the years and the recent increase in minoritized people in leadership coincides with the decline in the number of congregations and funding.

We also asked our interviewees to name current barriers to overcoming racism. They cited lack of experience with people of different races, white privilege in the church and the country, political climate of the country, and connecting this work with Scripture, among other obstacles. One respondent said there are still many within the denomination who are not aware of current racism in the church: "we just have too many people who don't know and don't understand the problem and so trying to figure out how to, how to help them see." This unawareness and denial in some cases were also related to the marginal support Reconciliation Ministry receives.

Finally, we asked for strategies for moving forward. Four interviewees called us to remember that we are the church. As one respondent put it, "I think we got to have some sense of Scripture that might help us hear the voice of our Christ and of our God. That God made out of one nation all people." Another said, "We have to continue to be prayerful. Be prayerful with one another, be prayerful for one another, be prayerful for those who oppose."

Continuing the Journey

The Christian Church (Disciples of Christ) has a complex history in the journey to become an answer to Jesus's prayer "that they may all be one" (John 17:21). This denomination must continue to hold in tension the complexity of growing from a movement whose members were reported in 1851 as owning more slaves per capita than any other religious body in the United States, to a church with a diverse racial and ethnic membership speaking multiple languages. More than 180 years after the union of followers of Stone and the Campbells, the call of the first African American general minister and president is historic, and something that should be celebrated. At the same time, this historic call must be held in tension with the monumental task she has before her as the denomination has dwindled as Disciples congregations are declining. Disciples are closing sixty-five to seventy congregations per year, and funding is also declining.[36]

A common theme among our interviewees was the perception that the initiatives of the past century had been steps toward becoming an anti-racist/pro-reconciling church. More than one interviewee said there needs to be more space where white people can work with white people on white supremacy and how it manifests itself in our systems and institutions. Others believed that more interaction and relationship building between people of different races and ethnicities is the way forward.

The issue of racism must continue to be put before the church so the church can keep working at it. One respondent stated, "I think it's time for critical conversation and to move from conversation to action because we are I think at our most vulnerable. I mean I see it as crisis level and I believe it's also at a great level of opportunity." This quote seems to coincide with

36. "Best Practices for Establishing Vital Disciples Congregations" can be downloaded from Hope Partnership for Missional Transformation, accessed January 5, 2017, http://www.hopepmt.org/wp-content/uploads/2013/01/Best-Practices.pdf.

the feelings of many of the nineteen leaders interviewed. Acknowledging that the Christian Church (Disciples of Christ) has not overcome racism, all the interviewees affirmed with differing measures of confidence, joined with realism and hope, that the Christian Church (Disciples of Christ) has made progress and is called by God's grace in Jesus Christ to continue the journey toward wholeness.

Appendix

After receiving a signed consent form from the interviewee, we emailed a copy of the twelve "Initiatives to Overcome Racism in the Disciples of Christ" to the interviewee to allow him or her time to think about the initiatives ahead of the interview. Hall Sharp conducted each interview by phone. The interviews began with the following questions:

1. How long have you been identified with the Christian Church (Disciples of Christ)?
2. How did you come in to the Disciples of Christ?
3. What are some of the positions you have held as a Disciple?
4. Can you tell me what you understand by race and racism?
5. What is the racism that the Disciples have been trying to overcome?

The authors believed these questions were necessary to learn more about the background of the interviewees. Capturing how each person understood race and racism was also essential in establishing our baseline data. The interviewees were given the option to hear each initiative read to them or to read it for themselves. After the reading of the initiative, the interviewer asked participants if they believed the initiative was effective in overcoming racism in the Christian Church (Disciples of Christ). They were given four possible responses to the question: very effective, somewhat effective, not effective, or no opinion. After discussing all the initiatives, interviewees were asked if they believed racism still existed in the denomination. If they answered yes, which all participants did, they were then asked to provide some contemporary evidences of it. Participants were also asked to identify any barriers to overcoming racism that have yet to be effectively addressed, and to offer recommendations for achieving the goal of "becoming an anti-racist/pro-reconciling church." Every interview was recorded, and a written transcript was produced. The responses to each question were documented and summarized.

The results are presented in the following table.

Interview Responses

INITIATIVES	VERY EFFECTIVE	SOMEWHAT EFFECTIVE	NOT EFFECTIVE	NO OPINION
1. A General Organization Free from White Control	3	12	2	2
2. An Integrated Disciples Convention	2	12	2	3
3. Admission to Disciples Seminaries	3	11	3	2
4. National Council of Churches Call for Civil Rights	4	13	1	1
5. Call for Opportunities in Housing and Church Employment	1	12	3	3
6. Call for Social and Economic Responses to Racism	5	11	3	0
7. Merger	6	10	3	0
8. Affirmative Action	5	13	1	0
9. New Congregations	0	7	10	2
10. Growth of Hispanic Ministries	4	14	1	0
11. Growth of North American Pacific/Asian Ministries	3	14	1	1
12. Becoming an Anti-racist/Pro-reconciling Church	3	15	1	0

Proposals for the Future

Resisting White Supremacy

RICHARD T. HUGHES

If the heart of Jesus's preaching was his concern and compassion for disenfranchised and oppressed people, then the first step toward becoming his disciple is to listen carefully and attentively to what those people wish to tell us about the contours of their lives. In America, oppressed and marginalized black people have testified almost unanimously to the twin realities of white supremacy, on the one hand, and the racial failures of white Christianity, on the other.

The great abolitionist Frederick Douglass offers a case in point. "Between the Christianity of this land, and the Christianity of Christ," he wrote, "I recognize the widest possible difference—so wide, that to receive the one as good, pure, and holy, is of necessity to reject the other as bad, corrupt, and wicked. . . . I love the pure, peaceable, and impartial Christianity of Christ: I therefore hate the corrupt, slaveholding, women-whipping, cradle-plundering, partial and hypocritical Christianity of this land. Indeed, I can see no reason, but the most deceitful one, for calling the religion of this land Christianity."[1] Some one hundred years later, many white churches were still complicit in racial oppression, leading Martin Luther King Jr. to ask regarding those churches, "What kind of people worship here? Who is their God?"[2]

1. Frederick Douglass, *Narrative of the Life of Frederick Douglass, an American Slave* (Boston: Anti-Slavery Office, 1845; New York: Signet Books, 1968), 120.

2. Martin Luther King Jr., "Letter from Birmingham City Jail," in *A Testament of Hope:*

This essay draws from two of my books: *Myths America Lives By: White Supremacy and the Stories That Give Us Meaning*, rev. ed. (Urbana: University of Illinois Press, 2018), which centers on the myth of white supremacy, and *Christian America and the Kingdom of God* (Urbana: University of Illinois Press, 2009). It also draws from my essay "Civil Rights and the White Churches of Christ," in *Reconciliation Reconsidered: Advancing the Conversation on Race in Churches of Christ*, ed. Tanya Smith Brice (Abilene, TX: Abilene Christian University Press, 2016), 85–100.

There seems no point—and it would not serve us well—to rehearse the racial failures of America's churches at any great length here. What will serve us well is an honest recognition that what caused and sustained those failures on the ground were deep and far-reaching theological failures. In this chapter I want to ask about the nature of the racist culture that seduced evangelical Christians in particular, about the kind of theology that allowed the seduction to occur with such apparent ease, and about the kind of theology that can empower Christians of every stripe to resist the racist seductions of our culture and pursue justice and equality for oppressed and marginalized people.

My own tradition, the Churches of Christ, offers a window into the way in which American evangelicals have all too often succumbed to the racist dimensions of American culture. A product of the American frontier in the early nineteenth century, Churches of Christ devoted themselves to restoring the primitive church of the apostolic age.[3] For that reason, they typically rejected evangelical churches as "man-made" traditions, born of the womb of human history instead of Scripture and the primitive church. Since the 1960s, however, Churches of Christ have increasingly embraced American evangelicalism.[4] But the racism Churches of Christ shared with the larger evangelical world predated the 1960s by many years.[5] Three vignettes from the history of Churches of Christ offer important clues into the nature of that tradition's theological failures with respect to race.

First, *Gospel Advocate*[6] editor James Allen reported in 1925 that "many of the preachers" of Churches of Christ belonged to the Ku Klux Klan.[7]

The Essential Writings and Speeches of Martin Luther King, Jr., ed. James Melvin Washington (San Francisco: HarperSanFrancisco, 1986), 299.

3. On Churches of Christ, see Gary Holloway and Douglas A. Foster, *Renewing God's People: A Concise History of Churches of Christ* (Abilene, TX: Abilene Christian University Press, 2002).

4. Richard T. Hughes, *Reviving the Ancient Faith: The Story of Churches of Christ in America* (Grand Rapids: Eerdmans, 1996; Abilene, TX: Abilene Christian University Press, 2000), 373.

5. On racism in Churches of Christ, see Foster, "Justice, Racism, and Churches of Christ," in *Unfinished Reconciliation: Justice, Racism, and Churches of Christ*, ed. Gary Holloway and John York, rev. ed. (Abilene, TX: Abilene Christian University Press, 2013), 115–33, and Wes Crawford, *Shattering the Illusion: How African American Churches of Christ Moved from Segregation to Independence* (Abilene, TX: Abilene Christian University Press, 2013).

6. The *Gospel Advocate*, begun in 1855, was a popular gospel paper serving the Churches of Christ.

7. James Allen, "Scripture Studies," *Gospel Advocate* 67 (May 14, 1925): 457.

Second, famed Churches of Christ preacher G. C. Brewer recalled that as a young man growing up in Tennessee in the early twentieth century, "None of us thought of inviting Negroes into our homes as guests or of sitting down to eat with them at the same table; we felt, as a matter of course, that they should have the same food that we ate, but that they should eat in the kitchen or in the servants' quarters." He continued, "This was the condition that prevailed and this we accepted as right and satisfactory," but concluded, "We were not prejudiced against the Negroes."[8]

Third, Anne Moody reported that in the aftermath of the murder of Medgar Evers in Jackson, Mississippi, in 1963, on the Sunday after Evers's funeral, young black activists visited numerous churches in the city of Jackson. Moody recalled that "at each one, [the churches] had prepared for our visit with armed policemen, paddy wagons, and dogs." On the second Sunday, the group visited a Church of Christ where the ushers "offered to give us cab fare to the Negro extension of the church." When the young blacks resisted that advice, the ushers "threatened to call the police if we didn't leave. We decided to go."[9]

These three reports should set off in our heads the alarm bells of a theology gone badly awry. What kind of theology would allow self-professed followers of Jesus to hold membership in the Klan? What kind of theology would allow a disciple of Jesus to practice racial discrimination and then claim, "We were not prejudiced against the Negroes"? And what kind of theology would allow Christians to refuse to worship with other believers, even to call the police if those "others" did not leave?

The answer to those questions is clear: a theology that offers believers no means of resistance against the bigotry of the popular culture. Before we explore the contours of such a weak and listless theology, we first must ask, what is it about American popular culture that pulls professed disciples of Jesus so easily into the sinkhole of racial bigotry and prejudice?

The Racialized Contours of Popular American Culture

The answer to that question is something that most white Americans, including most white American Christians, neither recognize nor understand,

8. G. C. Brewer, "Saved by a Moonbeam; or, Facing Death for Saying a Negro Has a Soul" (unpublished paper, n.d.), 2-3. Paper in possession of author.

9. Anne Moody, *Coming of Age in Mississippi* (New York: Dell, 1968), 283-84.

and something to which they typically give little or no thought, simply because it is hidden from their eyes, even though it pervades American culture. I am speaking of the myth of white supremacy.

When I use the word "myth," I do not have in mind a story that is untrue, but rather a story that gives us meaning. John Westerhoff III helps us understand the meaning of myth when he writes, "We need a story to see in the dark," for "stories are the imaginative way of ordering our experience."[10] When I speak of "white supremacy," I am not speaking of the Ku Klux Klan or other white nationalist groups that proclaim white supremacy from the rooftops. I am speaking, rather, of virtually all white Americans, including myself, for the myth of white supremacy is the very air we breathe, an ideology so deeply embedded in our common culture that we can escape the power it wields over our minds, emotions, and actions only with great difficulty, if at all.

While many whites might find this claim preposterous, even offensive, most blacks, in my experience, acknowledge this claim as the central truth about the meaning of black life in the United States. If we wish to know the truth, therefore, we must listen carefully to their assessment of white supremacy.

White supremacy, obviously, is not a story shared in common by *all* Americans. Most blacks understand that myth because they have suffered its bitter fruit and know no other way to explain that experience. Whites, on the other hand, embrace the myth but, for the most part, do so unconsciously. Nothing in their experience has forced them to recognize this myth, much less to regard it as America's primal narrative.[11]

While David Billings's experience might have been more blatant and direct than that of most American whites, his story is, for the most part, typical. Reflecting on his childhood in Mississippi and Arkansas in the 1950s and 1960s, Billings recalls:

> As a white person, even in my youth, I was taught that everything of significance that had happened in the United States had been accomplished by white people. . . . I was brought up to think and see my white world as normal. Everybody else around me seemed to me

10. John H. Westerhoff III, *A Pilgrim People: Learning through the Church Year* (Minneapolis: Seabury Press, 1984), 3–4.

11. The central argument of my book *Myths America Lives By*, in its revised edition (2018), is that white supremacy is not one American myth among others, but rather is the primal American myth that informs and drives all the others.

to see the world in the same way. . . . My worldview, shaped by this internalized sense of racial superiority, meant that I saw history, morality, the will of God, and scientific truth as the special province of white people, usually white men. . . . More than [to] laws or customs, my very understanding of myself was bound to the idea of white supremacy.[12]

Billings goes on to explain that in his world, "whites were not self-reflective about race."[13] But why should they have been? Some of them—perhaps many of them—had experienced hardship and persecution. But not a single negative dimension in their lives was due to the color of their skin. To the contrary, the color of their skin ensured that most of them would not face the same limitations that they themselves imposed on their African American neighbors. There was simply no incentive for them, therefore, to reflect on what it meant to be white, on the privileges to which white skin entitled them, or on the myth of white supremacy, which they simply took for granted.

Blacks, on the other hand, have been forced to think deeply about the notion of white supremacy, for that myth alone could provide to their minds the rationale for the realities of slavery, for Jim Crow segregation, for beatings and lynchings and castrations, and for denial of equal opportunity in a nation that claims that "all men are created equal."

White supremacy has worked powerfully not only on the bodies but also on the minds of blacks in the United States. A young woman—one of my students in recent years—told how a teacher once asked her a question that pierced to the marrow of her being: "Why do you always draw white girls?" the teacher queried. Later that evening, my student recalled, "The image of my teacher kneeling down to ask the impossible question stomped through my mind and raged through my ears like a violent storm. The weight of the question bent me, splitting my mind and my heart." And then she said this:

When I was in high school, I would often do what many girls did. I would imagine myself years from now, getting ready for work early in the morning. The house was quiet, I would be tranquil but moving quickly to beat the traffic. I'd check the mirror in the foyer before

12. David Billings, *Deep Denial: The Persistence of White Supremacy in United States History and Life* (Roselle, NJ: Crandall, Dostie and Douglass, 2016), 13–14.
13. Billings, *Deep Denial*, 14.

leaving, straighten my perfectly pressed collar, twist the ring on my wedding finger so that the beautiful carved diamond would face the right way. I'd check my long and silky hair for any strands that had fallen out of the elaborate style I'd wrapped it in. I'd check my skin for imperfections.

It was always the skin that grabbed me, that pulled me away. It was always then that I realized the beautiful, successful, loved woman in my dreams was white. I have never felt more gut wrenching shame than those times, when I was suddenly torn from my unreachable dream to face a reality that was impossible to ignore. I could not be white. I wasn't white. . . .

It is harrowing to live with a stress you can never escape . . . —the fear that you will never be fully accepted.[14]

In her novel *The Bluest Eye*, Toni Morrison tells a similar story about a young girl named Pecola to whom "it had occurred . . . some time ago that if her eyes . . . were different, that is to say, beautiful, she herself would be different. . . . Each night, without fail, she prayed for blue eyes. Fervently, for a year she had prayed. Although somewhat discouraged, she was not without hope. To have something as wonderful as that happen would take a long, long time."[15] In one way or another, Pecola's experience reflected reality for millions of American blacks.

Over twenty years after writing that novel, Morrison reflected on its meaning. "*The Bluest Eye*," she wrote, "was my effort to say something about . . . why she [Pecola] had not, or possibly ever would have, the experience of what she possessed and also why she prayed for so radical an alteration. Implicit in her desire was racial self-loathing. And twenty years later, I was still wondering about how one learns that. Who told her? . . . Who had looked at her and found her so wanting, so small a weight on the beauty scale?"[16]

These kinds of experiences, so common to blacks in the United States, help us understand why the black appraisal of the American nation is so different from that of most whites. The poet James M. Whitfield (1822–1871), born in New Hampshire to free parents, spoke for millions of American blacks when he described black life in this country in the starkest of terms:

---

14. Lesley Walker, "Words," essay in "Learning to Tell Our Stories," an honors first-year seminar at Lipscomb University, Fall 2016.

15. Toni Morrison, *The Bluest Eye* (1970; reprint, New York: Plume, 1994), 46.

16. Morrison, *The Bluest Eye*, 209–10.

America, it is to thee,
Thou boasted land of liberty,—
It is to thee that I raise my song,
Thou land of blood, and crime, and wrong.
It is to thee my native land,
From which has issued many a band
To tear the black man from his soil
And force him here to delve and toil
Chained on your blood-bemoistened sod,
Cringing beneath a tyrant's rod.[17]

If one is tempted to think Whitfield's judgment extreme, that white supremacy has never been as pervasive as he suggests, consider the role that white supremacy played in the thinking of America's founders and many other leaders of this republic. It is common knowledge that when the founders affirmed that "all men are created equal," they limited the meaning of "all men" to white men (not women) who held property. Further, the man who actually wrote the words "all men are created equal"—Thomas Jefferson—offered something very different in his *Notes on the State of Virginia*. There he affirmed "that the blacks, whether originally a distinct race, or made distinct by time and circumstances, are inferior to the whites in the endowments both of body and mind." Like the promise of "Life, Liberty, and the pursuit of Happiness," Jefferson regarded the inferiority of black people as a self-evident truth, also grounded in nature. "It is not their condition, then, but nature, which has produced the distinction."[18]

Likewise, Abraham Lincoln, in a debate with Stephen A. Douglas five years before he would sign the Emancipation Proclamation, affirmed this regarding blacks:

I am not, nor ever have been, in favor of bringing about in any way the social and political equality of the white and black races; that I am not, nor ever have been, in favor of making voters or jurors of negroes, nor of qualifying them to hold office, nor to intermarry with white people. . . . There is a physical difference between the white and

17. James M. Whitfield, "America," History Is a Weapon, accessed October 30, 2017, http://www.historyisaweapon.com/defcon1/whitamer.html.
18. Thomas Jefferson, *Notes on the State of Virginia*, ed. William Peden (Chapel Hill: University of North Carolina Press, 1955), 138–43.

black races which I believe will forever forbid the two races living together on terms of social and political equality. And inasmuch as they cannot so live, while they do remain together there must be the position of superior and inferior, and I as much as any other man am in favor of having the superior position assigned to the white race.[19]

And Andrew Johnson, Lincoln's vice president and the man who succeeded him in office, wrote to Missouri governor Thomas C. Fletcher that "this is a country for white men, and by God, as long as I am President, it shall be a government for white men."[20]

Decades later, President Woodrow Wilson resegregated the federal civil service that had been integrated for years following Reconstruction and held in the White House a private screening of *Birth of a Nation*, a film that praised the rise of the Klan as symbolic of the white South's resurgence after Reconstruction.[21]

Then, in 2016, 81 percent of America's white evangelical Christians voted to place in the seat of the presidency of the United States a man who had built his political career on the utterly false and disproven claim that the nation's first black president had been born in Kenya and therefore occupied the White House illegally, and a man whose racist comments and actions have been publicized so widely that, while some might ignore them, no American can deny them.[22]

If we are beginning to grasp the depth and breadth and power of the myth of white supremacy in American life, and if we are willing to acknowledge the failures of the church in this regard, then we now must ask, what is it about the theology that many American Christians have embraced that has permitted—and even sanctioned—such complicity in the bigotry and racial oppression that are so much a part of America's popular culture?

19. Abraham Lincoln, "Fourth Debate: Charleston, Illinois," National Park Service, September 18, 1858, https://www.nps.gov/liho/learn/historyculture/debate4.htm.

20. Quoted in Hans L. Trefousse, *Andrew Johnson: A Biography* (New York: Norton, 1989), 236.

21. William Keylor, "The Long-Forgotten Racial Attitudes and Policies of Woodrow Wilson," Professor Voices: Commentary, Insight and Analysis, March 4, 2013, http://www.bu.edu/professorvoices/2013/03/04/the-long-forgotten-racial-attitudes-and-policies-of-woodrow-wilson.

22. For a list of Trump's racist statements, see David Leonhardt and Ian Prasad Philbrick, "Donald Trump's Racism: The Definitive List," *New York Times*, January 15, 2018, https://www.nytimes.com/interactive/2018/01/15/opinion/leonhardt-trump-racist.html.

Reading the Biblical Text through the Lens of the Dominant Culture

In his important book *The End of White Christian America*, Robert Jones writes that "no segment of White Christian America has been more complicit in the nation's fraught racial history than white evangelical Protestants."[23] Two gross misreadings of Christian theology have allowed evangelicals, including members of Churches of Christ, to buy into the myth of white supremacy and to participate in the racist behavior that myth inevitably spawns.

First, many American Christians read the biblical text through the lens of American popular culture while they should read the culture through the lens of the biblical text. And through that misreading, they allow the American nation, its values and its dominant culture, to take the place of the only reality to which, as Christians, they should pledge their allegiance: the biblical vision of the kingdom of God.

The statement by G. C. Brewer, cited earlier in this chapter, typifies that reversal of priorities. Recalling how he and others routinely humiliated blacks when he was growing up in the early twentieth century, Brewer concluded, "This was the condition that prevailed, and this we accepted as right and satisfactory."

Brewer was a Christian minister who preached the gospel with extraordinary power. Yet in the question of race, he read the gospel through the lens of the racial biases that had defined his culture. Accordingly, "the condition that prevailed" apparently transformed the humiliation of blacks into "right and satisfactory" behavior, regardless of anything Jesus or any writer of the biblical text might have said to the contrary. Christians like the young man Brewer—and there were many just like him—apparently found "the condition that prevailed" in the popular culture so overwhelming, so irresistible in the shaping of their hearts and minds, that they could somehow view racist behavior as thoroughly compatible with the Christian faith.

Or consider Landon Garland, the first chancellor of Vanderbilt University, an institution related at that time to the Methodist Episcopal Church South, who expressed in 1869 his hope that this new Christian college would always exhibit "a proper conformity to the conventionalities of society."[24] The "conventionalities of society" in the American South at the time Garland wrote were rooted in the principle of white supremacy.

23. Robert Jones, *The End of White Christian America* (New York: Simon and Schuster, 2016), 167.
24. Landon Garland, in *Nashville Christian Advocate* 29 (February 27, 1869): 2.

One of the factors that allowed so many evangelical Christians to transform the Christian faith into a handmaiden for the popular culture was the conviction common among Christian people that the United States was a Christian nation.[25] And if the nation was Christian, it would be difficult to admit to the racial oppression, even the racial crimes, that the majority of America's citizens sanctioned.

How else can we explain the fact that professed Christians—thousands and thousands of them—took part in the lynching, the burning, the castration, and the brutalizing of thousands of blacks throughout the United States between 1880 and 1940?[26] How do we know that many of these people identified themselves as Christians? Because lynch mobs almost always drew from a cross section of the community in which the lynching occurred, and because most lynchings occurred in America's "Bible Belt." As Leon F. Litwack wrote, "The bulk of the lynchers tended to be ordinary and respectable people . . . , not so different from ourselves—merchants, farmers, laborers, machine operators, teachers, lawyers, doctors, policemen, students; they were good family men and women, good, decent churchgoing folk who came to believe that keeping black people in their place was nothing less than pest control, a way of combating an epidemic or virus that if not checked would be detrimental to the health and security of the community."[27] Indeed, "the mobs who meted out 'summary justice' were pronounced by one Georgian as 'composed of our best citizens, who are foremost in all works of public and private good.'"[28]

These racial zealots sometimes turned out by the thousands, as if lynching were some sort of spectator sport, and then gathered up souvenirs—fingers, toes, even genitals—to take back to their homes. Reflecting on the fact that Christians participated in these atrocities, James Cone, in his powerful

25. On the United States as a Christian nation, see Martin E. Marty, *Righteous Empire: The Protestant Experience in America* (New York: Dial Press, 1970); Robert T. Handy, *A Christian America: Protestant Hopes and Historical Realities*, 2nd ed. (New York: Oxford University Press, 1984); John Fea, *Was America Founded as a Christian Nation? A Historical Introduction* (Philadelphia: Westminster John Knox, 2011); Steven K. Green, *Inventing a Christian America: The Myth of the Religious Founding* (Oxford: Oxford University Press, 2015); Kevin M. Kruse, *One Nation under God: How Corporate America Invented Christian America* (New York: Basic Books, 2015); and Hughes, *Christian America and the Kingdom of God*.

26. The Equal Justice Initiative has documented approximately five thousand lynchings nationwide between 1877 and 1950. *Lynching in America: Confronting the Legacy of Racial Terror*, 3rd ed. (Montgomery, AL: Equal Justice Initiative, 2017), 4.

27. Leon F. Litwack, "Hellhounds," in *Without Sanctuary: Lynching Photography in America*, ed. James Allen et al. (Santa Fe, NM: Twin Palms, 2004), 19, 34.

28. *Savannah Morning News*, as cited in Litwack, "Hellhounds," 19–20.

book *The Cross and the Lynching Tree*, leaves us to ponder this massive contradiction—that Christians who believed in an innocent Jesus, lynched for their sins, lynched thousands of innocent blacks on a comparable tree while never discerning the obvious similarity that connected both crimes or the obvious contradiction between their faith and their deeds.[29]

Half a century or so later, their conviction that the United States was a Christian nation led many evangelicals, including members of Churches of Christ, to regard the freedom movement, led by Martin Luther King Jr., as an unjustified complaint. How could this Christian nation have possibly denied equal rights and equal opportunity to any of its people? Martin Luther King and those for whom he spoke, therefore, were nothing more than agitators, inspired more by communism than by anything resembling the Christian faith to which King so often appealed. A 1968 letter from Reuel Lemmons, editor of the *Firm Foundation*,[30] written to Jennings Davis, dean of students at Pepperdine University, made this point unmistakably clear. Lemmons wrote, "A lot of people wanted to compare Martin Luther King to Jesus Christ, while in reality, King was a modernist, and denied faith in Jesus Christ as taught in the Bible. . . . If he was not an outright Communist, he certainly advocated Communist causes. His absolute disregard for law and order except those laws and orders which he wanted to obey leaves me cold. . . . J. Edgar Hoover branded King as a notorious liar and Harry Truman said he was a troublemaker. This kind of man, black or white, I cannot conscientiously praise."[31] Significantly, when Lemmons sought to appraise King's character, the standard he erected was not one provided by Christian theology but a standard provided by the director of the Federal Bureau of Investigation and a former president of the United States.

Those Christians who took their cues from this "Christian nation"—whether those who hanged blacks on the lynching tree or those who opposed the profoundly Christian work of the freedom movement—had substituted the nation for the only reality to which Christians are called to pledge their allegiance: the kingdom of God, a reality whose theological significance we shall explore below. For now, suffice it to say that the people who waged the struggle for equal rights, for equal housing, and for equal access to food, education, and clothing were some of the people Jesus envisioned when he

---

29. James M. Cone, *The Cross and the Lynching Tree* (Maryknoll, NY: Orbis, 2011).

30. The *Firm Foundation* was a popular religious paper serving the Churches of Christ.

31. Lemmons to Davis, May 23, 1968, in John Allen Chalk files, Harding School of Theology library.

said, "He has anointed me to bring good news to the poor . . . and . . . to let the oppressed go free" (Luke 4:18).[32] But many evangelicals, including many in Churches of Christ, simply failed to make that connection.

There is a second misreading of Christian theology that has allowed evangelicals to buy into the myth of white supremacy. For the past 125 years at least, evangelicals have more often than not envisioned the gospel as a strictly private affair, involving just "Jesus and me," and a religion that has little to do with the affairs of this world but everything to do with other-worldly visions of an afterlife to come.[33] The theological problems with such a vision are immense. A privatized gospel completely severs the social or communal implications of the Christian message, and a gospel that is defined in purely otherworldly terms makes no room for social justice in the here and now. In cutting Christians off from the social implications of the gospel, these perspectives, even though they are embraced by millions of American Christians, essentially reject the heart of Jesus's teachings.

If one imagines that the Christian life is nothing more than a private, daily walk with Jesus, there can be no compelling theological motive for judging white supremacy and racist behavior to be fundamentally at odds with the core principles of the Christian faith. And if the goal of the Christian life is nothing more than securing an abode in the world to come and avoiding the fires of hell, then the Christian faith provides no compelling reason to come to terms with the pervasive power of white supremacy or to work to undermine racism in the larger society.

The Root of the Problem in Churches of Christ

While Churches of Christ, like the larger evangelical world, have often read the biblical text through the lens of American popular culture, have often worshiped a private Jesus, and have often defined the Christian faith chiefly as a journey to an otherworldly abode, there were other, additional factors that blinded them to the realities of white supremacy.

It was surely not the case that Churches of Christ were unfamiliar with the Bible, for the Bible has been the singular focus of Churches of Christ from the time of their inception in the early nineteenth century. But it is the case that

---

32. Biblical quotations in this chapter are taken from the New Revised Standard Version.

33. James Davison Hunter explains why this has been true in *Evangelicalism: The Coming Generation* (Chicago: University of Chicago Press, 1987), 40–41.

Churches of Christ forced questions and concerns onto the biblical text that, at best, were marginal to the biblical witness. And it is also the case that Churches of Christ read the Bible in ways that simply obscured its central message.

Alexander Campbell set the agenda for Churches of Christ when he vigorously promoted the restoration of primitive Christianity. The problem was not the idea of restoration in its own right, since that is an inherently useful vision. The problem lay in the fact that Campbell, indebted as he was to the principles of the Age of Reason, defined restoration in strictly rational terms. And the rational quality of Campbell's thought led him to view the New Testament not as a theological and ethical treatise that offers a vision of the kingdom of God, but as a scientific manual upon which rational and un-biased people might reconstruct in scientifically precise and accurate ways the forms and structures of the primitive church.

The notion of forms and structures is crucial to this conversation, for Campbell seldom asked what the Bible said about the poor. Instead, he asked about the biblical pattern for worship. He seldom asked what the Bible said about marginalized people. Instead, he asked about a rationally constructed plan of salvation. He seldom asked what the Bible said about people oppressed by imperial powers. Instead, he asked about the biblical model for the proper organization of the local church. In all these ways, Campbell diverted the eyes of Churches of Christ from the driving themes of the Christian gospel.

But there is more, for in his zeal to restore the forms and structures of the primitive church, Campbell argued that the Christian age began, not with the birth of Jesus, but with the birth of the church, an event recorded in Acts 2. Everything prior to Acts 2 belonged to what he called the "Mosaic dispensation," which had no relevance for the grand task of restoring the primitive church. In effect, then, Campbell minimized the importance not only of the Hebrew Bible but also of the gospels. Over time, that action would essentially sever Churches of Christ from the prophetic vision one finds especially in Jesus and the Hebrew prophets.

There is still more, for even in the lifetime of Campbell, some in Churches of Christ had transformed Campbell's goal of restoring the primitive church into a fixed and settled conviction that they had in fact restored the one true church and that, outside of that church, there could be no salvation. By the 1950s and 1960s, the notion that one's salvation depended on one's belonging to the one true church had become for many members and congregations in this tradition the most important consideration of all.

Having obscured the central themes of the biblical message, the white Churches of Christ, at the time of the Freedom Movement, were wholly unprepared to embrace their brothers and sisters of color who asked for nothing more than to be treated with respect as human beings. Indeed, they were wholly unprepared to discern in the freedom movement the faces of the kingdom of God.

Theological Resources

I know of no way that we can resist the shaping and defining power of the dominant culture unless we possess two assets. First, we must occupy a vantage point that allows us to look into our culture, as it were, from outside the culture itself. And second, that vantage point must provide us with a set of values that are foreign to the culture, that stand in judgment on the culture, and that challenge the culture's values in radical ways.

The Gospel of Grace

The fact is that every Christian has access to precisely that sort of vantage point. The New Testament describes that vantage point with the simple word "gospel"—the good news that God loves us infinitely more than we can fathom, has accepted us, and has said yes to us in spite of our inevitable failures, our brokenness, and our sins.

That is the gospel message, the heart of biblical faith. But there is a corollary to this central message—a corollary to which the New Testament writers return time and again. No one puts it better than John. "We know love by this, that he laid down his life for us—and we ought to lay down our lives for one another. How does God's love abide in anyone who has the world's goods and sees a brother or sister in need and yet refuses help? Little children, let us love, not in word or speech, but in truth and action" (1 John 3:16–18).

The gospel message, then, has two components. First, God extends his radical, self-giving love and grace to each of us, has accepted us, and has said yes to us in spite of our inevitable failures, our brokenness, and our sins. And second, God's love requires that we extend love and grace to others and say yes to them in spite of their inevitable failures, brokenness, and sin. The first component—God's own love and grace—is the driving, enabling power behind the second component, the grace we must extend to our neighbors.

But what happens when a Christian tradition seldom preaches the gospel of God's free and unmerited grace? What happens when a Christian tradition identifies God's grace with God's commands? What happens when a Christian tradition defines the "plan of salvation" not in terms of what God has done for us but rather in terms of the human response to divine commands? What may happen is this—the Christian tradition that fails to proclaim God's unmerited grace has severed the driving force behind the love and grace that, according to the gospel message, we must extend to others. And that is precisely what happened in Churches of Christ for 150 years—from the 1820s when Churches of Christ first began to identify God's grace with God's commands to the 1970s when Churches of Christ finally discovered and began to preach widely the gospel of unmerited grace.

When the freedom movement emerged in the mid-1950s, Churches of Christ almost entirely lacked the vantage point that might have allowed them to bring to that moment the insights of 1 John 3: "How does God's love abide in anyone who has the world's goods and sees a brother or sister in need and yet refuses help?" Indeed, they almost entirely lacked the vantage point that might have prompted them to extend unmerited grace to their neighbors just as God had extended his unmerited grace to them.

The Gospel of the Kingdom

In addition to the gospel of grace, the New Testament offers Christians another vantage point from which we can resist the sirens of the dominant culture. Matthew describes that vantage point as "the gospel of the kingdom": "Jesus went throughout Galilee, teaching in their synagogues and proclaiming the good news [i.e., *the gospel*] of the kingdom and curing every disease and every sickness among the people" (Matt. 4:23).

Matthew's phrase "the gospel of the kingdom" offers an early introduction to a theme that resonates throughout the gospels, namely, "the kingdom of God." While New Testament scholars differ over the meaning of that phrase, one of its meanings seems clear. In most of the instances where the phrase "kingdom of God" appears in the New Testament, the context links it to concern for the poor, the dispossessed, those in prison, the maimed, the lame, the blind, and all who suffer at the hands of the world's elites. In other words, the kingdom of God is where the powerless are empowered, where the hungry are fed, where the sick are healed, where the poor are sustained, and where those who find themselves marginalized by the rulers of this world are finally offered equality and justice.

Put another way, the "gospel of the kingdom of God" is the corollary to the "gospel of grace." It tells us that just as God has said yes to us in spite of

227

our failures, we must say yes to others in spite of their failures. Or, in the words of John, "We know love by this, that he laid down his life for us—and we ought to lay down our lives for one another" (1 John 3:16).

In this limited space, we cannot explore the biblical vision of the kingdom of God in great detail, but a handful of New Testament passages will help us grasp the point.

In the second chapter of Luke, an angel appears to shepherds in the field by night and proclaims "good news of great joy for all the people: [for] to you is born this day in the city of David a Savior, who is the Messiah, the Lord."

In the context of imperial Rome, the angel's proclamation was both revolutionary and seditious, for its two key words—"Savior" and "Lord"—were titles routinely applied to the emperor Caesar Augustus. Indeed, Caesar's titles included "Divine," "Son of God," "God," "God from God," "Redeemer," "Liberator," "Lord," and "Savior of the World."

It is one thing to proclaim that Jesus is Savior and Lord, but it is something else to ask what that Savior and Lord requires, and that is the question Luke answers with incredible clarity in Luke 3—a passage that contrasts the humble kingdom of God with the all-pervasive power and splendor of the Roman Empire. Luke sets up the contrast beautifully, referring first to the ruling elites of his day. "In the fifteenth year of the reign of Emperor Tiberius, when Pontius Pilate was governor of Judea, and Herod was ruler of Galilee, and his brother Philip ruler of the region of Ituraea and Trachonitis, and Lysanias ruler of Abilene, during the high priesthood of Annas and Caiaphas, the word of God came . . ." (3:1–2).

Came to whom? It came, Luke tells us, "to John son of Zechariah in the wilderness." Here Luke subtly contrasts the wilderness where John resided with the imperial courts of Tiberius Caesar, Herod, Philip, and Lysanias. Later in his gospel, Luke was not so subtle, since he reports that Jesus himself contrasted John's poverty with the luxury of imperial power. "What then did you go out to see?" Jesus asked the people. "Someone dressed in soft robes? Look, those who put on fine clothing and live in luxury are in royal palaces. What then did you go out to see? A prophet? Yes, I tell you, and more than a prophet" (7:25–26).

Finally, what message did John proclaim? Did he preach the American gospel that "God helps those who help themselves"? Hardly. According to Luke, John preached a message of radical compassion for those in need. And when the crowds asked him, "What then should we do?" John replied, "Whoever has two coats must share with anyone who has none; and whoever has food must do likewise" (3:10–11).

The point is this—John the Baptist, both through the life he lived and the message he preached, offered those around him a vantage point that allowed them to look into their culture, as it were, from outside the culture and to claim a set of values that would challenge the culture in radical ways.

Jesus did the very same thing when he came to Nazareth and there, in the synagogue, announced his mission and his vocation. According to Luke,

> When he came to Nazareth, where he had been brought up, he went to the synagogue on the sabbath day, as was his custom. He stood up to read, and the scroll of the prophet Isaiah was given to him. He unrolled the scroll and found the place where it was written:
>
>> "The Spirit of the Lord is upon me,
>>> because he has anointed me to bring good news to the poor.
>> He has sent me to proclaim release to the captives
>>> and recovery of sight to the blind,
>>> to let the oppressed go free,
>> to proclaim the year of the Lord's favor."
>
> And he rolled up the scroll, gave it back to the attendant, and sat down. The eyes of all in the synagogue were fixed on him. Then he began to say to them, "Today this scripture has been fulfilled in your hearing." (4:16–21)

The gospels record only one other instance when Jesus defined the concerns that would characterize his mission and vocation. Matthew reports that John the Baptist, languishing in prison, heard of the work Jesus was doing and "sent word by his disciples and said to him, 'Are you the one who is to come, or are we to wait for another?'" And Jesus replied, "Go and tell John what you hear and see: the blind receive their sight, the lame walk, the lepers are cleansed, the deaf hear, the dead are raised, and the poor have good news brought to them."

By framing his mission and vocation in these terms, Jesus lined out the contours of what he often called "the kingdom of God." That kingdom provided then—and still provides—a transcendent point of reference that allows Jesus's followers in every time and place to look into their culture, as it were, from outside the culture and to claim a transcendent set of values that can challenge the culture in radical ways.

Numerous other passages flesh out this vision of the kingdom of God. In Luke, for example, those who are first—the rich and the powerful—will be last, while those who are last—the poor and oppressed—will be first (13:29-30). Only those who are humble like little children can enter the kingdom of God (18:16-17). And Luke reports Jesus's comment, "How hard it is for those who have wealth to enter the kingdom of God" (18:24).

Driving Out the Myth of White Supremacy

The myth of white supremacy is alive and well in the United States. The pressing question for Christians, then, must be this: "How can we resist?"

Our resistance will be stillborn unless we recognize that the problem we face is both real and pervasive. That will be difficult to do, simply because in the lives of most American whites, there is nothing to compel them to reflect on the meaning of race, the meaning of white privilege, or the meaning of white supremacy. And without cause for reflection, it is easy enough to imagine that white supremacy thrives only in white nationalist organizations forthrightly committed to white control and dominance.

The sobering truth, however, is that white supremacy thrives in every nook and corner of the United States, including the nation's churches. Indeed, if we are honest, we will confess that it thrives even within our very own minds and hearts. Only when we come to terms with that reality can we effectively resist.

Once we admit that white supremacy is both real and pervasive in American culture, even in our churches, and even in our very own lives, we are then in a position to discover in the Christian gospel the great resources it offers for resistance: the gospel of grace and the gospel of the kingdom. Those truths assure us that God is love, that God has freely given his love and grace to each of us, and that God requires, in turn, that we extend that same love and grace to all human beings—those who live next door and those who live on the other side of the world. Indeed, the gospel requires that we love even our enemies.

If we internalize those great truths, they will drive the myth of white supremacy out of our hearts, out of our minds, and out of our churches. Indeed, the notion of white supremacy will cease to serve as a myth, will cease to function as a story that gives us meaning. For we will have built our lives on a story with infinite meaning—the gospel story of God's magnificent grace.

Racial Reconciliation as Professional Practice

JERRY TAYLOR

Like religion, matters of race are very personal. We often engage the issues of racial disunity in response to the grand sweep of history and with society at large in our view. This is appropriate, since so much of the struggle involves embedded social structures, past wounds, malignant policies, and the flawed habits of institutional life. However, people encounter the pain of religious and racial discord as individuals first of all, and the damage they suffer as a result is personal. Furthermore, for all the hope we may place in the transformation of policies, legislation, and institutional cultures, the goal is the changed minds, hearts, and habits of people in their relationships to their neighbors. With that in mind, engaging issues of race is not only personal but also contextual, the work of committed souls within their local churches, neighborhoods, and workplaces, including university faculties.

Putting the spotlight on personal factors and context invites us to think about specific circumstances and particular individuals. The history of race and religion in North America reveals time and again that the character and actions of a particular person in a given place can be a watershed for renewal. This chapter focuses on the work and impact of one religious scholar in particular: the church historian Douglas A. Foster. Foster has a particular background—raised in a milieu of white privilege and racial segregation in mid-twentieth-century Alabama; a particular religious heritage—white Churches of Christ[1] within the Stone-Campbell tradition; and a particular profession—teacher and scholar of the history of Christianity

---

1. In this chapter, "Churches of Christ" refers to the fellowship of churches, white and African American, that is historically connected to the reform tradition known as the Stone-Campbell Movement but is distinct from the related independent Christian Church/Church of Christ fellowship; see Thomas H. Olbricht, "Church of Christ," in *The Encyclopedia of the Stone-Campbell Movement*, ed. Douglas A. Foster et al. (Grand Rapids: Eerdmans, 2004), 212–20.

in North America in a private liberal arts university and seminary.[2] Yet the particularities of this scholar's work and context show how one's personal and professional activity, born out of a commitment to religious unity, can shine light on the problems of systemic racism and mitigate its pain. It is not the intent of this chapter to eulogize Foster, a careful scholar who would himself warn us against passing off hagiography as history. Instead, I wish to offer testimony, based on personal experience and the collegial relationship of two religious scholars—one white and the other black—who have partnered together in the task of racial reconciliation out of a shared Christian conviction.

One in Christ: Prophetic Voice on a University Campus

Even though it grew out of a heritage committed to unity,[3] in the mid-twentieth century the religious tradition known as Churches of Christ claimed with Pharisaic fierceness to be the only one true church and unmercifully condemned all other religious bodies beyond Church of Christ borders as being false and human-made.[4] All the while this divided religious body decried the imperfections and shortcomings of other denominations, it quietly excused itself from its inattention to the Christian gospel that called for the total eradication of the dividing wall of hostility between Jew and gentile.[5] Churches of Christ conveniently ignored the gospel mandate that called for

2. Foster received the PhD in church history at Vanderbilt University (1980). After teaching in the history department at Lipscomb University in Nashville, Tennessee, in 1991, he joined the faculty of Abilene Christian University in Abilene, Texas.

3. The Stone-Campbell Movement, of which Churches of Christ are a major part, had as one of its early guiding principles the quest for religious unity; see Foster, "Unity, Christian," in Foster et al., *The Encyclopedia of the Stone-Campbell Movement*, 754–58.

4. On the history of the tensions between ideals of unity and expressions of a sectarian mind-set in the heritage, see D. Newell Williams, Douglas A. Foster, and Paul M. Blowers, eds., *The Stone-Campbell Movement: A Global History* (Saint Louis: Chalice, 2013), 44–45, 164, 367–78; also Foster, "The Nature of Christian Unity: Historical Understandings of Churches of Christ," *Lexington Theological Quarterly* 46, no. 3–4 (2016): 87–98.

5. Although scholars in Churches of Christ have often boasted that the Stone-Campbell Movement was the only Christian fellowship that did not divide over the issue of slavery and as a consequence of the Civil War, recent scholarship has drawn attention to the clear and divisive impact of sectionalism and issues of race within the heritage. See Foster, "The Effect of the Civil War on the Stone-Campbell Movement," *Stone-Campbell Journal* 20, no. 1 (Spring 2017): 5–16.

the "true church" to live in radical defiance of the fabricated walls of racial segregation erected in a society where the dominant culture through racial narcissism worshiped the whiteness of skin as its true god.

It was at the One in Christ Conference held on the campus of Abilene Christian University (ACU) in the fall of 1999 that I first met Douglas A. Foster. ACU was founded in 1906 in Abilene, Texas, as a college affiliated with Churches of Christ.[6] Although it has educated tens of thousands of students, the school did not admit African Americans until 1962. Like many other Christian colleges and universities, ACU has a history of racial discrimination. Attempts to address racial inequities had been slow in coming, inconsistent, and largely ineffective, mirroring the situation in Churches of Christ generally.[7] The One in Christ Conference was designed with the good intention of bridging the Grand Canyon–sized, visible division between black and white Churches of Christ.[8]

Foster played a pivotal role in planning this significant event. He was professor of church history in the Graduate School of Theology and director of ACU's Center for Restoration Studies. In his academic career Foster had distinguished himself as an expert in the history of the Stone-Campbell Movement, especially Churches of Christ.[9] His deep engagement with the ideals of that heritage had imparted to him a passion for religious unity.[10] As a historian committed to the Christian gospel and the ideals of religious unity, he had become very conscious of the history and ongoing saga of ra-

6. See Foster, "Abilene Christian University," in Foster et al., *The Encyclopedia of the Stone-Campbell Movement*, 1–2.

7. For a brief account of racial issues at colleges and universities associated with Churches of Christ, see Foster, "An Angry Peace: Race and Religion," *ACU Today*, Spring 2000, 8–20, 39.

8. For the history of race relations in the movement, see Don Haymes, Eugene Randall II, and Douglas A. Foster, "Race Relations," in Foster et al., *The Encyclopedia of the Stone-Campbell Movement*, 619–22; the history of African American leaders and institutions in the movement is sketched out in Williams, Foster, and Blowers, *The Stone-Campbell Movement: A Global History*, 46–60, 204–9.

9. Alongside his many publications and conference presentations, Foster's status as a scholar of the movement is shown by his leadership in authoritative landmark projects, such as Williams, Foster, and Blowers, *The Stone-Campbell Movement: A Global History*, and Foster et al., *The Encyclopedia of the Stone-Campbell Movement*; see also Michael W. Casey and Douglas A. Foster, eds., *The Stone-Campbell Movement: An International Religious Tradition* (Knoxville: University of Tennessee Press, 2002).

10. Foster's early research focused on the history of American religious unity movements: "The Struggle for Unity during the Period of Division of the Restoration Movement, 1875–1900" (PhD diss., Vanderbilt University, 1980).

cial division in churches and Christian institutions, particularly within the Stone-Campbell Movement.[11]

Royce Money, then president of Abilene Christian University—he served from 1991 to 2010—convened the conference to talk about constructive ways that racially and doctrinally estranged brothers and sisters could reach across the deep chasm and experience an authentic racial connection, with Christ serving as the mediating centerpiece.[12] Attending the conference were ACU administrators and faculty, members of ACU's board of trustees, and the most prominent ministers and church leaders, young and old, in African American Churches of Christ.[13]

I vividly remember sitting on one side of the discussion table at the conference with many of the senior black ministers whom I had admired as icons and fathers in the Christian faith all my religious life. Two of the most prominent and influential voices in African American Churches of Christ were Jack Evans and W. F. Washington. Jack Evans at the time was the longest-serving president of Southwestern Christian College in Terrell, Texas, founded in 1948, the only historically black college among Churches of Christ. I attended the school for four years and was profoundly impacted and influenced by the life and example of Jack Evans. I was eleven years old in 1973 when I, for the first time, heard W. F. Washington preach at the Vance Avenue Church of Christ in Memphis, Tennessee. Dr. Washington was a widely traveled preacher and influential man in African American Churches of Christ. His preaching was so impressively impactful that it inspired in me, as an eleven-year-old kid, a desire to preach.

Much of my perspective about white Christians and their white churches and schools was shaped by these two powerful voices in African American Churches of Christ. I had come to accept the conviction, prevalent among many members and leaders in African American Churches of Christ, that white Christians for the most part were racist. This conviction for me had

---

11. Foster tells the tale of how his intensive research on the history of the movement revealed to him many "unknown stories" about black Christian leaders and forced him to confront the presence of racism in his own heritage, in "What I Learned about African-Americans," *Stone-Campbell Journal* 16, no. 1 (Spring 2013): 5–16.

12. For a brief account of the meeting, see Michelle Morris, "The Right Thing to Do: A Special Report," *ACU Today*, Spring 2000, 2–7.

13. On African American leaders in Churches of Christ, see Edward J. Robinson, "African Americans in the Movement," section 2.2, "Churches of Christ," in Foster et al., *The Encyclopedia of the Stone-Campbell Movement*, 15–17.

become a permanent mental fixture by the time I had come to sit around the discussion table at ACU in 1999 to talk about racial oneness.

I viewed the location of the conference to be somewhat ironic. Black Churches of Christ for years had considered ACU a major crime scene where the black spiritual psyche in Churches of Christ had been assaulted. Abilene Christian University's denial of enrollment to African Americans until 1962 left scores of blacks spiritually scarred for life. Having grown up hearing stories about ACU's "whites only" racial policy made me skeptical and doubtful that the One in Christ Conference would yield any lasting fruit in terms of genuine racial unity.

As I sat at the roundtable discussion in a serious state of skepticism, I heard the emergence of a prophetic voice ringing with sincerity and boldness. It was the first time in my life that I had heard a white male speak with such candor and courage about white supremacy. Douglas Foster's bold speech came from a place of honest introspection. His tone of voice was passionate, and backed with the heavy artillery of a first-rate intellect. He had not only researched the matter closely but he was also confessional, and convincingly conveyed his sense of responsibility for the ways his own establishment perpetuated the status quo. With the searching light of penetrating truth, Foster ripped open the internalized myths and inherited false propaganda about white supremacy.[14] He exposed the poisonous diet that had been fed to most whites on a daily basis since their early childhood. Here was scholarship and status in the service of reconciliation, with the potential of helping a white institution own its complicity in racist practices and the promise of helping African American colleagues dare to hope that things might truly change.

At the end of the conference, the group decided that ACU would issue a written apology for its past practices of racism.[15] A couple of months later, Royce Money read the apology before a predominantly black audience at Southwestern Christian College's annual lectureship. As I sat in the audience

14. In his presentations and publications, Foster has sought to expose the reality and consequences of white supremacy in his own religious heritage, e.g., Foster, "Justice, Racism, and Churches of Christ," in *Unfinished Reconciliation: Justice, Racism, and Churches of Christ*, ed. Gary Holloway and John York (Abilene, TX: Abilene Christian University Press, 2003), 129–51, and Foster, "1968 and the Reshaping of the Separation between Black and White Churches of Christ," in *Reconciliation Reconsidered: Advancing the National Conversation on Race in Churches of Christ*, ed. Tanya Smith Brice (Abilene, TX: Abilene Christian University Press, 2016), 29–41.

15. Morris, "The Right Thing," 3.

listening to the written apology, little did I know that three years later I would be invited to join the all-white faculty in the College of Biblical Studies at ACU. What influenced me was my recollection of what I and other African Americans had experienced at ACU during the One in Christ Conference, the apology that President Money made at Southwestern Christian College, and the bold and courageous statements Douglas Foster made at the conference about the sin of white supremacy. All these major components worked congruently to influence me to accept the teaching post at ACU.

Since the formal apology was a practical step in the right direction, I believed that someone from the ranks of black Christians in response to the public apology had to translate forgiveness into a practical step. I also believed that forgiveness had to provide meaningful and courageous assistance in the process of encouraging institutional repentance. It appeared to me that Foster was someone committed to the same ideals of embodied repentance, someone willing to use his scholarly abilities and academic leadership to work toward meaningful change on a university campus and in the church.

United by Faith: Academic and Pastoral Leadership

During my first year at ACU (2002), I looked for proof that the institutional apology President Money made three years prior was truly legitimate. I had now relocated my young family to a majority white environment that had historically been hostile toward and rejecting of the presence of black bodies. I leaned in with intensity, seeking to peer into the hearts of my new white colleagues as they spoke or lectured about race and racism. My cautious and vulnerable optimism led me to search beneath the honorable rhetoric about racial reconciliation to see if there was a disconnection between the mouths that spoke these righteous words and the hearts that produced them. Upon my arrival at ACU, a colleague advised me to "watch what they do and not what they say." This became my guiding evaluative paradigm as I sought to navigate a predominantly white world as a freshman faculty member of color.

I both listened to the words and watched the actions of university leaders. I was also very attuned to the actions of the outstanding colleague who had caught my attention before, Douglas Foster. They all displayed a strong commitment to dismantling institutional racism while seeking to guide ACU in finding ways to show visible fruits of repentance as an institution.

The intentional steps they took to increase racial diversity among students and the aggressive steps they took to hire administrators and faculty of color went far beyond merely giving a false appearance or making fake attempts at seeking diversity. Their unwavering commitment revealed a genuine desire to disrupt the religion of white supremacy that had long lived at the core of the Christian university.

However, rooting out ingrained systemic habits is not easy. Academic knowledge, vision, and institutional introspection leading to formal statements help, but transformed habits and transformative leadership are crucial. The investment of ACU's provost, Dwayne VanRheenen, eventually gave birth to a multiracial campus discussion group centered around the book *United by Faith*.[16] As a follow-up to the influential and convicting *Divided by Faith*,[17] the book proposes that intentionally multiracial local communities built on the Christian gospel can reduce racial division and inequality in our society.[18] From 2004 Foster led the group. The discussion eventually moved off campus into the homes of colleagues, moving from house to house. We met the first Monday of each month during each semester. Participants shared a meal at each gathering. The intention was to discuss matters of race while using the model of the first-century church as the inspiration for sharing life together (Acts 2:42–47). Foster had helped us move the discussion about race from the roundtable to the dinner table!

Through mutual testimony and honest conversation over meals, the participants quickly came to perceive the legacy of racial division in their minds and in their midst. The group concluded that an effective way to dismantle the external racial barriers that stood between Christians of all races was to engage in the demolition of internal spiritual barriers that had been inherited and erected by the gods of racism, fear, and rage. Eating and sharing life together became an effective method of sewing and knitting colorless souls together into an external, attractive tapestry reflected in the authentic union of diverse bodies drawn together by the living Jesus.

Foster was the convener and facilitator of these house fellowships that afforded people a safe space to deal honestly with their inner demons of racism as well as the deep rage often experienced by people of color in response to white supremacy. These conversations were tender, sincere, and

16. Curtiss Paul DeYoung et al., *United by Faith: The Multiracial Congregation as an Answer to the Problem of Race* (New York: Oxford University Press, 2003).

17. Michael O. Emerson and Christian Smith, *Divided by Faith: Evangelical Religion and the Problem of Race in America* (New York: Oxford University Press, 2000).

18. DeYoung et al., *United by Faith*, 3.

sometimes tearfully painful. Nevertheless, there was a display of courage to dive deeper into the inner space where the seeds of racism and rage had been planted many years before. In these gatherings Foster readily contributed his knowledge of the religious tradition and his solid grasp of the history of American culture. But his leadership ran deeper than academic expertise. When strong emotions abruptly appeared, Foster's nonanxious presence enabled him wisely to integrate those strong emotions into our group conversations. His fearless spirit and tenacious commitment to addressing the sin of racism empowered the United by Faith Fellowship (UBFF) to deal with a controversial topic that the broader church and society often simply avoided talking about.

As the UBFF moved from house to house, people were invited to share their personal stories about their first and most impressionable memories of race and racism. As a historian who saw the importance of archiving testimonial evidence, Foster asked people to put their stories into writing. His aim was to collect the written stories for future publication, but the value of these testimonials was much more immediate. This was a powerful exercise in that it invited people to plunge deeper into the region of the unconscious and tap into the underground emotions associated with race that had lain dormant there and had in some cases hardened into distorted spiritual formations. It was touching to see the profound effect these personal stories had upon all who heard them. Tears flowed from eyes as indicators that feelings frozen cold for a lifetime were now finally melting like ice under a heat lamp. Under Foster's leadership, UBFF participants gained knowledge of racism and greater capacities for relating across racial divides in ways that do not easily come outside the practices of deeply shared community.

Peacemaking in Practice

Foster is what I would call a public scholar/historian. Though he is a major academic voice in his discipline, his status did not keep him confined behind the guarded gates of the ivory tower. His research on the Stone-Campbell Movement had produced within him the desire to be an advocate for the religious unity that expressed some of the best instincts of the movement. He worked not only to understand and share knowledge of the movement's historic unity impulses,[19] but also to embody them in his own professional

19. Publications that focus on the unity aspects of the Stone-Campbell Movement include

life—especially since that very movement had come to be associated with religious division throughout much of the twentieth century. It was not enough to diagnose the legacy's errors or even accuse it of going wrong. Foster actively sought to remedy sins of the past by directing professional energy toward the aims of mutual religious understanding and ecclesial reconciliation. He invested in practices of religious peacemaking early in his career, thereby acquiring capacities for racial peacemaking that he would display in years to come.

For example, Foster is one of the founding members and codirector of the Stone-Campbell Dialogue.[20] The dialogue was established in 1999 to encourage noncombative conversations among the three major estranged fellowships that make up the Stone-Campbell tradition: the Christian Churches/Churches of Christ, the Christian Church (Disciples of Christ), and the Churches of Christ.[21]

Foster, "The Nature of Christian Unity"; Glenn T. Carson, Douglas A. Foster, and Clinton J. Holloway, eds., *One Church: A Bicentennial Celebration of Thomas Campbell's Declaration and Address* (Abilene, TX: Abilene Christian University Press, 2008); Foster, "The Understanding and Impact of the Declaration and Address among Churches of Christ," in *The Quest for Christian Unity, Peace, and Purity in Thomas Campbell's Declaration and Address: Texts and Studies*, ed. Thomas H. Olbricht and Hans Rollmann, ATLA Monograph Series 46 (Lanham, MD: Scarecrow, 2000), 389–409; Foster, "The Disciples' Struggle for Unity Compared to the Struggle among Presbyterians, 1880–1989," in *A Case Study of Mainstream Protestantism: The Disciples' Relation to American Culture, 1880–1989*, ed. D. Newell Williams (Grand Rapids: Eerdmans, 1991), 236–59.

20. See Foster, "Stone-Campbell Dialogue," in Foster et al., *The Encyclopedia of the Stone-Campbell Movement*, 720–21; "Stone-Campbell Dialogue," Council on Christian Unity, accessed December 18, 2017, http://councilonchristianunity.org/stone-campbell-dialogue. See Douglas A. Foster and Robert K. Welsh, "Stone-Campbell Dialogue (1999–2016): A Dialogue of Hope," *Lexington Theological Quarterly* 46, no. 1–2 (2016): 1–8; also Foster, "Efforts at Repairing the Breach: Twentieth-Century Dialogues of the Churches of the Stone-Campbell Movement with Baptists and Presbyterians," *Discipliana* 63, no. 4 (Winter 2003): 99–111.

21. See Williams, Foster, and Blowers, *The Stone-Campbell Movement: A Global History*, 371. Foster has coauthored numerous books to help lay audiences within different branches of the movement understand better their shared heritage: see Gary Holloway and Douglas A. Foster, *Renewing the World: A Concise Global History of the Stone-Campbell Movement* (Abilene, TX: Abilene Christian University Press, 2015); Douglas A. Foster, Gary Holloway, and Mark Toulouse, *Renewing Christian Unity: A Concise History of the Christian Church (Disciples of Christ)* (Abilene, TX: Abilene Christian University Press, 2011); W. Dennis Helsabeck, Gary Holloway, and Douglas A. Foster, *Renewal for Mission: A Concise History of Christian Churches and Churches of Christ* (Abilene, TX: Abilene Christian University Press, 2009); Gary Holloway and Douglas A. Foster, *Renewing God's People: A Concise History of Churches of Christ*, rev. ed. (Abilene, TX: Abilene Christian University Press, 2006).

Foster also became a key leader in the World Convention of Churches of Christ (which still serves all three Stone-Campbell streams), begun in 1930 and existing for the purpose of connecting Stone-Campbell churches around the globe.[22] In 2000 Foster began serving on the board of trustees of the World Convention; by 2010 he was a vice president. From 1998 to 2006 he served on the Disciples of Christ Historical Society Board of Trustees. In 2011 he became an ecumenical member on the General Board of the Christian Church (Disciples of Christ). In addition to his scholarly presentations at national academic conferences and his leadership on the board of Stone-Campbell International,[23] Foster accepted many invitations to speak in churches on the subject of Christian unity. He organized lecture series and enrichment opportunities on the subject at denominational gatherings. He was a key leader in the Great Communion (2009), a communion service on the bicentennial of Thomas Campbell's call for religious unity (1809), involving people from all streams of the Stone-Campbell Movement in thousands of places around the world.[24]

Foster's commitment to the visible unity of Christians went beyond the Stone-Campbell tradition. In 1990 Foster became a member of the Faith and Order Commission of the National Council of Churches (NCC), a body composed of many different Christian traditions collaborating to represent God's love and Christian unity in the public square.[25] Participating as a representative of Churches of Christ posed some challenges, due to that fellowship's lack of formal denominational structures on the one hand, and the suspicions of some within his own heritage on the other. Some believed that involvement in such ecumenical efforts threatened congregational autonomy and sectarian orthodoxy. Foster navigated the territory of his nondenominational context and became an effective representative of Churches of Christ in the NCC, graciously but firmly combating the criticisms he faced from those within his own religious fellowship.

Foster often involved his students in these activities, seeking funding for their travel and mentoring them in their participation. More than a teacher,

22. See Lorraine Jacobs and Lyndsay Jacobs, "World Convention of Churches of Christ, The," in Foster et al., *The Encyclopedia of the Stone-Campbell Movement*, 785–86; "World Convention," accessed December 18, 2017, http://www.worldconvention.org.

23. "Stone-Campbell International," Stone-Campbell Journal, accessed December 18, 2017, http://www.stone-campbelljournal.com/about_us/stone_campbell_international.

24. See Carson, Foster, and Holloway, *One Church*, for an exploration of ways to bring Campbell's unity ideals into the twenty-first century.

25. See National Council of Churches website, accessed December 18, 2017, http://nationalcouncilofchurches.us.

he was a mentor and exemplar in the practices of informed religious peace-making. As his ecumenical activities demonstrated his desire to integrate knowledge and action through practice, he showed the same integrity by his involvement in racial initiatives, such as the One in Christ Conference and UBFF.

It was shortly after my arrival at ACU that Foster invited me to join the Stone-Campbell Dialogue as a member representing Churches of Christ. I soon discovered that his mission was to bring racial and gender diversity to this mostly white group. It became clear to me that everywhere his life was invested he was committed to advancing the cause of racial diversity, racial justice, and racial and gender inclusion. When UBFF decided to go public in the Abilene community with the call for greater fellowship across racial boundaries, Foster was willing to play a major role in leading such an effort. He helped UBFF conduct public lectures at the Abilene Public Library and provide scholarly presentations for the community covering topics about race.

Back on campus, Foster exemplified how a scholar and teacher can translate ideas and values about race into habits that produce concrete re-sults. He and I collaborated on campus presentations and led faculty dis-cussion groups of Martin Luther King Jr.'s book *Where Do We Go from Here: Chaos or Community?*[26] When one talks with black students at ACU, they re-veal their enormous respect and appreciation for Foster. I witnessed faculty and students alike experience transformation as a result of their encounter with UBFF and Foster's leadership. By his selection of graduate assistants and student workers for his classes and for the Center of Restoration Stud-ies, Foster showed a strong commitment to racial diversity and minority empowerment. One could be certain that Foster and his wife, Linda, would be present at campus and community events put on by minority students. It is no surprise that major black student organizations at ACU came to utilize Foster as a sponsor or adviser. His commitment to the well-being of black students and other students of color in visible ways served as an example for all who witnessed it.

Racially motivated incidents can be among the most damaging and po-larizing events in a community. Whenever racial incidents occurred on the ACU campus or students raised concerns about remarks and policies that made them feel uncomfortable, Foster could be depended upon to respond

---

26. Martin Luther King Jr., *Where Do We Go from Here: Chaos or Community?* rev. ed. (Boston: Beacon, 2010).

quickly as a courageous ally of the injured and marginalized. His intervention went beyond the campus borders. Foster opened his home for small groups to meet to think strategically and prayerfully about how to address racial incidents constructively. Sometimes these meetings would run late into the night, but the Fosters always expressed an unhurried hospitable spirit.

The Fosters also routinely opened their home to African graduate students. Foster chose to spend many of his summers teaching in schools in Ghana, Swaziland, and other nations on the continent of Africa. His visits not only brought superb teaching and scholarship to underserved populations but also endeared the Fosters to many Africans, some of whom eventually became Graduate School of Theology students. After graduating and leaving Abilene, those students often stayed in the Foster home whenever they came back to the United States for a visit.

Integrity can be even more persuasive than a well-reasoned argument. The concerns and suspicions I originally had at the One in Christ Conference and when I originally arrived at ACU were alleviated when it became clear to me that in Douglas Foster I was seeing up close and personal one whose manner of life was in sync with his manner of speech. Making real progress in the area of racial reconciliation depends on leaders who display such lives of integrity.

Foundations of Faith and Spirituality

The themes of unity, hospitality, mercy, justice, and reconciliation prominently ran through Foster's personal life and professional activity. Yet it is evident that his practices of friendship and compassion toward people of different races and nationalities were not based on a political agenda or required by his academic institution, but were an expression of a deeply held personal faith fulfilling a mandate of the kingdom of God. Like many others who have labored for racial reconciliation, Foster's faith and Christian spirituality were foundations of his work. Examples drawn from his congregational investments, his willingness to take risks due to his convictions, and his use of spiritual practices to create community for peacemaking show this.

Foster's presentations and publications for the sake of the church and lay audiences are many.[27] These include his appeals that believers should

27. Some outstanding examples include: Foster, *Will the Cycle Be Unbroken? Churches*

seek visible religious unity as a matter of Christian discipleship[28] and pursue racial reconciliation as a matter of Christian witness.[29] Foster's commitment to advancements in diversity and racial inclusion was also seen in the local church where he served as an elder. For instance, he started a Bible class at his congregation consisting of young adults. He developed a robust curriculum addressing the topic of white privilege. People were introduced to books and videos that detailed the historical process whereby the illusion of race and the negative racial stereotypes of blacks became embedded in the psyche of white Americans. The class was difficult for some and eye-opening for others. Some in the mostly white class perceived the information as overwhelming and one-sided, and they pushed back against it. Foster regarded their resistance as healthy feedback and used it to recalibrate his approach to presenting the information. Transforming people's hearts was more important to him than defeating religious opponents—too important not to rethink his approach so that it would be more effective.

However, Foster's hunger and thirst for justice did not flinch in the face of taking political risks. I have heard Foster say on many occasions that his allegiance is not to his tribe or an institution. This became evident to me in a personal way when I shared with him my concerns about a face-to-face meeting I was to have with some individuals to discuss a potentially explosive and racially charged matter. Not only did Foster not seek to dissuade me from addressing the matter directly, but he accompanied me so that we could seek a healthy resolution to the situation together. There was not one second in which I felt he made any political calculations as to his decision to accompany me.

The importance of this should not be missed. It is at times like these that minorities feel the need for white allies like Foster who are not driven

---

of Christ Face the Twenty-First Century, rev. ed. (Abilene, TX: Abilene Christian University Press, 2007), and Foster's service as chief editor of ACU's Heart of the Restoration Series, a multivolume series designed to assist church leaders in reflecting theologically on issues of ecclesial identity for the twenty-first century. Foster also coauthored two volumes in the series: Jeff W. Childers, Douglas A. Foster, and Jack R. Reese, *The Crux of the Matter: Crisis, Tradition, and the Future of Churches of Christ*, Heart of the Restoration Series 1 (Abilene, TX: Abilene Christian University Press, 2002); Mark Love, Douglas A. Foster, and Randall Harris, *Seeking a Lasting City: The Church's Journey in the Story of God*, Heart of the Restoration Series 4 (Abilene, TX: Abilene Christian University Press, 2005).

28. E.g., Foster, "Attack the Enemy, Not the Sisters and Brothers," *New Wineskins* 10 (January–April 2006); Foster, "What Churches of Christ Might Have Done Differently in the Past," *Mid-Stream* 40, no. 4 (2001): 1–5.

29. E.g., Foster, "The Point of Christianity 2: Racial Reconciliation," *Christian Standard* 144 (May 2009): 357.

politically or imprisoned by a spirit of fear but operate out of deep conviction. Too often minorities feel they get "thrown under the bus" at the most crucial times, when they need their white friends to take a stand with them as allies against racial insults. I had seen Foster's integrity and courage on many occasions prior to this painful crisis. I had no doubt that he would stand with me in seeking a good resolution. He risked his privileged status in the eyes of those who could have attacked him for standing with me. He did not seek to protect or defend his racial tribe. He proved that his allegiance superseded race and his commitment was to pursue righteousness in a complex situation.

This is why it is imperative that people of different races be spiritually and socially connected to one another. In my experience, it is harder to hate a perceived enemy when that person bears a physical resemblance to your close friend. Despite all the polarizing voices in our culture challenging me to do so, how can I as a black man hate all white people for the racial insults I suffer, when I know that my close friend, risking his privilege and status to stand with me as an ally, is the same color as my perceived enemy? Foster's example taught me that the stance for racial justice and racial equality has no color.

In 2014 I was granted a sabbatical to work on bridging the great religious divide between blacks and whites, starting with the racially divided Churches of Christ in my own heritage. The vision entailed getting leaders in both fellowships to come together in a sustained way. The project evolved into what became known as the Racial Unity Leadership Summit (RULS), a racial unity retreat held at congregations and on university campuses.[30] From the beginning I knew I wanted Foster as my ally in this work. He helped me persuade the leaders of the Highland Church of Christ in Abilene to fund the project. Along with a few other key people, Foster would become one of the staple presenters at the gatherings conducted across the nation with church leaders, laity, university administrators, students, and others.

Brilliant minds with expertise in various academic disciplines offered their creative research on racism and white supremacy. But Foster's presentation, "Race as an Illusion," served as the core content. His material was given at the front end of the RULS events and went straight to the core of the issue of racism and white supremacy. Foster guided participants in appreciating how racism and white supremacy developed in the context of a

---

30. See Jerry Taylor, "The Racial Unity Leadership Summit," *Charis* (blog), June 1, 2015, http://char.is/blog/2015/06/01/racial_unity_leadership_summit.

historical process. Foster explained that black Churches of Christ came into existence in response to white racism and Jim Crow segregation.[31] Periodicals, books, and religious papers published in white churches show that white members of Churches of Christ were eager to create churches for black people so the white churches could remain a closed and exclusive fellowship for whites only. White churches sought to maintain the visible absence of black bodies in their white pews. Foster helped RULS participants see the hypocrisy in black and white Christians who both shared the joint claim to be members of the one true church. They adamantly claimed to be members in the same body while maintaining social lines of separation between black and white bodies.

From Fresno, California, to Oxford, Mississippi, people expressed appreciation for the enlightening material. It was powerful but also disorienting, especially for participants hearing it for the first time. Having Foster present on the painful history of the brutal mistreatment of blacks in this country since the arrival of the first African slave was not intended to cause attendees to feel guilty. But it is difficult to create positive history going forward unless we overcome our shameful denial of the history that lies behind us. Church history in America bears out the fact that in the harshest forms of racial brutality and during the height of southern lynchings, the white church often stood by silently, as Saul did at the stoning of Stephen (Acts 7:58; 8:1). The white church held the cloaks of those who carried out these atrocious acts in the name of white supremacy.

It would have been unrealistic to expect black and white Christians to embrace one another immediately, even in the face of such shameful history, after having been cut off spiritually and socially for years. There was a blockage of spiritual energy between blacks and whites. As long as the body remained divided, the spirit within the members of that body would be frustrated and overwhelmed by a state of racial despair. Only a rediscovery of the spiritual nature within members of the church would enable them to rediscover their spirituality. Extricating the human spirit from the murderous captivity of racism would require more than the intellectual component alone. Healing the historic wounds caused by the evil of racism would require more than a first-rate academic team. It would require a radically spiritual approach equipping participants to address racism as a pervasive and elusive state of sickness in their souls and in the church.

31. See Foster, "Justice, Racism, and Churches of Christ," and Foster, "1968 and the Reshaping of the Separation between Black and White Churches of Christ."

Some whites are afraid to say anything that may be considered inappropriate or insensitive. They would rather remain silent than take the risk of being branded a racist. Some African American Christians refrain from talking about race because they fear losing control of their black rage. They have learned to keep their anger and rage concealed under the external demeanor of friendliness. This type of silence is not constructive because it is practiced out of fear and anger; it is not an intentional silence practiced in contemplation. It was in the face of these challenges that I knew we would need to create a spiritual, contemplative component to complement the academic and social components of RULS.

I had full confidence that Foster would be the perfect partner in this as well. Having watched him and listened closely to the things he had spoken from his heart, I had noticed a healthy balance in his life between the academic and the spiritual. I knew he had a high view of the Holy Spirit and a serious appreciation for spiritual disciplines. My emphasis on the need to root our work in Christian contemplative practices resonated deeply with him. We talked often about the need for leaders to remain reliant upon the guidance of the Spirit in their efforts to dismantle white supremacy. When we held the first RULS Contemplative Prayer Retreat at the Saint Columba Retreat Center in Memphis in December 2016, Foster was right there on the front line, helping an interracial group of about fifty who gathered to practice silence, dwell contemplatively in Scripture, and participate in spiritual exercises related to race and reconciliation.

Most people only notice the public activism seen throughout the civil rights movement. They fail to see the private and personal spiritual activism that took place underground in the prayer life of those who led the movement. Lewis Baldwin's book on the prayer life of Martin Luther King Jr.[32] helped me understand more clearly how many civil rights leaders were drawing from a deep spiritual well that inspired and motivated them to do extraordinary things in the ugly face of extraordinary odds.

Somehow during the journey of seeking racial justice and racial unity, the wagon of activism became unhitched from the horse of divine power that once pulled it up the hill of injustice. Too often the church lost its belief in God's power to bring about racial healing, so that we turned more and more to our own intellectual devices and methods of rational discourse without a conscious reliance upon the Spirit. We sought to remedy a spiritual malady

---

32. Lewis V. Baldwin, *Never to Leave Us Alone: The Prayer Life of Martin Luther King Jr.* (Minneapolis: Fortress, 2010).

through our own intellectual strength and social action. I have become convinced that if progress is to be made today in the areas of racial justice and racial harmony, it will be undergirded by a strong connection to the divine. In my experience, God works powerfully through those who avail themselves of his divine power through such spiritual practices as public and private solitude, meditation, fasting, spiritual reading of Scripture, and contemplative prayer. Foster's effectiveness as a scholar and churchman who advocates for racial justice was grounded in the same convictions and practices.

Scholarship Practiced with Integrity

The RULS Contemplative Prayer Retreats normally close with communion. This practice reminds us that the rules we observe at the Lord's Table should also serve as the rules of engagement at the discussion table. Learning to listen to our Savior in community helps establish the discipline of listening to one another over the difficult topic of race. Practices of integrity are practices binding together mind, will, heart, speech, action, and social presence.

One of the greatest gifts I have received in my life is the gift of friendship with Douglas A. Foster and his particular model of scholarship practiced with integrity. Despite his great standing in an academic world often saturated with white male privilege, personally and professionally he practiced habits that enabled him to be an academician and spiritual activist in terms of the race issue. We are in need of such people in the twenty-first century, who not only assent to the ideals of racial harmony and advocate loudly for justice, but also will devote to them their personal time and their professional labor, reflecting on the issues, acquiring the capacities, and cultivating the relationships necessary to be agents of reconciliation. For Foster, that entailed a blend of scholarly activity, academic and ecclesial leadership, and investment in personal relationships, all built on a foundation of personal faith and Christian spirituality.

Racial Reconciliation Workshops from the 1960s for Today

Tanya Smith Brice

In 2006, my family and I relocated to Abilene, Texas, from Columbia, South Carolina, when I accepted an administrative and faculty position in the newly minted School of Social Work at Abilene Christian University (ACU). I was invited to participate in the United by Faith fellowship group, composed of ACU administrators, faculty, staff, and students, along with Abilene community members. This small group engaged in monthly fellowship over a meal in each other's homes. This multiracial, intergenerational group met to discuss the concept of "racial reconciliation." We read books together like Lena Williams's *It's the Little Things*[1] and had difficult yet rewarding discussions about this thing called "racial reconciliation."

Racial Reconciliation Defined

During my first meeting with United by Faith in Abilene, I was fascinated by the discussion around racial reconciliation. I was a bit skeptical about this largely white group discussing race issues. I was even more skeptical when they began to explore the concept of racial reconciliation. I asked the group, "How can there be reconciliation when there has never been conciliation?" Reconciliation suggests that we were once in accord, and some force divided us, and now we are seeking to come back together. My understanding of US history prevented me from buying into the concept of racial reconciliation as such. It was in the group's handling of my question, and the ensuing discussions, that I came to appreciate the potential value of such efforts as United by Faith.[2]

---

1. Lena Williams, *It's the Little Things: Everyday Interactions That Anger, Annoy, and Divide the Races* (Wilmington, MA: Mariner Books, 2002).

2. My early experiences with United by Faith also solidified my deep admiration for Douglas A. Foster, who was a leading presence in the meetings and whom this book honors.

I am a third-generation member of the Churches of Christ. My grandfather, Albert Lemon Smith, was a church planter throughout South Carolina and Georgia in the 1970s and 1980s. I had known only of the Church of Christ when growing up. However, it was not until moving to Abilene that I realized that I was only really familiar with the black Churches of Christ. I knew that there were white Churches of Christ, but from my perspective they were not in true church fellowship. My grandfather would take me with him to midweek services at white Churches of Christ where he taught them—what I assumed to be—new songs. As an adult, I would occasionally visit a white congregation when traveling or during the periodic "unity" fellowship events between black and white congregations. But until moving to Abilene, I never even considered placing membership at a white Church of Christ. If asked, I would have stated that whites and blacks worship differently, and that I prefer the way blacks worship. Very seldom was I asked. The lack of true fellowship and the intentional separation of congregations by race were how I saw the Churches of Christ.

As a child growing up in Greenville, South Carolina, I was raised to be unapologetically black. I have met African Americans who talk about having feelings of inferiority to whites. I have never experienced those feelings. While I attended majority white schools throughout my primary and secondary education, and was often the only black child, or one of a few, in my classes, I was nurtured to be secure in my identity by my large, extended family; my black community; and my black church. As a classically trained social worker, my focus has always been on the African American community. My doctoral studies afforded me the skills to engage in historiographic work to further understand the plight of black people in the United States. I have crafted a research agenda examining the impact of structural violence on black women and children, specifically, and on the black community broadly. It was in this context that I asked the United by Faith group about "reconciliation." My racialized experiences in the Churches of Christ coupled with my upbringing characterized by race pride made me skeptical of true reconciliation among our fellowship.

While living in Abilene, I came to realize that there are a number of divides, both doctrinal and racial, among the Churches of Christ. According to Leroy Garrett, within the Churches of Christ there are six identified branches: (1) mainline, (2) noncooperatives, (3) one-cuppers, (4) premillennial, (5) non-Sunday school, and (6) black churches.[3] We could add others

3. Leroy Garrett, *The History of the Stone-Campbell Movement* (Joplin, MO: College Press, 1981).

to the list, including, more recently, congregations that use musical instruments in corporate worship.[4] However, there remain a distinct black Church of Christ and a distinct white Church of Christ, which, though they do not observe any formal divisions, rarely have anything to do with each other and practically exist in different worlds. They are functionally estranged. It is not unusual, in either black or white churches, to hear sermons or to engage in Bible studies about doctrinal divides among the fellowship. Very rarely does one hear sermons or engage in Bible studies about the racial divide. I would argue that the racial divide is the more devastating of the two to the future of the church. It impacts every aspect of our relationship with each other, which impacts every aspect of our relationship with Jesus Christ.

Racialized Context of Churches of Christ

The racialized history of the Church of Christ is well documented. We know that there was an intentional effort, by white members of the Churches of Christ, to plant black Churches of Christ. For example, Alexander Bigby Lipscomb (1876-1940), a renowned Church of Christ minister, editor of the *Gospel Advocate*, and president of the board of education in Valdosta, Georgia, once advocated for the continued funding of black church plants because this work produced "better farm hands, better porters, better cooks, better housemaids than ever before."[5] In other words, the black Church of Christ seemed to him and many others to be a mechanism for maintaining subservience among African Americans.

It is important to remember the social and political context of the late nineteenth and early twentieth century. It was during this time of "American apartheid"[6] that African Americans were legally relegated to second-class citizenry. The southern states were recovering from economic ruin brought on by the Civil War, which resulted in the emancipation of their largest labor force, formerly enslaved Africans. Poor whites found themselves competing with the formerly enslaved Africans for scarce resources.[7] Tensions between

4. In the context of this chapter, "Churches of Christ" refers to the fellowship of churches in the Stone-Campbell Movement that have traditionally worshiped a cappella.

5. A. B. Lipscomb, "It's Not Keeble, but the Bible Is Right," *Christian Leader* 45 (August 25, 1931): 6.

6. Douglass Massey and Nancy Denton, *American Apartheid: Segregation and the Making of the Underclass* (Cambridge, MA: Harvard University Press, 1998).

7. W. Cohen, "Negro Involuntary Servitude in the South, 1865-1940: A Preliminary

the two races became more and more intense. Policies such as slave codes, black codes, and Jim Crow laws were enacted to control African Americans and to maintain their inferior status.

African Americans responded to these unjust policies by developing parallel social and economic systems. For instance, this period saw the founding of most of the historically black colleges and universities still in existence today.[8] Further, there were thriving African American communities throughout the country, where one could find social and economic success that rivaled that in white communities.[9]

It was also during the late nineteenth century that African Americans left traditionally white Christian denominations and formed what we now know as the black church. The black church was central to the African American community. The black church was not just a place for religious rituals, but often served as a support mechanism for businesses, schools, and charitable organizations associated with African American communities.[10] The black church became an institution of social uplift, racial pride, and mutual aid among the African American community.[11]

Analysis," *Journal of Southern History* 42, no. 1 (February 1976): 31–60, reprinted in *African American Life in the Post-Emancipation South*, vol. 12, *Black Southerners and the Law, 1865–1900*, ed. Donald G. Nieman (New York: Garland, 1994), 35–64 .

8. Travis J. Albritton, "Educating Our Own: The Historical Legacy of HBCUs and Their Relevance for Educating a New Generation of Leaders," *Urban Review* 44, no. 3 (2012): 311–31; W. E. B. Du Bois, *The Talented Tenth* (New York: James Pott and Co., 1903); Du Bois, *The Education of Black People: Ten Critiques, 1906–1960* (1973; reprint, New York: New York University Press, 2001).

9. Brandee Sanders, "History's Lost Black Towns," *The Root*, January 27, 2011, https://www.theroot.com/historys-lost-black-towns-1790868004; Charles Gerena, "Opening the Vault," Federal Reserve Bank of Richmond, Spring 2007, 46–49, https://www.richmondfed.org/publications/research/econ_focus/2007/spring/economic_history_weblinks; Lila Ammons, "The Evolution of Black-Owned Banks in the United States between the 1880s and 1990s," *Journal of Black Studies* 26, no. 4 (1996): 467–89.

10. C. Eric Lincoln and Lawrence Mamiya, *The Black Church in the African American Experience* (Durham, NC: Duke University Press, 1990), 519; Andrew Billingsley, *Mighty Like a River: The Black Church and Social Reform* (Oxford: Oxford University Press, 1999); Andrew Billingsley and Cleopatra Howard Caldwell, "The Church, the Family, and the School in the African American Community," *Journal of Negro Education* 60, no. 3 (1991): 427–40.

11. Iris Carlton-LaNey, "African American Social Work Pioneers' Response to Need," *Social Work* 44, no. 4 (1999): 311–21; Kevin K. Gaines, *Uplifting the Race: Black Leadership, Politics, and Culture in the Twentieth Century* (Chapel Hill: University of North Carolina Press, 2012); Peter J. Paris, *The Social Teaching of the Black Churches* (Minneapolis: Fortress, 1985); Lincoln and Mamiya, *The Black Church in the African American Experience*.

It was in this context that Lipscomb encouraged the continued funding of Marshall Keeble (1878–1968), a renowned African American preacher who has been credited with establishing over two hundred African American Church of Christ congregations and baptizing upward of forty thousand people.[12] Lipscomb wrote about the significance of Keeble's ministry during the Great Depression, a time when whites and African Americans competed for limited jobs,[13] leading to increased racial tensions. Domestic terrorism abounded, resulting in a record number of lynchings of black bodies.[14] African Americans were in the midst of what is termed the Great Migration,[15] during which they fled the rural southern states in record numbers in search of safety in the urban centers of the Midwest and Northeast. African Americans were empowered to speak out against white supremacy through their institutions,[16] including the black church. This empowerment was a threat to the sociocultural norms of the Churches of Christ. White church leaders saw Keeble as a humble preacher who did not appear to seek to rock the pro-

12. Darrell L. Broking, "Marshall Keeble and the Implementation of a Grand Strategy" (MA thesis, East Tennessee State University, 2003); Paul D. Phillips, "The Interracial Impact of Marshall Keeble Black Evangelist, 1878–1968," *Tennessee Historical Quarterly* 36 (1977): 65; Edward J. Robinson, *Show Us How You Do It: Marshall Keeble and the Rise of Black Churches of Christ in the United States, 1914–1968*, Religion and American Culture (Tuscaloosa: University of Alabama Press, 2008), 252.

13. Cheryl Lynn Greenberg, *To Ask for an Equal Chance: African Americans in the Great Depression*, African American History Series (Lanham, MD: Rowman and Littlefield, 2009); Robert S. McElvaine, *The Great Depression: America, 1929–1941* (New York: Broadway Books, 1993); Milton Meltzer, *Brother, Can You Spare a Dime? The Great Depression, 1929–1933* (New York: Knopf, 1969).

14. James Allen et al., *Without Sanctuary: Lynching Photography in America* (Santa Fe, NM: Twin Palms, 2000); Elwood M. Beck and Stewart E. Tolnay, "The Killing Fields of the Deep South: The Market for Cotton and the Lynching of Blacks, 1882–1930," *American Sociological Review* 55, no. 4 (1990): 526–39; Stewart E. Tolnay, Ellwood M. Beck, and James L. Massey, "Black Lynchings: The Power Threat Hypothesis Revisited," *Social Forces* 67, no. 3 (1989): 605–23.

15. Neil Fligstein, *Going North: Migration of Blacks and Whites from the South, 1900–1950*, Quantitative Studies in Social Relations (New York: Academic Press, 2013); Stewart E. Tolnay and Elwood M. Beck, "Racial Violence and Black Migration in the American South, 1910 to 1930," *American Sociological Review* 57, no. 7 (1992): 103–16; Stewart E. Tolnay and Elwood M. Beck, "Black Flight: Lethal Violence and the Great Migration, 1900–1930," *Social Science History* 14, no. 3 (1990): 347–70.

16. Andrew Billingsley, *Mighty Like a River: The Black Church and Social Reform* (Oxford: Oxford University Press, 1999); Lincoln and Mamiya, *Black Church in the African American Experience*; James H. Cone, *For My People: Black Theology and the Black Church*, Bishop Henry McNeal Turner Studies in North American Black Religion 1 (New York: Orbis, 1984).

verbial racial boat.[17] Lipscomb and other white ministers and civic leaders saw the planting of African American Churches of Christ as a means to maintain the social order of white supremacy. Many black Church of Christ leaders eventually rejected white paternalism and were forced to create independent institutions and structures where they could worship free of white control and racism.[18]

I was reared in the black Churches of Christ that descended from this sordid racialized history. So when United by Faith participants and I talked about racial reconciliation, I saw reconciliation through the lens of an intentional racialized oppression perpetrated by white Christians under the guise of Christianity. So, how does a white Christian talk with an African American about racial reconciliation? Productive ways to engage this discussion begin with actions as much as with words. Douglas A. Foster, a leader of United by Faith, modeled what racial reconciliation looks like in his personal life and has pointed us to certain historical events in the history of Churches of Christ from which we might learn valuable lessons going forward.

Race Relations Workshops

Foster has contributed to the scholarly literature by examining the sordid history of race relations in the Stone-Campbell Movement, broadly, and in Churches of Christ specifically. He has investigated this movement with a clear target on the role of the white church in maintaining a social order of white supremacy. In his study entitled "1968 and the Reshaping of the Separation between Black and White Churches of Christ,"[19] Foster reminds us of efforts made by members of black and white Churches of Christ to address race relations in its societal context. Among these efforts was a Race Relations Workshop at the Schrader Lane Church of Christ in Nashville, Tennessee, held March 4–8, 1968. This workshop was followed by the Atlanta

---

17. Wes Crawford, *Shattering the Illusion: How African American Churches of Christ Moved from Segregation to Independence* (Abilene, TX: Abilene Christian University Press, 2013), 223; Phillips, "Interracial Impact," 65; Robinson, *Show Us How*, 252.

18. Crawford, *Shattering the Illusion*.

19. Douglas A. Foster, "1968 and the Reshaping of the Separation between Black and White Churches of Christ," in *Reconciliation Reconsidered: Advancing the National Conversation on Race among Churches of Christ*, ed. Tanya Smith Brice (Abilene, TX: Abilene Christian University Press, 2016), 29–39.

Race Relations Workshop in June 1968.[20] At these meetings strategies were suggested for addressing race relations among members of the Churches of Christ, specifically, and among evangelical Christians, broadly. In what follows, we will examine these meetings more closely, looking for clues that can help us chart better paths in race relations for the future.

The initial Race Relations Workshop at the Schrader Lane Church of Christ, an African American congregation, was well attended, with an average of 548 attendees each evening, broken into about 60 percent African American and 40 percent white.[21] Black and white speakers alternated in addressing the racial problems faced by the church.

The purposes of the event, as delineated by Dr. David Jones, the pulpit minister of Schrader Lane, were as follows:

To come to a candid understanding of each other
To reveal many unspoken truths about the Negro and Christianity in
    America
To emphasize the position of Jesus Christ in the race issue
To initiate actions that will correlate in practices with true Christianity
To explore various aspects of religious problems as related to the race
    problem. (2–3)

The speakers at this workshop included black and white ministers of local congregations, as well as black and white students from the local universities. They each shared their experiences with race and gave suggestions for improving race relations among the Churches of Christ. David Jones acknowledged that during the time of this workshop, Churches of Christ were experiencing a significant growth in membership. He pondered why this growth had happened:

Is it because we are doing a superior job at proclaiming true Christianity to the world? Or is it that we are doing a superior job at convincing the world that we are rapidly becoming the only remaining segregated religious institution in the world? Think about it. Are we

20. It is important to note that between the dates of these two workshops, Dr. Martin Luther King Jr. was assassinated (April 4, 1968) and Marshall Keeble died (April 20, 1968).

21. "Report on Race Relations Workshop," in Walter E. Burch, ed., *Supplement to Christian Chronicle*, May 10, 1968, 3. The supplement is available at http://digitalcommons.acu.edu /sc_arc_journals/16. Hereafter, page references from this work will be given in parentheses in the text.

growing because denominations are becoming too liberal? Do we really believe that bigots and racists and "Uncle Toms" can flock to the Church of Christ, continue their "southern way of life," and "go sweeping through the pearly gates"? I would hope it is because we are doing a superior job in evangelism, but I wonder. Are we growing or simply swelling? (4)

Jones raised a compelling set of questions that speak to the nature of the Church of Christ and the racist ideology motivating much of its history. In effect, he asked this multiracial audience if the Church of Christ attracts those, both black and white, who are comfortable with racist ideology that divides the church along racial lines.

In response, Lawrence "Bud" Stumbaugh, a white Nashville business-man and a member of the Madison Church of Christ, confirmed the senti-ments expressed by Jones. Stumbaugh provided a stirring history of Africans brought to this country by white Christians under the guise of "saving the African savage" through Christianity. He went on to lament the impact of this history on the church:

> As already suggested, so-called white Christianity was and is the main cause of the racial problems we face today. The church started the doc-trine of race separation and worked so vigorously for it that segregation became a part of Christian dogma. White supremacy was literally de-fended with Bible in hand. Passages of Scripture were so twisted out of context until even today, to many people, the true defender of "pure religion" is he who screams most vociferously for eternal separation of the races in the church and general society. But while claiming to uphold the teachings of the Bible, the segregationist's stance has been in direct conflict with what the Bible really teaches. (6)

In highlighting the conflation of racist ideology with Christianity, Stumbaugh asserted that "white Christianity was and is the main cause of the racial problems we face today." He went on to admonish white Christians for sustaining racist behavior such as moving out of a neighborhood when "too many" African Americans moved in or referring to African Americans by disparaging names. Stumbaugh called this behavior "moral bankruptcy" that made him "want to throw up" (7).

James Dennis Sr., minister of the Fifteenth Avenue Church of Christ, an African American congregation in Nashville, similarly provided a perspective of how African American Christians felt about their treatment by white Christians. He delineated the continuum of responses to racist behavior, from a more conservative, prayerful response to a more radical, demonstrative response. Dennis argued for the legitimacy of all these responses based on the historical relationships between African Americans and whites in the United States. Dennis provided an illustration of why it is important that African Americans and whites get to know each other. He stated, "You remember when Cain killed Abel and God asked him, 'Where is Abel, thy brother?' and he said, 'I know not.' This was an indictment of Cain, an indictment he made himself, against himself, because he should have known where his brother was. All of us Negroes need to know what white people feel about us. They need to know what we feel about them. We need to know it in the church. We need to know where each is. We need to know it in the church, because here is where it is so important" (14).

Dennis articulated the frustrations that African American Christians had with their white coreligionists, who could send money and missionaries to Africa while ignoring the plight of African Americans. Dennis pointed out that African Americans, at that time, constituted one-fortieth of Church of Christ membership but made up 12 percent of the general population, "because segregation has made it so" (15). He identified the silence of white Christians and their participation in the racial segregation of schools and public accommodations, and in other forms of structural oppression, as a source of concern for African American Christians. Dennis concluded that the church needed to teach Christian love as a solution to the race problem.

Don Finto, minister of the Una Church of Christ, a white congregation in Nashville, and a faculty member at David Lipscomb College (now Lipscomb University), proposed a simple response to race relations in the church: "But the problems are here. What can be done to balance the scales? Let me suggest four ways which may help: (1) Knowing each other; (2) Praying for wisdom; (3) Courage and determination; and (4) In all things, love" (18). While simple, Finto's suggestions clarify the Christian obligation toward others. He also called upon his audience to challenge the intergenerational transference of racist ideology, arguing that following these four steps would help to break that generational cycle.

The workshop participants also heard the voices of the next generation of Christian leaders about race relations in the church. Among those who participated there were three African American students, Fred Leon Hill of Tennessee A&I State University (now Tennessee State University), Joseph Tucker of the University of Tennessee (Knoxville), and Perry Wallace of Vanderbilt University, and two white students, Phillip Roseberry and Joe Tomlinson, both of Lipscomb College. These local students echoed the sentiments of the other speakers. They expressed frustration with the slow progress made by Christians (20–24).

The final speaker of the workshop was Walter E. Burch, a white public relations consultant from Long Island, New York, and a self-described "outside agitator." He spoke about Christianity from a public relations perspective. He made the following provocative statement: "The problem of image becomes sticky when our doing the will of God runs counter to the prevailing community opinion. If, in the process of trying to save all persons, regardless of race or social standing, we 'allow' the church's reputation to become tarnished, then we must accept the consequences. The church cannot consciously choose only those areas of ministry or actions that are in agreement with the consensus of community beliefs and outlooks" (26). Burch observed that the church had allowed itself to reflect the world instead of being the light of the world. He invited the audience to consider 2 Timothy 3:12, which states, "Indeed, all who desire to live a godly life in Christ Jesus will be persecuted" (ESV). Burch suggested that the church must be countercultural. A church that supports racist ideology is clearly of the world, not a light in a world of darkness.

By the end of the workshop, its participants had agreed to a number of next steps that they called "Suggested Guidelines for Improving Race Relations":

1) Call an interracial meeting of church leaders to discuss and implement remedial actions as soon as possible against obvious practices of racial discrimination;

2) Preachers should immediately begin to preach some biblical sermons on the subject—not sermons to justify our sinful positions but sermons telling the truth of the matter;

3) Conduct interracial work projects such as personal work teams, workshops, community service projects, etc., so Christians can come to know each other as persons and not simply as "members" of a racial group;

4) Prepare congregations for integration. . . . A serious educational program on the truth of the gospel on race relations should be launched immediately in every congregation;

5) Have more race relations workshops at other congregations, especially white churches;

6) Correct existing segregated church related establishments, such as the "Hobby Shop," camps, church related businesses such as publishing

houses and bookstores. It is not a sin to hire [an African American] clerk in church related bookstores;

7) Hold smaller interracial group fellowships on a regular basis (monthly);

8) Plan teaching ads on the race problem on radio, TV, and newspapers;

9) Encourage Christian school officials to have a lectureship with race relations as a theme and invite a cross-section of [African American] and white speakers;

10) Provide a speaker's bureau, making available a group of men to conduct race relations workshops in churches;

11) Plan to worship at a church of another race, either as a visitor or permanently;

12) Clearly indicate that the church is open for men of all races . . . ;

13) [African Americans] should develop plans to be independent—building their own buildings, buying their own songbooks, refusing to buy church buildings vacated by the "white brethren";

14) Compile a suggested book list on the subject of race relations; and

15) Show disapproval by withdrawal of fellowship from those congregations and/or individuals who refuse the Christian way in this matter, in keeping with New Testament principles. (10)

What do we learn from the Schrader Lane workshop? David Jones emphasized that the two groups simply did not know each other: "By this I mean that we are not really aware of the feelings, attitudes, habits, and customs of the other group. . . . We only have notions about what we're supposed to be like, and how we are supposed to act while around each other." Insisting that all participants open their minds, he called for them to show mutual respect, if not agreement, speaking and behaving only "in the spirit of Christian love." For him, the gathering underscored that it was "high time for mature Christians [to] be able to come together and sit down and really look at where we are" (2–4). The need for white Christians and black Christians within their communities to meet and do the hard work of becoming better acquainted so that they can learn how to honestly but respectfully discuss their issues is no less pressing today than it was in 1968.

Following up on the Schrader Lane meeting, the Atlanta Race Relations workshop was a smaller, invitation-only event of approximately forty attendees. This interracial group of men included the presidents of Abilene Christian University and Harding University, as well as the directors of two Christian publishing houses. After meeting for two days, the group produced a document that acknowledged the sin of racial prejudice existing in churches and other Christian institutions before providing nearly thirty proposals to Churches of Christ. The proposals, which sought spiritual equality and racial justice in the churches, were grouped into six categories—local churches, church-related institutions, Herald of Truth (a radio and television ministry), publishing companies and Christian bookstores, Christian-owned businesses, and all Christians. Key emphases running throughout the proposals were integration of congregations, fellowship meetings, colleges, and other institutions; educational programs and workshops on racial relations; intentional hiring of black people at all institutions; use of media platforms to speak against racial discrimination; the seeking out of nonwhite voices when planning events, missions, and other efforts; and the inclusion of black speakers and teachers in all institutions. The final section urged all Christians to affirm that equal opportunities in housing, jobs, and schools should be granted, and all should employ their political, social, economic, and religious influence to support these convictions.[22]

Agreement was not unanimous among the attendees at the Atlanta workshop. All the attendees, except five, agreed to sign the document in support of it. Yet in his analysis of the workshops and other significant 1968 events, Foster notes that relationships remained basically the same after the events, or were even more entrenched. He writes, "rather than bringing black and white members of Churches of Christ together on an equal basis, instead [the workshops] reshaped the long-existing separation."[23] In the Atlanta meeting, among the five who chose not to make overt and formal commitments by signing the proposals were the two college presidents and the two publishers. While the number of participants of this invitation-only meeting was smaller than at the Nashville meeting, the reach of the participants was potentially greater. The college presidents and publishers had a broad reach across the fellowship. Unfortunately, they seem to exemplify the struggle of some Christians not to take on the prevailing opinions of the community. Gathering for conversation and relationship-building is indispensable, but it remains fruitless without commitments to changed actions and concrete follow-through.

22. "Conference on Race Relations," *Mission* 2, no. 3 (September 1968): 24–26; "Atlanta Race Relations Conference Lists Recommendations for Improvement," *Christian Chronicle*, July 12, 1968, 4; see Foster, "1968 and the Reshaping," 33–34; Herald of Truth, "Statement of Acknowledgement of Racial Prejudice and Proposals for Improving Race Relations in Churches of Christ" (1968), Herald of Truth Documents, Paper 214, http://digitalcommons.acu.edu/hot_docs/214.

23. Foster, "1968 and the Reshaping," 38.

A Sankofa Experience

Events of a half century ago teach us important lessons about race and religion in America. As we draw on those and other experiences, we have an opportunity to have what I call a Sankofa experience in American Christianity. *Sankofa* is a word in Twi, a language spoken among the Akan people of Ghana, West Africa. Sankofa is symbolized by a bird whose feet are traveling forward but whose head faces backward. In its beak is an egg. The Sankofa bird reminds us that we take our past with us as we move toward the future.

While the focus of this chapter has been on Churches of Christ specifically, the concept applies to evangelical Christian churches generally. Our elders in the faith have struggled with race relations from the inception of the church in America. The Race Relations workshops of 1968 demonstrate the seriousness with which evangelical Christian leaders understood the social, political, and historical relevance of race in the practice of Christianity. They embodied practices that we can profitably emulate—taking initiative rather than remaining complacent, gathering for honest conversation, showing mutual respect for the sake of love. They developed suggestions and guidelines still relevant today. In the spirit of Sankofa, the church can take the suggestions from the past, as delineated in both workshop reports, and carry them forward into the future of the church. Perhaps simply revisiting each of the suggestions is what is needed, holding each other accountable to ensure that we are intentional about working toward improved race relations.

Foster has been instrumental in helping us to revisit these suggestions. He cautions us that we cannot take the suggested steps without sincere repentance. He places the responsibility of repentance and reconciliation squarely on white Christians as the perpetrators of the sin of racism. He writes: "Race hatred and racial discrimination and segregation is not a mistake; it is sin. It is sin now, and it was sin then. If that sin was not recognized in times past by members of Churches of Christ in America, then God's grace will have to cover it. But *we* can see it, I pray. And we can do something about it."[24] Historians who, like Foster, raise the voices of those who came before us to guide us as we move forward do us a great service. For the future of the church, it is imperative that we listen.

24. Douglas A. Foster, "Justice, Racism and Churches of Christ," in *Unfinished Reconciliation: Justice, Racism, and Churches of Christ*, ed. Gary Holloway and John York, rev. ed. (Abilene, TX: Abilene Christian University Press, 2013), 133.

Index